MW00817741

The Great Pyramid Robbery

The
Great
Pyramid
Robbery

John Minahan

W·W·Norton & Company
New York · London

Copyright © 1987 by John Minahan
All rights reserved.
Published simultaneously in Canada by Penguin Books Canada Ltd., 2801 John
Street, Markham, Ontario L3R 1B4.
Printed in the United States of America.

The text of this book is composed in Times Roman, with display type set in
Trump Bold. Composition and manufacturing by The Haddon Craftsmen, Inc.

First Edition

Grateful acknowledgment is made to Hachette Littérature, Paris, for permission
to quote short excerpts from *Féerie Nocturne des Pyramides* by Gaston Bonheur,
copyright © Hachette, 1961.

Library of Congress Cataloging-in-Publication Data
Minahan, John.
The great pyramid robbery.
I. Title.
PS3563.I4616G75 1987 813'.54 86-23642

ISBN 0-393-02433-4

W. W. Norton & Company, Inc., 500 Fifth Avenue, New York, N.Y. 10110
W. W. Norton & Company Ltd., 37 Great Russell Street, London WC1B 3NU

1 2 3 4 5 6 7 8 9 0

Acknowledgments

I want to express my appreciation for the technical advice of the Police Department of the City of New York, the Miami Police Department, and the Central Security Force of the Arab Republic of Egypt.

J.M.

To Jim Mairs,

friend, editor, mentor (in that order),
whose sense of humor started this series.

Provided a man is not mad, he can be
cured of every folly but vanity.

JEAN JACQUES ROUSSEAU

1712–1778

The Great Pyramid Robbery

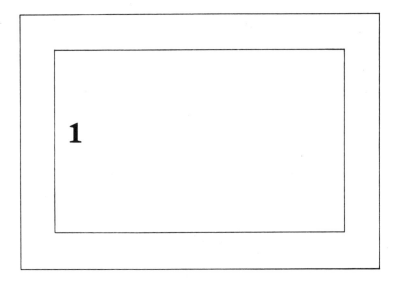

1

WHEN I WAS A KID, growing up on the Lower East Side
of Manhattan in the 1940s, there was a certain dependable
"feel" about New York, because it was still made up of real
neighborhoods, so it had a different atmosphere in more ways
than one. I love this city, always have, always will, and I know
that change is the price of progress, but sometimes I have
problems adjusting to change. Case in point, here's this story
I cut out of the *Times,* July 16, 1985, headline reads: "New
Police Station, New Perspective." Tells about the Nineteenth
Precinct. Tells how we had to move out of our historic old
station house at 153 East Sixty-seventh and into a modern
building at 312 East Ninety-fourth. Reason? Renovation that's
expected to take at least three years. Tell you the truth, I hate
this new dump. No character, no tradition, just two rede-
signed floors of a four-story building that used to be a social
services office. Also, there's no place to park; we got cars and
scooters double-parked for blocks. Plus, if you commute from
Long Island like me, you're into serious downtime. Get into

Penn Station, hop the stinkbag subway up to Times Square, squeeze aboard the shuttle to Grand Central, wait at least ten minutes for the express to Ninety-sixth, then you either wait for a crosstown bus that's jammed to the doors, or hoof it like me (forget about cabs in this neighborhood), all the way east from Lexington to Ninety-fourth between Second and First. Try it in winter with the wind nailing jagged icicles through your coat.

Now, the old house, built in 1887, one of the last police stations designed by Nathaniel D. Bush, it's a New York City Landmark. They can't change the exterior. All they can do is gut the inside, which they're doing, and it'll cost $10 million to the taxpayers. Don't get me wrong, I'm not saying it didn't need renovation. I mean, it was ninety-eight years old, it had no air conditioning, no central heating, no elevators, the plumbing didn't work, some of the ceilings were caving in, the mice were taking over. All I'm saying, when we move back in (and it won't be as early as three years), when that time finally comes, we'll go back to a station that, inside, is an exact duplicate of all the others—an ultramodern, high-tech, computerized, color-coded, impersonal, antiseptic emergency ward in a mental hospital. Fine, if you like hospitals.

"New Police Station, New Perspective." Tell me about it. We go from a Landmark in a quiet, tree-lined neighborhood with townhouses and embassies and elegant shops, all the way up to a modern yawn in the northeastern corner of our precinct, between Yorkville and East Harlem, a noisy hellhole of housing projects and tenements. A haven for drug dealers before we got here. That's our new perspective, right? First thing we move in here, the drug dealers slash the tires on our vehicles out front. Welcome to the neighborhood. Have a nice three, four years.

Story in the *Times* didn't come out until about a month after we moved, that's how important we are to the media, but I cut it out because it's one of the few articles I've ever read that gives specific details about the old place. Seems like nobody appreciates historic stuff like this until it's too late. Me, I do. I spent fifteen years in that house, exactly half my career, it was like a home to me. Gave me a comfortable feeling every time I walked in there. So, what I'm trying to bring out, this move really gets to me. Really hits me hard. Surprising, because I usually take change in stride. Delayed reaction, takes a couple of months to sink in, then I begin thinking: What the hell am I doing here anyway? What the hell am I doing in this crowded modern psycho ward, surrounded by cops who look like they just got out of the Academy, in a neighborhood that makes *Fort Apache* seem tame? What am I, a masochist? I'm fifty-two years old, for Christ's sake, I've been a cop for thirty years. Maybe it's finally time to hang it up, draw my full pension (I was eligible for it ten years ago), step back and smell the roses for a while. Then, if I get bored, I can always get one of those cushy nine-to-five corporate security jobs I hear so much about, where they pay big bucks for experience like I got. Couple of months ago, my wife and I finally sat down and discussed it at some length. First time we ever seriously considered it. Decided to hold the idea in abeyance, look around, see what my options are.

Then something happens that changes my mind completely, starts the adrenaline pumping again, makes it fun to go to work, just like the old days. Monday, December 16, 8:45 A.M., we're in the squadroom catching up on paperwork when I get a call from Doris Banks, Chief Vadney's classy executive secretary.

"Is this the infamous John Rawlings?"

"Guilty as charged."

"Sex symbol of the mighty Nineteenth?"

"Your words, Doris, not mine."

"You sure have a memory for voices. It's been a while."

"Too long. How's it going down there?"

"This morning? Total bedlam since I walked in the door."

"What's happening?"

"Chief wants you and Brendan in his office, nine-thirty sharp."

I glance at my watch. "We'll be there. What's up?"

"I can't tell you on the phone, John. Orders."

"That big, huh?"

"Believe it. We've got so much brass running around here, you need Porsche-Carrera sunglasses."

"Happen to have a pair."

"Knew you would."

I pull Brendan Thomas away from his typewriter, tell him to grab his coat. Stands up, towers over me at six-foot-four, 220, not an ounce of fat, belly flat as they come. Top of that, he's handsome and almost six years younger than me. Originally from Ireland, if you please, still has a wee bit of a brogue. Best partner I ever had. We go downstairs, stop in Lieutenant Barnett's office, tell him where we're headed, he wants to know why, all we can do is shrug. Puts his head down on the desk, starts laughing; he's familiar with Vadney's antics. Can't help noticing how gray Barnett's hair's turned since we moved into this efficient modern crisis center here.

Out we go into our elegant new neighborhood, hands deep in our topcoat pockets, collars turned up, temperature's about 40°F this morning, wind from the East River's rattling all the stately rows of garbage cans. Brendan's got our unmarked four-door '84 Chevy double-parked on First Avenue near Ninety-third. Nice car, we've had it about a year now, good heater, only thing about it, they gave us a black one again. Excellent color choice for undercover work, especially when we're on surveillance duty. Only better choice that comes to mind, they could've given us NYPD blue, clamped the emergency lights on top, and painted the word COPS on the doors in Day-Glo.

It's 8:55 when we jump inside, breath hanging in the air like cigar smoke. Brendan hits the defroster, heads straight up

First to Ninety-sixth, hangs a right, finally hits the heater as we take FDR Drive south in fairly heavy traffic. Long drive down to headquarters, but at least it's partly sunny this morning and there's a nice view of the river once you get out of the tunnel under Sutton Place South. After passing East River Park, FDR gives way to the Elevated Highway, heading almost due west around the horn, and we turn off just before the Brooklyn Bridge, then northwest on Wagner past St. James Place. Compared to our new digs on Ninety-fourth, 1 Police Plaza looks like a palace straight out of Disneyland. Fourteen floors of red brick and deeply recessed windows. Only twelve years old now and still one of the most modern police facilities in the country.

We park in the big underground garage and take the elevator up to the lobby. Spacious and gleaming. Show our gold to the officer at the desk, he checks our appointment, asks us to sign in, gives each of us a red plastic ID card to clip on our lapels. Every floor in this fortress is color coded; all visitors —police as well as civilians—wear a color-coded ID pass restricting admission to the floor of that color. Take the elevator up to the top floor, fourteen, walk down one of the long, bright, antiseptic hallways, and into Doris Banks's office, a reception area just outside Vadney's corner office.

Can't help smiling when I walk in here. Before Doris was hired in October 1983 (Chief calls that age B.D.), this area looked like your typical family dentist's waiting room— fluorescent lights, framed but forgettable prints, ratty plastic furniture, six-month-old magazines. Now we're two years into A.D. and you wouldn't believe this whole routine here. I mean, we're talking Life-styles of the Rich and Famous Chief of Detectives here. And it didn't cost him a dime. Just get a load of this. You walk in, soft gold light glows from three corners where real black-marble lamps adorn real white-marble tables like something straight out of a Greek temple. You blink, you look around, you pick up on tastefully framed, individually lighted, real original oil paintings of old and new Manhattan street scenes. Far left corner's occupied by Doris's exquisite glass-and-chrome desk, which is actually a table. Sitting area, you're almost afraid to sit down over there, she's got spotless white matching couches and armchairs surrounding a large square glass-and-chrome coffee table. Take a wild guess what's on that coffee table? *Current* copies of a variety of newsmagazines and periodicals, arranged in a perfect fan, together with this morning's final editions of the *Times* and the *Journal,* neatly folded, of course. Sparkling clean cut-glass ashtrays. Under the coffee table, the final touch: Long fluffy-white sheepskin rug from New Zealand (genuine sheepskin, too, I sneaked a look at the label).

Who paid for all this class? Doris's husband, J. W. "Will" Banks, retired self-made multimillionaire. Financial wizard of some kind, I don't know. Met him one time about a year ago. Tall, lean, distinguished gentleman, originally from Canton, Ohio (Doris's hometown, too), looks you straight in the eye, grips your hand in a vise. Obviously says what he means, means what he says, that type guy, no nonsense. Bears a strong resemblance to Ty Cobb, in my opinion, same beak on him, same penetrating eyes. Probably a mean son of a bitch in business, wouldn't surprise me, you don't find many multimillionaire pussycats. Will, he got in an argument with Chief Vadney one time, couple of years back, just after Doris started. I wasn't there, Doris told me about it. Seems Will was picking her up after work, they were going to dinner and a Broadway show. Chief had some routine crisis, wanted her to work late. Will tells him very politely that they have reservations for dinner and tickets to a show. Chief tells him very politely to stick it in his ear. Will walks up to him very politely, smiles his thin-lipped Ty Cobb smile, delivers a very quiet message. Says, "Now I want you to listen to me carefully, you weird little fuck, because I'm only gonna say this once. If you ever so much as *annoy* me again, you slimebag pigfucker, I'm gonna pinch your head off," snaps his fingers fast, "like a fuckin' *bug!*" Chief's face goes pale, according to Doris, and a peculiar odor fills the air, reminds her of rotten eggs and beer. Chief smiles, shrugs, clears his throat. "Well," he says, "you two have a nice evening now." Best of my knowledge, Doris is never told to work late again. *Asked,* but never told. There's one thing the Bankses seem to have in common, must be from their puritanical upbringing in Canton, Ohio: Doris and Will, they don't take no shit from *nobody.*

All right, okay, in fairness to Vadney, you got to take into consideration how hard he worked to persuade Doris to take the job in the first place and how paranoid he is that she might up and walk out on him. I mean, this Tiffany-type talent was executive secretary to the president of American Airlines some years back, before they moved their corporate headquarters to Dallas; she "retired," then got bored, answered Vadney's ad in the *Times* that didn't mention anything about NYPD. Well, the Duke, he'd interviewed dozens of girls by then (wife Samantha insisted the successful candidate had to be a married woman), he takes one look at Doris's résumé, does a triple-take on her, wines and dines her for two solid weeks, promises her the moon with him yelping at it, finally convinces her to give it a shot. Today, story goes, he's got more respect for this little charmer than he does for Commissioner Reilly, she's effectively changed his whole professional profile. Rumor around the department, and I can easily believe it, Doris shoulders much more responsibility than any executive secretary. What she's become, in just over two years, is his strong right arm, his key assistant. Deputy Chief Mat Murphy, who should know, comes right out and says it: Doris runs the day-to-day administrative operations, all the mountains of paperwork and telephone calls that were always Vadney's weakest points. Today, story goes, he asks her advice on virtually everything, she's the only person in his department who actually has all the facts and figures at her fingertips at any given time, she even writes his speeches.

Which, predictably, almost inevitably, gives rise to another rumor, a far juicier rumor that, frankly, I have trouble swallowing. That they're having an affair. Somehow, I just can't seem to buy that. Duke and Doris? Naw. No way. Tell you the honest truth, I just don't believe Doris would give him a second look in that regard. Still, the rumor's alive and kicking, fast and dirty. Basis of it, apparently he takes her out to lunch frequently. Good restaurants, too. Business lunches, puts 'em all on the expense account. Reason I happen to know that, one of Mat Murphy's responsibilities is reviewing all expense account vouchers for the department's headquarters personnel before he submits them to the accounting office. Mat and me, we go way back, twenty-five years or so, we keep in touch. That's how I know it's the truth, he takes her out to lunch a lot. But that's not all. Nowadays, when the Duke has to work late, which is much more frequently than back in B.D., he takes her out to dinner, too. Yeah. Expensive little hideaway restaurants, mostly French, according to Mat. Big tabs, too, Chief's no cheapskate when it comes to Doris. Hate to spread rumors like this. Especially when they're so deliciously tacky. Hate to do it. Particularly about a bona fide asshole like the Duke. One thing gives me pause. Can't help wondering what a nifty little number like Doris sees in him.

But again, in fairness to Vadney, after all is said and done, he actually *does* look a hell of a lot like John Wayne. That's a fact. "The Duke" in his more mature years. And, let's face it, millions of women go for that image, they turn on to it, gives 'em multiple orgasms just seeing guys like that in action. So maybe that's what turns Doris on: Big, strong, rawboned, two-fisted, foulmouthed, fearless all-Americans. I mean, look at her husband Will. Which brings up a question I'd rather not think about. What if it's all true, what if the Duke and Doris are having a torrid affair, and what if Will gets wind of it? Horrible thought. Horrible. Listen, I met the guy, right? Says what he means, means what he says. Believe it. So what happens when *two* big, strong, rawboned, twofisted, foulmouthed, fearless all-Americans confront each other over the honor and affections of petite damsel Doris? Hot damn, Vietnam. Stallone versus Schwarzenegger. Ty Cobb gets his shot at Duke Wayne. I mean, somebody could get hurt here. Somebody could get his head pinched off like a bug. Stay tuned.

Back to reality. So now Brendan and I walk in, it's 9:25, Doris is studying the screen of her brand-new Apple IIe word processor. She glances up, gives us a fast smile, blond hair lustrous as ever, hazel eyes framed by those thick Liz Taylor lashes, about five-foot-four, 120 pounds poured curvaceously into a slim white designer pants-suit. As she stands to shake our hands, I think I catch just the hint of a sparkle of mischief in her eyes. But, hell, I could be wrong, right?

"Nice to see you, John, Brendan. Long time."

"Must be at least a year," Brendan tells her.

"So whatcha been up to?"

I take off my topcoat. "Same old stuff, Doris. Catching crooks, kicking butts. Moved into a new station house last summer."

She makes a face. "Oh, John, I heard about it, I read about it. Must've been tough for you, you loved that old house, right?"

"You should see the new one," Brendan says. "Charming neighborhood, delightful people."

"I'll bet. Hang your coats in the closet over there, I'll tell Chief Vadney you're here."

Next ten minutes, there's a continual stream of brass rushing in and out of Vadney's office, all very serious, plus a handful of FBI agents I worked with some years back. Obviously, something big is brewing. Get called in at 9:35, Jerry Grady of Press Relations is just leaving with a worried puss and a couple of boxes of NYPD "Press Packages" in blue Duo-Tang folders. Looks like he's been up all night.

So does Vadney. He's sitting at the far end of his long teakwood desk, which is actually a conference table (seats twelve), sleeves rolled up, tie yanked down, big shoulders hunched, hands to his forehead as he studies Grady's press release. Glances up at us, sky-blue Duke Wayne eyes slightly bloodshot, obviously hasn't shaved or showered. Motions for us to sit in the chairs closest to him, tosses a couple of copies of the release across the table: "Read it first, get up to speed, then we'll talk."

As I lean forward to pick up my copy, I reach under my seat and feel for his ever-present Sony TCM-600 Cassette Corder; Brendan does the same. Now we glance at each other in shocked disbelief; it's not under either seat. If the Duke's that preoccupied, we know we're about to sink our Guccis into some unusually heavy shit.

 POLICE DEPARTMENT
NEW YORK, N Y 10013

CONTACT: DET. JERRY GRADY   FOR IMMEDIATE RELEASE

PRESS RELATIONS

(212) 477-9777

GUNMEN ROB BRONX FIRM OF RECORD $8 MILLION

NEW YORK, December 16--The biggest cash robbery in United

States history took place last night in the Bronx when two

ski-masked men armed with shotguns, burglary tools, and

sophisticated electronic alarm-foiling equipment broke
into an armored-car courier company and took at least $8
million in used, untraceable bills, Chief of Detectives
Walter F. Vadney announced today.

The gunmen, who broke into the building by cutting a hole in
the roof, got away with 15 to 17 canvas bags containing $50
and $100 bills that were stacked on handcarts in the money
room at the New York Armored Car Courier Company in the
Williamsbridge section. But, according to company
officials, the holdup men left behind $20 million in $50 and
$100 bills that were also stacked on handcarts in the
building at 108-29 Cambridge Road.

The cash in the money room had been picked up by the firm
over the weekend from many clients, including $1 million
from Yonkers Raceway. It was scheduled to be delivered to
various banks today. The FBI is cooperating in the
investigation because all of the banks involved are
federally insured.

Chief Vadney disclosed that the robbers apparently used
sophisticated electronic equipment to disconnect a silent
alarm system on the roof and elsewhere in the building that
was intended to alert a private security company in another
part of the Bronx.

The fortress-like white brick building has a ground floor,
a lower level, thick steel doors, and no windows. It is
located in a mixed commercial and residential area at the
corner of Cambridge Road and Queensland Avenue in the north
Bronx.

From tire marks found in the snow, detectives believe that

late Sunday night the thieves parked a van or small truck alongside the building on the Queensland Avenue side. The robbers are believed to have climbed from the top of the truck onto the 18-foot-high roof of the structure.

After disconnecting the alarm system, the robbers used a power drill or similar tool, plus a saw, to create a circular hole, two feet in diameter, through the flat six-inch-thick steel and tar-paper roof. The thieves then tied a rope to an air-conditioner compressor on the roof, lowered themselves through the hole and down six feet to a false ceiling. After removing lightweight ceiling panels, they used the same rope to lower themselves another eight feet into an office.

In a security office next door, Russell A. Rumenik, 25, was the only guard on duty in the building. The security office contains a closed-circuit television monitor that scans the interior of the garage and the money room.

Rumenik told detectives that at 11:15 P.M., while he was watching the monitor and viewing commercial television, two men burst into his room. Both men wore dark ski masks, dark gloves, and carried shotguns, he said. Rumenik was disarmed, forced out of the room, and handcuffed to the top railing of a stairway leading to the lower level. The gunmen then went to the lower level that houses the garage and the money room.

At that point, Chief Vadney said, the robbers used a crowbar or similar tool to snap open two locks on the steel door of the money room. Inside, they apparently used bolt cutters to cut through a floor-to-ceiling chain-link fence enclosing the stacks of bags containing bills, coins, and food stamps. Lastly, the thieves dragged 15 to 17 moneybags about 25 feet through a door leading to the garage, then out the garage door to their truck.

   Mr. Rumenik had reported for work at 7 P.M. and was scheduled to be the only guard in the building until 7 A.M., Chief Vadney said. However, the robbery was reported at 2:32 A.M. today, when another guard, Fred Kells, 28, arrived and notified police. Company officials explained that the firm has a standard cross-check system that required Rumenik to make periodic telephone calls to other security personnel during his tour to verify that there were no problems. When Rumenik failed to call at the designated cross-check time of 2 A.M., Kells called him, received no reply, and, after several more attempts, rushed to the building.

When I finish reading the release, I flip through the rest of the Press Package. Not as comprehensive as others prepared by Grady, obviously not enough time to cover all the bases, but it includes a variety of good 8 × 10 B/W glossy photos of exteriors and interiors, complete with suggested captions attached. I also note that the chief appears in roughly half the photos, all taken by Grady, of course.

   Glance up, the Duke's still reading his copy, big lock of hair over his knitted brows. Notice he forms the words with his lips as he reads. Not obviously, in fairness, but he does it. Brendan's finished reading, we exchange smiles, then look around the office, see if anything's new. Same twenty-six steel-blue filing cabinets against three walls, all locked, one of which contains more than 900 Maxell UD-60 tape cassettes, all meticulously labeled and dated, of all major meetings, all important telephone calls, and "selected" visitors to his office. Which means every joker who walks in here. What he does, at least ostensibly, according to Mat, he studies the speech patterns and vocabularies of people, examines their verbal techniques, their strengths and weaknesses, for two reasons: Number one, to improve his own verbal techniques and vocabulary; number two, to get a handle on people. Mat's opinion, to get a "handle" on people means he concentrates on their weaknesses, so if he ever needs to, he can castrate the suckers verbally. Apparently got the whole idea from a management course he took in 1980, Effective Retention of Verbal Communication. FBI course, Mat took it with him. Mat suspects the real reason he tapes all this stuff, he's got a shit memory. Could be, but somehow I doubt it. Anyhow, Mat figures the guy's got at least 900 hours of conversations now, six years of 'em, he's seen the cassettes in the file. Doesn't have a clue how many people. Must be thousands by now. Brendan and me, we're on plenty of 'em.

Can't help wondering how many hours he taped Doris before she found out. Wonder what they talked about? Knowing Vadney, he'd be psychologically incapable of *not* taping her. Probably concealed it on his person during some of those intimate lunches and dinners, right? Maybe other places, too. Like bedrooms? Naw. Naw, nobody'd be that sick, to keep a tape recorder running in the bedroom, in your coat pocket, say, on the chair next to the bed. Naw. With all those passionate, juicy things being said? No way. Not even Vadney would stoop that low, pull a sicko-whacko stunt like that. Right? Must've made fantastic listening. Till she found out.

Chief finally gets to the last page of the release, Brendan and I exchange glances, flip to the last page, pretend to be reading as he snaps his folder shut. Now we can feel his lightning-fast speed-reading sky-blues on us as we struggle through to the bitter end.

He leans forward, clears his throat, speaks hoarsely. "Needless to say, this is a very major case here, I'm already starting to get pressure from Commissioner Reilly, and I've been up half the night. Reason I called—"

"We knew it was a big one," I tell him.

"Huh?"

"We knew it was a big one before we even read the release."

"You did?"

"Yes, sir."

He frowns. "Doris tell you? I gave her explicit—"

"No, sir, Chief. She didn't tell us anything."

"Who told you then?"

"Nobody, sir. Nobody told us anything."

"Then how the fuck did ya find *out?*"

"Intuition, sir. Sorry I interrupted, go ahead, I didn't—"

"Now, wait a minute, Rawlings." He blinks, frowns, rubs the stubble on his chin. "I've been up half the night, I'm a little groggy, forgive me. But how the fuck could your intuition tell you something like *that?*"

"Absence of your tape recorder, sir."

"Absence of my—?"

"Tape recorder. I know you always make it a strict rule to tape important meetings. Which, personally, I think is an excellent idea. Anyhow, I simply reasoned that if you were too preoccupied to tape this meeting, it must be an unusually big case, that's all. Sorry I interrupted, I don't normally do that, as you know."

He sits back now, closes his eyes, rubs the lids carefully. "Pressure at this level is tremendous, Rawlings. Tremendous. You got to learn to cover your ass nine ways from October." Opens his eyes, blinks at me. "Y'follow me, buddy?"

"Yes, sir."

"Nine ways from October."

"Yes, sir. So where is it?"

"Where's what?"

"Your tape recorder, sir."

"Oh." He gives in to a yawn now, almost luxuriously, an all-out, wide-open-mouthed, arms-stretching, eyes-watering, nose-snorting, teeth-gleaming, air-sucking, completely uninhibited extravagance. Then, following a long, loud exhale: "It's broken."

"I see." I yawn now, a quickie, can't help it.

Chief nods, gazes off into space. "Somebody broke the fucker on me. It was a good one, too, the best. Expensive piece of equipment. It's been a valuable part of this job for—about six years."

Brendan leans forward, all serious. "Chief Vadney, sir, may I offer a suggestion?"

"Yeah, sure."

"You say somebody broke it on you, sir. You should order that person to get it repaired at his own expense, sir. Or to buy you a new one, if it's beyond repair. It seems only fair, sir."

He turns to Brendan, eyelids at half-mast. "I'm afraid it's beyond repair, Thomas. Way beyond repair. It got thrown through a fuckin' window."

"Oh," Brendan says. "Ah, Jesus, I'm sorry to hear that, sir."

"Here?" I ask innocently.

"No." Stares into space again. "Fell twenty-two floors into an alley. Smashed to smithereens." Thinks about it a while, then sits up straight, glances at his Omega Astronaut Moon Watch, seems to collect himself. "It was a case I was working on, nobody's fault, just haven't gotten the time to buy another. Now, to get back to what I was saying, the reason I called you two men in, I've decided I could use your expertise on this robbery. Frankly, I liked the work you did on that big hotel robbery back in eighty-one, then that big diamond robbery in eighty-two, then you collared that mass-rapist killer back in eighty-three. Excellent investigative work all the way, very impressive."

We thank him modestly.

"Helluva team. *Hell*uva team." Picks up his folder, frowns at it. "You guys always—somehow, you guys always seem to stumble into the biggies. Must have the luck of the Irish. It's just unbelievable to me, it really is. You stumble in, you bumble around, you abuse every rule in the book, you disobey direct orders from me—I'm talking about you, particularly, Rawlings—and some way, somehow, you manage to pick up on some halfass, rinky-dink clues that everybody else and his brother overlooked, using your intuition or radar or whatever the fuck you use, and collar the perps. Total fuckin' blind luck, most of it, the blind leading the blind. But you get the job done, I'll give you that."

We maintain a humble silence.

Tosses his folder on the table. "This case, we got the Joint Robbery Task Force on it, we got the Bronx Robbery Unit on it. Total manpower allocation of twenty-seven detectives and eight crack FBI agents. Thirty-five experienced men. Know what they came up with so far? Although I admit it's early in the game, but you know what they came up with after working out there half the night and well into the morning?"

"What?" we ask.

"Squat."

"Squat?"

"Squat. Doesn't surprise me. Know why? I'll tell you why. Too many cooks spoil a stew, that's why. Particularly when some of 'em are FBI agents. That's why, as of this minute, I'm relieving both of you from all precinct duty to head up a special team. A special team to work *independently* from all the other clowns assigned to this case. I'm talking full-time here. I'm talking unlimited overtime, within reason. Rawlings, you're team supervisor. Thomas, you're assistant team supervisor. Select four more men. Report directly to me."

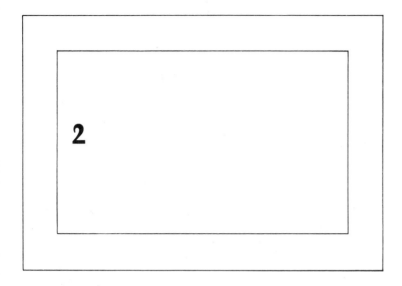

2

LIEUTENANT BARNETT doesn't exactly turn cartwheels when we tell him, especially when we request permission to borrow two more men from our own Nineteenth for the special-assignment team, Big John Daniels and Nuzhat Idrissi, but he's been through this routine before with the chief, he knows the politics and priorities involved. Next we select the two top detectives from the Seventeenth, Rick Telfian and Gene Thalheimer. We've all worked together on special assignments before, we have a lot in common, we always manage to have some fun. First order of business, 11:30 that morning, we all meet in the squadroom of the Nineteenth, Brendan and I give each of them a copy of the press release, sit them down, ask them to read it carefully. Give you a quick rundown on these guys. Big John Daniels, used to be my regular partner years ago before he got transferred to the Major Crimes Unit, he's fifty-three now, been a detective sergeant since 1957, came up the hard way, same as me. Big eloquent Irishman, six-foot-two, 205 pounds, terrific dry sense of humor. Ever see Daniel

Patrick Moynihan when he's telling a joke? Those elfin eyes and impish grin? That's him, that's Big John. Talk about diametric opposites, Nuzhat Idrissi is an Arab, born in Nazareth, raised in Jerusalem where his father was chief of police. Naturalized citizen, of course, been in the department around twenty-eight years. Early fifties, heavyset, dark complexion, neatly trimmed mustache. Still speaks with traces of an Arabic accent, but he's a classy dresser, excellent undercover man, no crook in his right mind would make this guy as a cop. Now, Telfian and Thalheimer, they're partners in the Seventeenth, they're always our first choice outside our own precinct, when they're available. Rick Telfian, known him for years, scrappy little Armenian, about thirty-nine or forty, still plays semipro baseball, shortstop, stays in top shape. Far as I know, he still doesn't smoke or drink, has a nice family, only one problem: Kid's a gambler. Swears he isn't, swears he's reformed now, but this kid will bet on anything that moves. I mean, he'll lay you odds on Billy Martin's next fight. To round out our all-WASP team here, Gene Thalheimer is Jewish, of course, went to Cardinal Hayes High with Rick, year ahead of him, hell of a football player, first-string all-city quarterback. Handsome guy, Gene, cerebral-type ladies' man, reminds me of Gene Kelly in his prime.

Soon as they read the release and study the photos, all of us get on the phones and check with our regular informants, dangle heavy bread, try to find out the word on the street. We come up empty. Nobody out there seems to have even a sniff on this one.

After lunch we drive up to the scene of the crime. We all pile in one of the undercover vans from the squad pool because, with no solid leads at all, we want to re-create the heist for ourselves. Telfian's the wheel-man, loves to drive, used to be a real car nut before he got married and had the three boys. Follows First Avenue up to Ninety-sixth, hangs a right, gets on FDR Drive, streaks north in relatively light traffic all the way to the mouth of the Harlem River, crosses over, takes Bruckner Boulevard across the Bronx River, then due north on the Bronx River Parkway all the way. Now we got snow all around us, that's what happens this time of year, soon as you get out of Manhattan. Passing through the big open areas around the Bronx Zoo and the Botanical Gardens, there's a solid layer of snow on the ground, result of a couple of small storms first week in December. Same storms hit Manhattan, of course, but, except for the parks, it doesn't stick. Off to our left, Woodlawn Cemetery has a blanket of it, still clean and white, but when we get off the parkway and head southeast on 233rd Street in the Williamsbridge section, forget it, streets are all plowed and clogged with dirty snow, slush, ice, few sidewalks are even shoveled, your typical north Bronx Christmas card.

Corner of Cambridge and Queensland, the New York Armored Car Courier Company sticks out like a clean white ice-cream factory in the midst of your basic soot-gray, rundown commercial-residential neighborhood. Must say, building inspires confidence, what can I tell you? Telfian pulls in the small parking lot. It's now 1:45, but the lot's still jammed with all kinds of police vehicles, TV equipment vans, other press cars, unmarked cars, parked at all angles, the usual chaos. We pile out, trudge through the slush and ankle-deep dirty snow (none of us had the smarts to bring boots), walk around the familiar NYPD wooden barricades out front. Two big steel doors. One to the right has no knob; other one is guarded by a young uniformed cop. Show him our gold, in we go, stomp the snow off our soaking-wet shoes in the little reception area. Well, I mean, the carpet in here, looks like it was once a clean tan, it'll never be the same, so we figure, hell, we're innocent latecomers, don't look at us. FBI probably started it.

Nose around a little first, get our bearings. Narrow hall leads to four small offices where about a dozen members of the intrepid JRTF are still sitting around, studying client files, drinking coffee, smoking, goofing off. Turn right, walk through an open steel door, we're into the security area, including the office with the closed-circuit TV monitors where the lone guard was stationed. Office next door is where the crooks entered. We know because it's filled with those nice polite ladies and gentlemen of the media. Ceiling panels are missing, we can see the hole in the roof exactly fourteen feet up and the heavy rope is still hanging from it, extending all the way to the floor. Seems like the crooks knew exactly the length rope they needed. Outside that office, open area leading to an open steel door to the lower level. Outside the door is the metal railing where they handcuffed the guard. We go down the stairs. Whole place down here is crawling with uniformed cops, detectives, FBI agents, reporters, photographers, TV cameramen, sound technicians, light technicians, correspondents, directors, the whole shot. I mean, we're talking major, major national news here, biggest cash heist in U.S. history, network TV lead-story stuff tonight by Brokaw, Rather, and Jennings; front-page splashes in the *Times, News, Post, USA Today*—who knows, maybe even the *Journal;* cover-story possibilities for *Time* and *Newsweek,* if Christmas stories don't preclude it. I stand back, take it all in, light a cigar, savor the excitement of the Big Apple at its best. Beats the crap out of sitting at my new tin desk.

Now a sad thought creeps into my happy brain. Sad. Oh, no, I don't want to think about this. *Chief* should be in the midst of all this, he'd be in his element right this minute, barking orders, giving statements, reluctantly granting exclusive interviews, directing the directors. I mean, you got to feel for him. Poor son of a buck just got here too early. Way too early. Major media people were obviously still asleep, three o'clock in the morning, second-string skeleton crews were goofing off, as usual: North *Bronx,* Grady? Y'gotta be kiddin'! Y'askin' us to get a full crew up to the north Bronx at three

o'clock in the fuckin' *mornin'?!* Chief probably waited out
here just as long as he possibly could, checking his watch,
pacing up and down, screaming at Grady to keep bugging the
networks, the papers, the magazines, the wire services, eating
his poor palpitating heart out. I can see him now, I can hear
him now: "Tell 'em to call 'em at *home,* for Christ's sake, tell
'em to get the lazy, worthless fuckers outa *bed!"* Sad. Very
sad. Hate to think about it. Blows his whole psychology of
effective press relations that he's worked his ass off to perfect
all these years: Maximum utilization of time and space within
given parameters of minimum leadtimes necessary for meeting
deadlines in both broadcast and print journalism. Blows it
right out of the snow. Truth is, this robbery just happened at
an inappropriate *time,* that's all. Caught police and press with
their collective pants down, literally. Inconsiderate ski-
masked amateurs. If they'd had a little more patience and
made the effort to steal all the remaining moneybags, all $20
million left behind, which would've made the grand total $28
million (keep that figure in mind), there's no question the extra
time required would've made a serious difference here. But no.
Not these clowns. They quit too early. Lazy good-for-noth-
ings. Never amount to anything.

More important, they got no sense of making heistory here.
I've been keeping stats on the subject for years, got the exact
dates, places, facts, figures, all that. Start with the smallest,
which was considered big at the time: January 1950, Brink's
armored-car robbery in Boston, they grab $2.5 million, but
just $1.2 million in cash; May 1981, The Great Hotel Robbery,
the Champs-Elysées heist in New York, they take $3.4 million
in cash, jewelry, and securities from safe-deposit boxes; October 1974, Purolator Security warehouse in Chicago, they lift
$4.3 million in cash; December 1978, Lufthansa cargo hangar,
JFK Airport in New York, they snatch $5.8 million in cash
and jewels; August 1963, England, The Great Train Robbery,
aboard the Glasgow-London Royal Mail Express, twenty to

thirty men get away with $8 million in cash and diamonds; July 1976, Société Générale Bank in Nice, France, they boost $10 million in cash, gems, and securities from the vault; and finally, the biggie of 'em all to date, April 1982, The Great Diamond Robbery, Heritage Gallery in New York, they get $11.5 million in diamonds, including the legendary North Star (72.4 carats), largest privately owned diamond in the world.

Of course, if you check *The Guinness Book of Records,* you find out they list the greatest robbery on record as that of the German National Gold Reserves, Bavaria, June 1945, but nobody's ever come up with an actual bottom-line figure or even proved it ever took place. Story goes, it was supposed to have been pulled by a combine of U.S. military personnel and German civilians and the take was said to be 730 gold bars, valued at roughly $8 million at the time, plus six bags of bank notes and twenty-five boxes of platinum bars and precious stones. Total? Nobody has a clue. And nobody was ever brought to trial. Fact is, historians today strongly suggest the whole thing was an elaborate hoax, a Soviet propaganda invention to embarrass and discredit the U.S. Administration during the early period of the quadripartite control.

In any event, the point I'm trying to bring out here, these two ski-masked men, it's obvious to me that they have no sense of making heistory. All right, granted, the $8 million in cold cash is a national (and probably a world) record, but how long can it last? My opinion, it'll be broken in our lifetimes, easy. On the other hand, if they hadn't been in such a hurry, if they hadn't lost their nerve, which I suspect they did, they could've grabbed all $28 million. Now, that's serious cash, that's a solid world-class record to last a while, right? What I'm saying, if you've got guts enough to pull a heist like this, if you're going to take the risk anyway, why not go all the way?

Sorry for the digression; happens to people as they grow old and approach senility. Let's see, where was I? Oh, yeah, so we're down in the lower level now, picking up on the media dream merchants as they record every dramatic detail for posterity. Floor-to-ceiling chain-link fence has a big jagged door cut into it. Dozens and dozens of white canvas money-bags still stacked in there on handcarts. Now I glance around, notice the large convex mirrors up in the four corners, for the closed-circuit TV cameras, have all been turned up to face the ceiling. Why go to all that trouble when you're wearing ski masks? Last part of the orientation, we stroll into the dimly lighted garage. Six dirty gray armored trucks, all neatly parked, spaces for two more.

Now we got our bearings, next order of business, we go back upstairs and through the security area into the hall with the four business offices. I figure the owner or general manager or whoever's in charge probably has the corner office, even though there aren't any windows. Turns out I'm right. Door's open and he's in there with a couple of FBI agents. Reason I know they're FBI men at a glance, seems funny in this day and age, but these guys are still wearing dark sincere suits and ties, just like they had to in the days of Edgar Hoover. FBI dress code's been relaxed since then, of course, but nine times out of ten, you see agents like these at the scene of a robbery, you know they're CPAs, they're studying the firm's books, they rarely get their hands dirty.

Don't know how long we'll have to wait, so I tell the others to go ahead, use the coffee machine in the reception area. Short time later, FBI agents stand up, put away their calculators, shake hands with the man, leave their cards, depart quietly. Now I go in, identify myself, the man does likewise. He's the owner, name of John Holland, tall, well-built man in his early forties, curly brown hair graying at the temples, high forehead, light brown eyes, very strong chin. Wears a white turtleneck sweater, brown cords. Thing about this guy, quick first impression, despite the fact that he has brown eyes, I just can't help connecting his face and general physical character-istics to those of Paul Newman. A young Paul Newman, maybe playing Fast Eddie Felson in *The Hustler.* Remember that, 1961? Not that this guy gives the impression of being a hustler, far from it, but remember those closeups of Newman's eyes, the transparent blue eyes? That's this kid.

"What can I do for you, Detective Rawlings?"

"I'm here with a special team from Chief Vadney's office. We'd like your permission to just go through the motions of reenacting the crime for ourselves. In other words, drive our van up to the side, climb on the roof, lower ourselves down the rope, see if we can add anything to what's already known."

He shrugs, speaks tiredly. "It's been done to death, but, sure, go ahead."

"Thank you. Afterward, we'd like to ask you a few questions, if it's convenient for you."

"No problem, I'll be here."

Okay, Telfian scoots off to get the van, the rest of us go outside, squeak through the snow to the Queensland Avenue side. We know exactly where the thieves parked their truck or van because, of course, the JRTF carefully dug up the hard-packed snow here to make plaster casts of the tire tracks, leaving two rectangles of wet black asphalt. All we have to do is guide Telfian in.

Sun peeks through for a short time, snow throws a dirty glare, can't tell my breath from my cigar smoke. Brendan gets on top of the van, tosses a grappling hook up over the low ledge that borders the roof, secures it easily first try. He climbs up the side first, makes it look effortless. In the apartment house across the street, people start appearing at the windows, women mostly, they've undoubtedly seen the same reenactment a number of times, I can almost hear them in my head: Hilda, c'meah, y'gotta getta load a deez assholes heah, doin' it *again,* awready, for Chrissake, just *lookit* 'em! I mean I gotta mind to call Ed Koch an ax 'im: *Dis* is wayah *tax* dollahs go?

Dis is wayah. Now it's my turn, I grab the rope, scuttle up

the side of the building, cigar clamped in my teeth, hang a leg over the edge, graceful as Rambo, I can almost hear the Bronx cheers from the windows. Brendan, he's a comfort, he breaks up as he grabs me. Telfian and Thalheimer, they're up in nothing flat, commando style. Nuzhat, he makes me feel better, he gives an unintentional imitation of Oliver Hardy (mustache and all) trying to climb nonchalantly up a wall of ice. Nuz and me, we're really too old for this crap, but we hang tough. Brendan pulls him over the ledge, he dusts himself off with great dignity as he catches his breath. Me, I give him a Stan Laurel nod of approval, feel like saying, "Good, Ollie," but somehow manage to control myself. Big John's last up, elfin eyes sparkling.

Most of the flat roof is covered by a thin layer of snow, of course, except for a series of wet tar rectangles where the JRTF dug out footprints for plaster casts. The rope used by the robbers is tied to a steel bar on an air-conditioner compressor that's around fifteen feet from the hole. I get down on my hands and knees and inspect the circular two-foot-diameter hole, just about wide enough to accommodate an average-sized man. What I see really surprises me. Words from the press release come back to me: ". . . the flat six-inch-thick steel and tar-paper roof." That's what I'd visualized, but it's not what I see. Instead, what we have here is about a six-inch-thick layer of tar, then a relatively thin layer of sheet metal. Grady obviously took some clown's word for it. Also, I'm not at all convinced the crooks used "a power drill or similar tool." My opinion, looks like they could've used a long Phillips screwdriver and a hammer just as easily; would've made less noise. Grady was right about one thing, they used a saw to join the punch-holes and lift off the slab of roof. Slab itself is missing, undoubtedly taken to the lab for examination.

First question that comes to mind: What building contractor would be dumb enough (or smart enough) to construct a solid brick and reinforced concrete fortress with no windows, thick steel doors, and a roof that could be penetrated with a screwdriver? As we lower ourselves down the rope into the building, I wonder vaguely if anybody else has asked that obvious question. Must have. Total of twenty-seven detectives and eight FBI agents working on the case for close to twelve hours now, orchestrated by Chief Vadney himself? You kidding?

Owner John Holland tells me no, as a matter of fact, nobody's asked the question as yet. He's intrigued by this angle, gets out the actual files, shows me himself. Building's fairly new, constructed in 1981 by R.T. Mustafa & Company Inc., large builder and contractor headquartered in the Time & Life Building, Manhattan. Architects were Harris & Levine. Three engineering subcontractors: Zimmer & Brody (mechanical); Trent & Wolfe (structural); Merton Associates (electrical).

Off we go in the dirty snow, back to the Nineteenth Precinct, switch to our regular cars, agree to meet back here in the squadroom to compare notes around five o'clock. Telfian and Thalheimer pay a visit to architects Harris & Levine; Daniels and Idrissi go to see structural engineers Trent & Wolfe; Brendan and me head down to the Time & Life Building to speak with R.T. Mustafa himself or a reasonable facsimile thereof.

If you remember when Avenue of the Americas was still officially called Sixth Avenue, you also know how drastically it's changed in the past twenty-five years. Back in the late 1950s, the Time & Life Building was the only real skyscraper on Sixth. I mean, today it's just another forty-eight-story aluminum-and-glass job in a canyon of similar modern office buildings, but back then it was considered special, a real tourist attraction. I actually saw it go up from a gigantic hole in the ground. Remember one time, autumn of 1960, I interviewed a *Time* magazine reporter in here, first time I ever went in the place, I'd only been a detective two years, I was twenty-seven then. This kid, he couldn't have been any older than I was, he had an office on the twenty-third floor facing due west. Real good view of the Hudson and the famous transatlantic cruise ships docked there from Forty-second Street to Fifty-seventh. What a sight that was. Don't recall much about the interview, but I remember those ships vividly.

Brendan and I double-park on Sixth (I still call it that, I don't give a shit), between Fiftieth and Fifty-first, stick the orange ID card up on the dash, stating we're on police business, walk through the little plaza and into the spacious lobby, look up R.T. Mustafa & Company on the big glass directory on the wall. Suite's on the forty-sixth floor, business must be booming for this guy. Up we go in one of the thirty-two elevators (in case you ever get that question in Trivial Pursuit), this one's an express to forty-five, stops my ears up, have to hold my nose and blow air all the way, gets a few raised eyebrows from MBA corporate Yuppies in the car, so I make it a point to blow harder, make it audible for 'em.

As luck would have it, Mustafa's suite occupies a part of the building's west side, so I'm anxious to see his view of the old docks, what's left of them. Floor-to-ceiling glass doors open to a tastefully appointed reception area with soft lighting, thick gray carpeting, and an attractive young receptionist at a glass-and-chrome table. She looks up from her magazine and smiles.

"May I help you?"

I show my gold. "Detectives Rawlings and Thomas from the Nineteenth Precinct. Like to see Mr. Mustafa, please."

"I'm sorry, Mr. Mustafa's out of town. Could anyone else be of assistance?"

"Who's in charge right now?" Brendan asks.

"Executive Vice President Orloski."

I give the kid my card. "Would you tell him we'd like to ask him a few routine questions?"

"Certainly. It's a woman, Susan Orloski." She picks up the phone, punches two buttons on the console, glances at my card. "Miss Orloski, Detective John Rawlings, Nineteenth Precinct, and another detective would like to see you." Kid listens. "I don't know, they wanted to see Mr. Mustafa. Right. Thank you." Hangs up. "Please have a seat, Miss Orloski will be with you in a minute. There's a coat closet over there to your left."

We thank her kindly, hang up our topcoats, straighten our ties, try to shine our wet shoes on the backs of our trousers. Take our seats now, admire the receptionist's legs from behind our magazines.

Short time later we have a pleasant surprise. Big mahogany door to the right swings open and out comes this kid with the face and figure of a top fashion model, makes the receptionist pale in comparison. Relatively short but thick sandy-blond hair, about five-foot-six, 115 pounds, wears a light-blue, exquisitely tailored designer pants-suit, matching medium-height heels. Smiles as she walks briskly toward us, face has a delicate architecture, high cheekbones, brilliant blue eyes, thin lips, almost perfect teeth. Goes directly to Brendan, of course, holds out a slender manicured hand.

"I'm Susan Orloski."

"Detective Brendan Thomas. Pleasure to meet you."

She turns to me, narrows her eyes, grips my hand very firmly. "And you're Detective Rawlings."

"Correct."

"Will you follow me, please?"

With pleasure. She takes my card from the receptionist, leads us through the mahogany door, walks with a graceful buoyancy down a wide, thickly carpeted hallway, turns left, turns right, her office is next to the big corner one that I assume to be Mustafa's. Talk about an office reflecting a person's personality? You walk in here, you get the immediate impression that you've stepped into her living room. Paintings, prints, watercolors, silk-screens, all against delicate blue wallpaper; no diplomas on these walls, although I'm sure she's earned her share. Aubusson carpets, glass display cabinets with art objects and Fabergé knickknacks. A screen cuts off a sitting area to our left: Matching pale-pink upholstered couches and three fancy chairs surround twin glass coffee tables, one holding an ashtray and a folded newspaper, the other holding a silver cigarette box and a table lighter. Soft lamplight only. Desk? Forget it. Closest she comes to that is an old marble-topped table near the three tall windows facing west. White curtains filter the late-afternoon sun. Before we sit, I part the curtains slightly and take a squint at the ravaged old docks. Exactly twenty-five years since I've seen them from this angle. Doesn't seem anywhere near that long. But it is.

Puts me in a melancholy mood. When we sit down, I take a close look at Orloski. Age? I'd guess early thirties. Conservative makeup, elegant but understated earrings, necklace, bracelet, watch. Who was it said, "We see, but we do not observe"? Tell you what, times like this, I'm glad I'm a trained observer. I try not to stare, of course, I leave that to Brendan. Orloski, you look at her eyes, you know she's used to all this.

"I know why you gentlemen are here." Picks up the neatly folded newspaper from the coffee table. "In fact, I've been expecting you." Snaps the paper open, hands it to me. "I've already called Mr. Mustafa and alerted him."

It's the early edition of the *Post,* which neither of us have seen. Big bold headline reads:

$8M BRONX HEIST
ALL-TIME RECORD
But Gunmen Leave $20M Behind!

Below that is a shot of Vadney climbing a ladder to the roof (courtesy of Grady), flanked by a schematic "cutaway" diagram of the building with arrows tracing the route taken by the gunmen. Story begins on page three with photographs of the interior. I hand the paper to Brendan.

"Naturally," I tell Orloski, "we're conducting routine investigations of every firm involved in the construction of the building."

She glances at the *Post*. "I read the entire article to Mr. Mustafa this afternoon. He wants to cooperate in any way possible."

"Where is he now?" Brendan asks.

"In Florida with his family. I'll give you his address and telephone number." She gets up, goes to the table by the windows, jots something on a pad, rips off the page, comes back and hands it to me:

Fontainebleau Hilton
4441 Collins Avenue
Miami Beach, FL 33140
(305)538-2000

Glances at her watch. "You can call him from here, if you want to. I'll be glad to leave the room and give you privacy."

"Appreciate it, but it won't be necessary," I tell her. "We have teams interviewing the architects and structural engineers right now. I'd rather wait for those reports before I talk with him."

"I see. All right, I plan to speak with him tonight anyway, so I'll tell him to expect your call—when?"

"Probably tomorrow morning."

She stands, hands each of us her card. "If there's anything else I can do for you, please don't hesitate to call."

We thank her, she walks us back to the reception area, waits for us to put on our coats, even sees us to the door. Classy little lady, Susan Orloski. Cool confidence based on bedrock granite. Not a pretentious bone in her body.

My wife's been telling me all about this "new" corporate

scene for at least ten years now. Trouble is, my line of work, you don't get many opportunities to see top women executives in their element. What you don't see, you can't observe. Dates me, I know, but it's more complicated than that.

Most of the time I love my work, but there are very serious side effects to being a cop in this city. Side effects you can't really see in true perspective until you've been around a while. When you deal with lowlife who represent the worst aspects of our society—and I mean the worst—and you do it on a day-to-day basis, routinely, for fifteen, twenty years, your perspective on society in general can get altered. Badly altered. I'm telling you. Ask any cop who's been around this city a while, male or female, they'll tell you. Only remedy that seems to work, for me, for most of the veteran cops I know, is to develop a sense of humor—which is to say, a better perspective. That's right. Not to make a joke out of the job, I've never done that, I'll never do that, I have far too much pride in my work, in my career, it's been my whole life. But, the thing is, you try not to let the job get you down. If you do, if you let it get to you, if you let it alter your perspective on ordinary people, then I say, forget it, turn in the badge and the gun. And I feel strongly about this. Because a seriously depressed cop can be a dangerous cop. I've seen it happen enough to know. So, what I'm saying, you try to develop a certain sense of humor about who you are, what you're doing, and why. Because, in the meantime, life goes on in this city, relatively "straight" life, and it changes constantly, just like the skyline, corporate life, social life, changing life-styles that cops like me just don't get many opportunities to observe at close range on a day-to-day basis. That's why days like this are a refreshing kick in the head to old grunts like me. Just wish I had more like 'em.

Drive back to the precinct, meet with the others, 5:15, now we get some very intriguing information, several extremely curious pieces of the puzzle to play around with. Can't believe this shit, things are happening much faster than normal, people involved in slapping up this building must be running scared, they're telling us stuff they'd normally filter through their attorneys in language it'd take us a week to translate. Or, better yet, and more logical, maybe their attorneys advised them to cooperate right up front, get it all out on the table before anybody gets the preposterous idea that somebody might've done something wrong here.

Here's what goes down: Telfian and Thalheimer find out from executives at Harris & Levine, the architectural firm, that final approved specifications for the roof called for a one-foot-thick layer of reinforced concrete topped by a six-inch-thick layer of roofing tar. They have the original blueprints and documentation to prove it. Daniels and Idrissi are told by executives at Trent & Wolfe, the structural engineers, that the building contractor, R.T. Mustafa & Company, was seriously over budget during the final stages of this project and ordered them to depart from the roof's blueprint specifications as a cost-cutting expedient. They have a series of memos signed by Mustafa himself to prove the point. Copies of which they've given us.

Last order of business for the day, we have to write our reports, of course, so while the others groan and grab available typewriters around the squadroom, I make a call to Chief Vadney's office to set up an appointment. I mean, as team supervisor, I get perks like this once in a while, I'm relieved of such time-consuming drudgery as pecking away at a broken-down reconditioned manual typewriter. Yeah, we *still* got *them* in this high-tech modern palace here. It's 5:25, Chief's regular shift is eight to four, same for Doris, but today, who knows?

"Chief Vadney's office."

"Hey, Doris, you sound tired."

"Tired? *Tired,* John? No. No, whatever gave you that idea?"

"As a detective, I detected a note of gravel in your voice."

"Gravel? Try cinders. I'm a total burnout."

"Know what you need?"

She laughs. "Yeah. Yeah, I *know* what I need. But tonight I'll settle for a couple of very dry vodka martinis."

"Now you're talking. Don't suppose the chief's still there."

"Ha! He went home at three. Basket case."

"How's he look for tomorrow morning?"

"Let's see. Commissioner at eight-fifteen; staff meeting at nine. I'll put you down for nine-thirty. All six of you?"

"The whole first team."

"Got a lead already, Sherlock?"

"Was Professor Moriarty the Napoleon of crime?"

You know how certain days come along once in a while, you don't want them to end? I'm walking west on Ninety-sixth toward Lexington, it's cold and dark, wind's whipping through my topcoat, I got my head down like everybody else, hands deep in my pockets, but I'm happy tonight, feel almost light-headed. Ninety-sixth Street is all Christmas lights, just like the posh neighborhoods. All the little shops and stores seem warm and bright. I don't even mind standing there with the crowds waiting for the traffic lights to change. Christmas spirit? No, although I feel that too. It's difficult to put into words. For the first time in months I'm alive, excited about my job, about my life, about this overcrowded, dirty, cold, fantastic city. Feeling doesn't fade when I get on the subway either. Surprises me, it really does. Don't mind the crush of bodies, the damp smell, the lurch and sway, the lights, the screech of steel when we brake. Glance around, people are reading the *Post,* and there's the headline, big and bold, and Vadney on the ladder. I'd be a liar if I didn't admit that's part of the excitement, being with these people, watching them read about the biggest cash heist ever, watching their faces, wondering what they're thinking. Knowing I'm involved, knowing we might already be on to something important. Kick in the head.

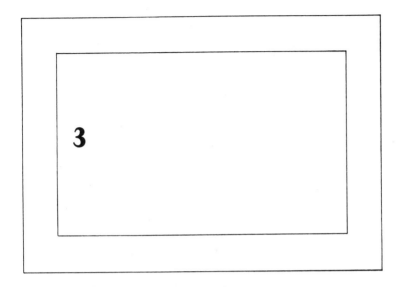

3

VENOMOUS VINNIE CASANDRA, managing editor of the *News,* draws first blood next morning, December 17, with a simple front-page monster headline designed to have a subtle, cerebral impact on the city's sophisticates:

HEY, RAMBO,
SO WHODUNIT?

Directly below that, occupying at least half the page, is an all-too-familiar *News* file photo, an all-too-candid closeup of Vadney, big eyes bulging, bent right forefinger inserted into his right nostril in such a manner as to suggest that the man might reasonably be engaged in probing the interior. Caption below that reads: "He's got a biggie! Chief of Detectives Walter F. Vadney contemplates his next move after record $8-million cash heist in Bronx. (Page 3)"

Typical cheap shot, my opinion, but you have to understand the sordid background. Casandra's had a smoldering beef with the chief since 1981, just after that robbery at the Hotel Champs-Elysées. What triggered it, among other things, was innocent enough. Casandra started a cartoon series to put pressure on Vadney and Mayor Koch to get their act together. Title was "How'm I Doin'?" Public response was fantastic. Even Koch liked it, not that he's ever been accused of being partial to friendly publicity. Chief, he's never been noted for his quick and easy sense of humor. Considers the series an unwarranted personal attack on his integrity. Thinks Casandra is out to get him, that his job might be in jeopardy. Makes the unfortunate tactical error of venting his spleen head-to-head. Calls Casandra directly, "demands" the series be dumped immediately for the good of the department. Casandra doesn't appreciate demands, cites the First Amendment. Chief blows his cool, calls him a nasty name. Casandra calls him one back. Before they're finished, quite a few genealogical pedigrees are hotly debated. Next day, cartoon series continues, of course, prime space now, till the case is eventually cracked. But no way is the hatchet buried. Casandra's always coiled for a biggie legit excuse to strike again.

Now he's got one. Turn to page three today, cheek by jowl to the news story, the cartoon series is renewed in tacky splendor, same thrilling cast of characters, but the title's been changed to reflect the trends: "Rambo Bambo: Bad Blood, Take One." This morning's opener shows our two heroes in the "money room," peering out from behind twenty gigantic moneybags, each marked "$1 Million." Duke-faced but musclebound Chief Rambo Bambo wears a headband to contain unruly shoulder-length locks, his glistening bare chest is crossed with a bandoleer stuffed with fat bullets, and he's holding what appears to be an oversized Uzi. Mayor's talk balloon says, "You sure they're coming' back tonight?"

Rambo Bambo's talk balloon says, "Ey, wimp, would I lie to ya?"

We show up at headquarters, 9:15, best sincere suits, armed with our three reports on yesterday's revelations, three Xerox copies each, all flawlessly typed, three-hole punched, looking as official as shit in NYPD-blue Duo-Tang 5-3558 presentation folders. Hang up our coats, straighten our ties, recline in the quiet elegance of Doris's softly lighted reception area. Staff meeting breaks up half a cigar later, Doris comes out with Mat Murphy and Jerry Grady, walks over to us in a figure-flattering pale-pink designer pants-suit, smiles like maybe she slept like a baby after those vodka martinis.

"Good morning, A-Team!" she says.

"Good morning," all six of us say.

I hold up a copy of the *News,* clear my throat. "What's his reaction to this?"

Rolls her hazel eyes. "Don't ask. It took the better part of a half hour just to calm him down." She glances at his closed door, lowers her voice. "What did it, finally, I told him I thought he looked kind of sexy as Rambo Bambo. He stopped ranting and raving, he said, 'Yeah?' I said, 'Absolutely.' He looked at the cartoon again, he said, 'You really think so?' I said, 'Ey, wimp, would I lie to ya?' "

Muffled laughter from the gallery.

"Well, that loosened him up a little," she tells us. "So I said, 'Walt, let's face some obvious facts here.' I said, 'Your face is familiar to millions of people in this city, they've seen you in the media for five solid years now, ever since that Champs-Elysées robbery hit the fan.' I told him, I said, 'Walt, that's when you hit the jackpot.' I said, 'Admit it, that's when you hit the media jackpot, you even had that long interview on "Sixty Minutes," for Christ's sake.' I said, 'That was the turning point, that's when you became the most visible chief of detectives this city's ever had.' I said, 'Look at the positive side of this thing in the paper today.' He said, 'Positive side?' I said, *'Positive* side.' I told him, I said, 'When the newspaper with the largest daily circulation in the country decides to do a cartoon series with you as the star—not Mayor Koch anymore, but you, Rambo Bambo—when that happens, that's when you know you've arrived. That's when you know you're a household name, that's when you know you've made the critical jump from private individual to public domain.' I said, 'Walt, think about that a minute.' I said, 'Do you realize how much money any public relations firm in this city would pay to get this kind of exposure for any of their clients—I'm talking actors, writers, directors, corporation presidents, the real heavyweights in this town?' I said, 'Hell, Walt, that kind of publicity is worth millions and millions of dollars, it's almost priceless, nobody could possibly afford to buy that kind of exposure, if it could be bought, which it can't, not at any price.' I said, 'Actors, writers, directors—hell, how about politicians? Don't forget them. Can you imagine how much they'd give for daily exposure like this?' Well, anyway, he seemed to calm down after that." She glances at the door again. "Till Commissioner Reilly arrived—late, as usual—and blew my whole pep talk."

All six of us ask: "What'd he do?"

She takes the *News* from my hands, unfolds it, flashes the front page. "He just pointed out the negative aspects, that's all. The man has a decidedly negative personality, what can I tell you? He storms in here waving the paper, Little Caesar, launches into a diatribe about how much the department is damaged by this kind of publicity. Goes into a song and dance about how much it hurts the morale of every average cop on the street, how it makes their job that much harder, how their authority and credibility is damaged when the press makes a joke out of the department."

"Doris," Rick Telfian says, "that's total garbage. Chief Vadney can't control what a newspaper wants to print any more than Reilly can or anybody else. It's a totally illogical argument."

"Tell me about it," she says. "I launched into my own diatribe when I heard it." She smiles now, hands the paper back to me. "God, I really lit into the little wimp, let him have it with both barrels. He was—shocked. Flabbergasted. I mean I didn't call him any names or anything, I didn't even raise my voice, I just pointed out how irrational and illogical his whole position was vis-à-vis practical reality. He called me insolent and impertinent, and ordered me out of Walt's office. As I left, I said, 'Commissioner Reilly, sir, if you check the definitions of the adjectives insolent and impertinent, you'll discover they're synonyms.' Then, just before I closed the door, I added, 'The same as adjectives such as—incompetent and unqualified.' "

Chuckles from the peanut gang; she's got us mesmerized.

"Naughty, I know, but I simply couldn't resist turning the scalpel." Looks at her watch, walks to her telephone console, presses a button, uses the squawk box: "Detective Rawlings and his team are here."

"Thanks, honey, send 'em in."

We walk to the door. Honey? Never heard him call her that before. Obviously didn't know he was on the squawk box. As we enter, Rambo Bambo's hunched over, writing laboriously on a yellow legal pad. Doesn't look up, doesn't stop writing, doesn't speak. We take our seats at the big conference table in silence. Teakwood table's polished to a deep luster, as usual, we can see our reflections in it. No ashtrays, no water glasses, not even the ever-present Sony TCM-600, poor little thing, I kind of miss it. R.I.P. Wonder who chucked it out of the window? No, *through* the window, that's right, that's what he said. Twenty-two floors into an alley. Some reason, that sounds like a hotel to me, don't know why. Naturally suspicious mind, what can I tell you?

Chief finally looks up. "Whatcha got, Little John?"

"Could be a lead." I slide the three reports to him.

He ignores them, stares at his legal pad. "Know what I'm doing here? I'll tell you what I'm doing here." Glances up, raises an eyebrow. "This is strictly confidential, men, your ears only, that understood?"

We all nod, say, "Uh-huh." Sounds to that effect.

"What I'm doing, I'm drafting a letter to that vicious little scrote Vinnie Casandra. Gonna psych 'im outa his fuckin' socks. Reverse psychology, don't know why I didn't think of it before. Naturally, this will go out under Jerry Grady's signature, official press relations stationery, all that crap. Wanna hear what I got so far?"

"Yeah, love to," I say for all of us.

Chief sits up, clears his throat, can't control a soft giggle. "Jesus, this shit's gonna tear him up. By the time he gets it, there's no way he can prove anything one way or the other. I thought it out carefully. Next, Grady and I'll contact everybody concerned, cover our asses upside-down and backwards. Okay, here's what I got. Of course, Grady's gonna go over it, y'know, polish it up, make it look professional, but here's what I got, first draft:

" 'Mr. Vincent Casandra, Managing Editor, The Daily News, Two-twenty East Forty-second Street, New York, New York, One-oh-oh-one-seven. Dear Mr. Casandra: On behalf of the entire department, I want to express my sincere thanks to you, and to your staff artist Al Swartz, for the imaginative characterizations of Mayor Koch and Chief of Detectives Vadney in the opening installment of your new cartoon series titled "Rambo Bambo."

" 'Today, in my random-sample survey of commanding officers at twenty-one representative precincts in all four boroughs, I was delighted to learn that eighty-two-point-seven percent of those polled believed the series to be "Very Positive" to police-public rapport; eight-point-four percent believed the series to be "Positive"; only six-point-one percent believed the series to be "Negative"; and two-point-eight percent were "Undecided."

" 'In the judgment of those polled, the overwhelming positive factor contributing to improved police-public rapport was your editorial decision to portray Chief Vadney as Rambo. Clearly, the psychological ramifications of equating Vadney with the single most popular character in the U.S. motion picture industry today have already triggered a ground-swell of public interest and support, as witnessed virtually all day at headquarters. According to a statistical report submitted to me late this afternoon by the desk sergeant on the eight-to-four-o'clock shift, exactly forty-seven girls, ranging in age from twelve to nineteen, and thirty-four boys, ranging in age from eleven to eighteen, appeared in the lobby of our building, individually and in small groups, all requesting to see Chief Vadney in person or, if this was not practical, to be given personally autographed pictures of him. Unfortunately, work precluded the chief from making personal appearances. However, I persuaded him to autograph eighty-one photos and directed them to be distributed to our young visitors in the lobby.

" 'By depicting Chief Vadney as the classic role-model hero to millions of youngsters in our city, the *News* has made a significant contribution to achieve more effective police-public relations. We appreciate your support in this matter and wish you continued success with your new series.

" 'If I can be of any assistance to you, please don't hesitate to call. Sincerely, Detective Jerry Grady, Director, Press Relations.' " Looks up quickly, narrows his eyes, studies our open-mouthed expressions. "Comments, suggestions?"

Silence. Five seconds. Ten. Somebody clears his throat.

"Excellent letter," I tell him. "Interesting example of reverse psychology. One question, Chief: What if Casandra decides to check it out, send in a team of investigative reporters?"

"We'll cooperate all the way, Little John. Be our pleasure. By that time, all asses will be covered, all twenty-one commanders contacted and thoroughly briefed on our rationale and official response to any and all hypothetical questions, all three shifts at the lobby desk briefed, alerted, and provided with copies of the statistical reports. What it'll boil down to, it'll be our word against theirs. Us against them. They wanna play hardball, I'll *show* 'em how to play hardball."

Big John Daniels is getting a charge out of all this now, eyes sparkling, lips tight with the impish grin. "Walt, the bottom line. Think he'll pull it?"

"The series?" Duke's forehead flattens a split second before his ears jerk back, followed by an all-out left-sided molar-shower smile. "Well, Big John, I—I'll tell you the honest truth, I think he'll be too frustrated, too humiliated to do that right away. My guess, he'll hide the letter and wait, see what happens next, maybe have his flunkies make a few calls to some precinct commanders, try to check out those stats. But, hell, I'll tell you my master strategy on this, might just as well. What you've heard so far is just the tip a the iceberg. All right, now, see, Grady has a lot of contacts in the media here, right? I mean, hell, it's his job, he knows all the key media men in town on a first-name basis. Drinks with 'em, goes to ball games with 'em, probably even whores with 'em for all I know. With the single exception of Casandra; he's given that little fucker a wide birth for five years now, orders."

"Silent treatment?" Big John asks.

"No, no. No. No, the *News* gets all our Press Packages, all the standard intelligence from here, same as everybody else. Matter of fact, Grady gives 'em VIP treatment all the way, has to. Has to, they got the biggest audience. No, all I'm saying, he stays away from Casandra on a social basis, on a personal basis. I mean, let's face it, the *News* has some of the best reporters, writers, and columnists in the whole country, they're not all like this little dipshit."

"Don't forget Jimmy Breslin," I add brightly.

"What?"

"Jimmy Breslin, my favorite writer, don't forget him."

Rambo Bambo knits his brows, thinks on it. "Little John, why's it you always seem to come from left field with a digression that doesn't have any significant connection to what's being discussed?"

"Jimmy Breslin's a significant writer with the *News.*"

"Well, I never said he *wasn't,* did I? God damn it, I read Breslin practically every *day!* Gimme a fuckin' *break,* will ya?"

"Sorry, Chief. Just trying to add something to the discussion."

Talk about uncharacteristic moves, Chief stares at his pad now, takes a deep breath, picks up one of our report folders, reaches over and taps my arm with it. "Forgive me, Little John, didn't mean to bite your head off. I know you were trying to add something to the discussion, you have every right to. Every right in the world. It's just I'm under a lot of pressure here right now, y'know? This little scumbag's trying to nail me again, the little sadist. Y'see that picture on the front page? Y'read that caption?"

"Very unprofessional behavior, my opinion."

He nods, looks at the report folder. "What the hell's this?"

"One of three progress reports on the case," I tell him. "I think we may have a lead."

"Yeah? That's the stuff, Little John." Tosses it aside, goes back to his yellow pad. "Let's see now, where the hell was I?"

"Grady knows all the media men," Big John says.

"Oh, yeah." Forehead flattens, ears jerk back, molar-shower smile, but not all-out. "Anyhow, what I'm gonna do, my strategy below the iceberg, so to speak, I'm gonna tell Grady to run off about twenty-five copies of this letter, I'm gonna tell him to mail a copy to every key media man he knows on a personal basis—local and network TV, radio, newspapers, magazines—along with a short personal note. Y'know, just something like, 'Bob, f.y.i., Jerry.' Okay? Now, my guess, one or more of these guys is gonna make a little news story out of this thing, based on our stats and all. Nice little human interest piece: 'Kids Discover New Role-Model Cop' type thing. Know why? These media people, they been fighting an image problem for years now, as we all know. The public keeps screaming, 'Why don't you run some *good* news for a change, why's all the news have to be so *bad,* so depressing?' Right? So, what I'm saying, I mean I'm no public relations wizard, but it just seems to me we're giving 'em a nifty little news peg here, a different angle, a refreshing little human relations sidebar. And I think they'll pick up on it, some of 'em, the real competitive ones, before somebody else beats 'em to it. And then—bingo. Huh? Get my drift? Then, when they do, when the story gets some local TV air time, say, or maybe one of those local little think pieces in the metropolitan section of the *Times,* then—bingo. Then we really got this subhuman little ratfucker by the *dork.* Twisting, twisting in the wind. Why? I'll tell you why. Because then we've established *credibility* for the whole tub a shit. Professional peer pressure. So Casandra's got no choice but to eat it whole and choke it down. He'll have to keep running the series *indefinitely.* And he'll have to order his schmuckbag artist to make me into— well, if not an out-and-out hero, then at the very least an attractive role model for all those kids out there. I mean, let's face it, he'd have no real choice. If he made me come off looking like a moron, his bosses at the *News* would be mortified, his fellow journalists would tie a tin can to his rat-ass tail, and the kids—hell, the kids'd *crucify* him. See what I mean? He'd wind up between a rocket and a hard place. Now, how'd he handle *that,* tell me *that?*"

Silence. Five seconds. Ten.

Nuzhat to the rescue: "Uh, Chief Vadney?"

"Yeah, Idrissi."

"May I have clarification on one point, sir?"

"Sure, what's that?"

Must say, Nuzhat looks fashionable as ever. Dark gray suit, white shirt collar, pastel blue shirt, dark blue tie with tiny white polka dots. Sits forward, pushes at the nosepiece of his aviator-style glasses, touches the side of his trim mustache. Frowns now, chooses his words with great care, still has traces of an Arabic accent after all these years. "I just want to clarify something in my mind. Forgive me if I'm mistaken, Chief Vadney. But I—from what you've said, I have the impression that you would like this—this cartoon series to continue. Is that correct?"

"Well, yeah, that's essentially correct, Idrissi. But with—I mean I'd like the character there to be *attractive* to the kids in the city, y'know?"

Nuzhat frowns, clears his throat carefully. "Yes. You are talking about the character—uh, Rambo Bambo, are you not?"

"Yeah, right, Rambo Bambo."

"Yes. Forgive me, Chief Vadney, but I honestly don't believe you should do that, sir."

"No, huh? Why not?"

"Perhaps I'm mistaken, but in my opinion, I do not believe you should—encourage such a thing to continue."

"No? Huh. Why's that, Idrissi?"

Poor Nuz, he clears his throat again, slips his left hand in his trouser pocket. Know what's in there? String of white worry beads. Now he answers just above a whisper. "It is not dignified, sir."

"What's that, Idrissi? Didn't hear ya."

"In my opinion, sir, this character does not have the stature to be associated with a respected police officer of your rank, however humorous or good-natured the intention."

Chief studies him. "Bet you didn't see the Rambo films, huh?"

"Yes, sir, I have seen them."

"Yeah? And that's still your opinion?"

"Yes, sir, it is."

"Idrissi, the kids out there *adore* the guy!"

"I understand that, sir."

"I mean, they go totally *bananas* about him!"

"I've observed that, yes, sir."

"And that's still your—?"

"That is my personal opinion, yes. Of course, I may be mistaken. Obviously, this is not what you want to hear, but I would feel negligent if I did not tell you what I honestly believe."

Chief nods slowly, narrows his eyes. "All right, Idrissi. Point well taken. You sure as hell ain't a *yes* man, are you?"

"I would hope not, sir."

"You're a good cop, Idrissi, I like your moxie, always have. Remember that time you shot me in the ass, back in eighty-three?"

Nuz closes his eyes fast at the horror of that memory. "Yes, sir, the shotgun pellet. I still have nightmares about it."

"Hell, man, you shouldn't feel guilty about it. I mean, we were in a deadly situation there, wild shootout in a dark little room. So one of your pellets banged me in the bum, so what? We were lucky to get outa there alive."

"I do not feel guilty about it, sir, not any more. And I still stand by my statement to the press concerning your actions under fire."

"Yeah? What'd you say again?"

"Simply that never in my career had I personally witnessed such courage."

"Oh, yeah, I remember now. Yeah, we really blasted the piss outa that prep. Little John, you were there, right?"

"Right. I remember you got nominated for the Combat Medal."

Chief nods, glances away. "Nominated, right. Then poli-

ticed out of it by Reilly and them. Jealous, gutless, chickenshit
civilians. But now, Idrissi, to get back to this series thing. If
you were me, you wouldn't mail copies of the letter to all those
media people, huh?"

"I would not, no, sir."

"Whaddaya think of the letter idea itself?"

"I believe it is tantamount to baiting a rattlesnake, sir. If I
were you, I would not attempt reverse psychology on such a
creature."

"Yeah? Why?"

"Number one, it is beneath your dignity to resort to men-
dacity as a strategy for combating vindictive behavior. Number two, strategy of this nature, however convoluted, would
be transparently obvious to a man of such paranoid persua-
sions. Number three, I call your attention to an old Arab
proverb that seems appropriate, a very rough translation, of
course: 'When once a man stoops to wrestle with pigs, that
man gets up with the penetrating odor of pigshit.' "

Chief's eyes widen as he ponders that. "All right, okay, I
think I got your drift there. Point well taken, Idrissi. God
damn, you really *ain't* a yes man, are you?"

"I would hope not, sir."

"Need to surround myself with more oddballs like you,
buddy-boy, breath of fresh air around here. Gotta make a note
of that last one, maybe I can hit Reilly with it." Turns to a
new page of his yellow pad, jots it down carefully: *When once
a man stoops . . .* Finishes, glances up. "All right, tell you
what, Idrissi, I'm gonna give your suggestions some thought.
I'm gonna talk it over with Grady and them." Checks his
watch. "Okay, men, that just about wraps it. Appreciate your
input this morning, thanks for coming in. Report directly to
me if you come up with anything promising."

I tap my finger on the reports in front of him. "That's
actually what we're here for, Chief. We wrote these reports
last night for this meeting."

He picks one up, flips it open. "Oh, yeah, sorry, Little John. Sorry. I got preoccupied here, I been juggling about a dozen things this morning. Okay, give me a fast rundown on this stuff, huh? I'll study it out later, of course. Please, go ahead."

Automatically, I reach for a cigar, then remember we're not allowed to smoke in here. "As briefly as I can put it, I'm afraid our press release had one important inaccuracy. Somebody told Grady the roof was six inches of steel and tar. It's not. We go up on the roof, we find out it's actually about six inches of tar with a thin layer of sheet metal under that. Seems very strange in a fortress like this, so we go to the owner, we ask him who built the place. Nobody's asked him that question. He pulls the files—"

"Wait a minute," Chief says. "Nobody'd asked that question?"

"No, sir. According to the owner, John Holland."

"Unbelievable."

"Surprised me, too. Anyhow, he pulls the files, gives us the name of the building contractor, plus the architects and various engineering subcontractors. We go downtown in three teams, check the firms out. Architects tell Telfian and Thalheimer their blueprint specifications called for a one-foot-thick layer of reinforced concrete topped by a six-inch layer of tar. They can prove it, they've got the documents, they gave us copies. Daniels and Idrissi go to the structural engineers, find out they departed from the blueprint specs on direct orders from the building contractor, firm by the name of R.T. Mustafa, because he was apparently way over budget. Engineering firm can prove it, we have copies of the documents in the file here. Now Brendan and me, we go to the office of R.T. Mustafa. He's not there, he's in Miami, so we meet with his second-in-command, happens to be a woman. She's already read about the robbery, she's called Mustafa, briefed him, he says he wants to cooperate with us all the way. We got his address and phone number. Plan to call him this morning. That's about it."

Chief gets a pained expression. "Nobody—*nobody* from JRTF or the Bronx Robbery Unit has the common sense to even ask who *built* the place. That's just great, isn't it? Fabulous investigative work here. Total of thirty-five robbery experts, hand-picked veterans, cream of the crop. Hell, I got reports from both units this morning, on my desk eight o'clock sharp. Thick reports. Exhibits, verbatim interview transcripts, photographs, diagrams, lab reports. They went over that building inch by inch with every sophisticated investigative tool and technique known to forensic science. They even gave me—here's a good example of what I'm talking about—they even gave me the precise thickness of the roof's tar and sheet metal, accurate to one one-hundredth of a centimeter. Measured the slab in the lab. Believe that? But not one, single, solitary word about *why*. Why a place like that would have a roof like that. A roof that could be peeled off with a fuckin' can opener. Official conclusion of both reports? They got squat leads, but they're working on it. Real heavyweight stuff. Real FBI shit. Know the real *reason* they got squat? Know *why?*"

Question hangs in the silence of shrugs.

"I'll tell you why. Because they've become technology addicts. That's right. We've trained and tested and groomed and created a whole new breed of cops, men. That's no exaggeration, you know it as well as I do. They're so hooked, so addicted, so mesmerized by all the high-tech, state-of-the-art, passive, computerized, electronic gadgetry we got now, they've lost the most important tool they ever had: Plain, simple, ordinary, everyday common sense. Or what Little John here likes to call 'intuition.' So what happens? The Silicon Valley boys strike out. Not swinging, not taking a good old-fashioned cut at the ball, but standing there passively with their bats on their shoulders, eyes as blank as their brains. So what happens? You guys go up there without any of their toys —that's what they are, toys, expensive toys—you go up there, you nose around, you absorb it all, you get down and inspect the hole with your own eyes, you use your common sense, you think, 'Hey, who the hell would build a roof like *this?*' You go to the owner, you ask him the most basic, obvious question imaginable: 'Who *built* this place?' Then you check it out. Methodical, step-by-step, patient, careful, logical, disciplined commonsense investigative work. And you come up with the one and only solid lead we got to date."

In the pause, I'm wondering what became of our famous stumbling, bumbling, total blind luck technique of only yesterday. How quickly they forget.

"All right," Chief continues. "I think you're on to something. In fact, there's no question in my mind that you're on the brink of something big. As far as the overall picture, I'm more or less convinced it was an inside job. Why? Because of the obviously extensive knowledge these men had about the layout, the alarm system circuitry, the security, and the roof. That's why, as of early this morning, I ordered the JRTF to begin round-the-clock surveillance on three men: Holland, the owner; Ruminek, the guard who was on duty; and Kells, the cross-check security man who discovered and reported the robbery. Meantime, follow up on this R.T. Mustafa, give him top priority, see what you can dig up on him, huh? This guy intrigues me, Little John."

"I'll call him this morning."

"Where'd you say he's at now, Miami?"

"Right. Miami Beach, actually."

"Convenient to be out of town. Vacation?"

"Don't know, Chief."

"Know where he's staying?"

"Fontainebleau Hilton."

Chief puts his hands behind his head, leans back, blinks at the ceiling. "Don't make that call." Swings around, opens a drawer in his teakwood cabinet, whips out his *Official Airline Guide,* swings back, studies it. "Pan Am flight four-twenty-seven. Departs JFK one-fifteen this afternoon, arrives Miami four-oh-three. You and Brendan be on it. Don't even bother to pack. Get a cash advance from Mat Murphy. I'll call Chief Haynes down there right now, ask him to have somebody meet you."

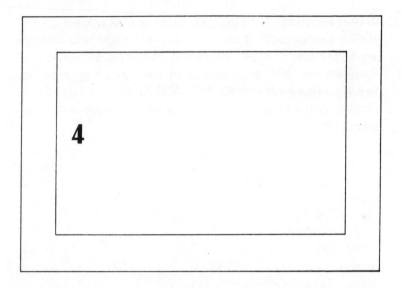

4

BRENDAN AND ME, we can't believe our good fortune here, couple of stumble-bumble blind-luck cops winging it down to warm Miami, middle of December, it's just totally unreal, we feel like kids playing hooky, living it up with the rich and famous. Spacious Pan Am 747, we got three seats in back all to ourselves, gracious young flight attendants serve cocktails, we buy two Beefeater martinis each, sit back, munch our peanuts, we're living like kings. Short time after our fashionably late lunch, about 3:45, we're starting our descent, we look out the window, there it is, just like I remember it, Miami Beach. Endless rows of big white luxury hotels bathed in bright sunshine, surrounded by sparkling turquoise dotted with yachts, sounds like a travel agent, but that's the way it looks today, what can I tell you? Now we're into a gradual turn west toward the mainland, we get a good view of the downtown skyline, and it really surprises me. I haven't been down here in about nine years, but I'm a fan of "Miami Vice," so I know the city's changed plenty since the last time I saw it. But somehow I'm not prepared for what I'm seeing. Only way I can describe it, this place looks brand-new, like an entirely different city. It's like they took the old downtown, leveled it, started from scratch, and now here's this ultramodern high-rise skyline that's like a big chunk of midtown Manhattan without the soot. Gigantic towers of glass and steel, granite and marble. Lots of construction still going on too—not out, but up.

Now we're moving past the downtown area, here's something else, new freeway system that snakes over, under, around, and through, reminds me of Los Angeles, except L.A. doesn't have a real downtown like this, at least not that I could find. Closer we get to the airport, going west, freeways feed into miles and miles of new streets crisscrossed in almost perfect geometrical patterns, like the farms they replaced, looks like all new residential-commercial developments. Maybe my memory's going, but nine years ago I don't think any of this was built yet. All I remember, the airport was being modernized back then and it seemed to be out in the boondocks. Gives me a strange feeling, hard to describe. Year after year, you read about this major migration to the Sun Belt, but it just doesn't mean much when you live in New York, you can't really visualize stats like that. Then you see a city like Miami from the air in daylight, December 1985, you get a clear idea of what's happening and how fast it's happening. Gives you pause. Really does. Cities like this, they're not just expanding rapidly, they're exploding. Makes you wonder how a place like this will look by the turn of the century. I'll be sixty-seven in the year 2000. Who knows, maybe I'll get fed up with the cold and dirt by then and retire down here, join the migration. Me? Naw. Love New York too much. Love the nonstop energy of the place. Like Jimmy Breslin always says, "There *is* no other city." Believe it.

Getting ready to land now, about 3:55, captain announces the temperature's seventy-seven degrees, clear skies, no chance of rain. Gets a resounding sitting ovation from the snowbirds. Smooth landing, pleasant taxi to the gate, we're met right inside the boarding bridge by Detective Mort Cooper of the Miami Police Department, maybe the biggest police officer Brendan and I have ever seen. Now, I know this sounds like bullshit, but I swear to God it's true: Mort Cooper is exactly six-foot-ten and weighs 385 pounds. I mean, we asked him, we couldn't help it, he gets the same question all the time. Remarkable thing is, Cooper's not fat and flabby at all, he hasn't even got a potbelly. Works out regularly, lifts weights, swims a lot. He's just a very big man, that's all, handles himself real good, wears a striped shirt open at the neck, blue blazer, light gray trousers. Reason he doesn't wear a tie, he'd be conspicuous outside of an office building, you don't see too many neckties on detectives down here. We ask him how he recognized us, he laughs, he says Chief Haynes got very detailed descriptions from Chief Vadney, sums up by calling us "Mut-'n'-Jeff." Ha-ha. Terrific analogy, Chief's developing a dynamite sense of humor in his twilight years.

We have no luggage, nothing to carry but our topcoats, so our first destination is a pay phone in the crowded terminal. Holiday decorations are all over, Muzak plays Christmas carols, palefaced New Yorkers in trendy winter togs shout earsplitting greetings to bronzed relatives in tony T-shirts and shorts: "*Goy*trude, *Boy*nee! Oh, my *Gawd!* Lookitcha, ya *black* awready, ya lucky schmucks, ya!" Salutations to that effect. Mort Cooper moves through this mob smooth as a buck elephant on the make, reminds me of that Chicago Bears' defensive lineman William Perry, except "The Refrigerator" weighs only 302, last I heard, so Mort's got him by eighty pounds easy. Makes Brendan look like a mere quarterback of a lad. Me? Frankly, I'm never intimidated by the size of a man. I mean, I raise myself up to my full five-foot-ten, 132 pounds, I feel like Paul Newman on a diet. I mean, us pygmies have our pride, right?

Now, technically, R.T. Mustafa's residence at the Fontainebleau Hilton places him under the jurisdiction of the Miami
Beach Police Department, separate city from Miami, but because Chief Vadney and Chief Haynes are old friends and all,
Haynes has already called the Beach and touched base. It's no
big thing anyway, we're not looking to collar the man. So
Cooper's cleared to call Mustafa at the hotel. Introduces himself, tells Mustafa he has two visitors from NYPD who want
to question him, asks what time would be convenient. It's now
about 4:10. Mustafa suggests 5:30 in his suite, if that's convenient for us. Fine and dandy. Gives us time to stop off at
headquarters on the way, meet Chief Haynes, brief him on the
case.

Cooper's old but clean-looking white Chevy Nova is parked
just outside the Pan Am arrivals area in a no-parking zone.
Walk out of the air-conditioned terminal into a refreshing
faceful of warm tropical air. Know how that feels? Coming
from the frozen north? Humidity from heaven, you can almost
hear your bones squeak in pure ecstasy. Me, I put on my classy
Porsche-Carrera sunglasses, toss my topcoat in back, slide in
front, nonchalant as Don Johnson. Wonder how Vice I'd look
in those collarless three-button pastel shirts, formless white
jackets, baggy trousers, white Guccis? Naw. Probably look
like Peter Lorre.

Maneuver out of the airport in heavy traffic, mostly taxis,
go east on the East-West Expressway (836), pick up speed as
we head downtown. First thing Cooper points out, Orange
Bowl off to our right. Says it's still the home of the Dolphins,
but they're building a new stadium north of here, should be
ready in a couple of years. Change to the elevated North-
South Expressway (95), head due south, fantastic view of the
new skyline. Short time later we see the headquarters building,
can't miss it, huge black letters on the northwest corner of the
roof: MIAMI POLICE DEPARTMENT. Relatively new,
Cooper tells us, finished in 1978, first building in the Govern-

ment Center. Occupies one full block between Northwest Second and Third avenues and Northwest Fourth and Fifth streets. Helicopter landing pad on the rectangular roof. Five graceful floors of reinforced concrete, all windows shaded by clean lines of slanted overhanging concrete slabs extending around the building. For some reason, this place doesn't seem cold or forbidding, probably because the high concrete wall surrounding it encloses a bright green courtyard of trees, mostly palms, and obviously well-watered grass.

Same is true of the parking lot to the south, also a full block long. Landscapers simply left many of the older trees where they were, then planted rows of new ones, so the majority of cars are in shade. Unfortunately, Cooper can't find a shady spot this late in the day, but he gets one reasonably close to the building. Long orange-tiled ramp to the front entrance is flanked by palm trees and the wide wall to the left of the glass doors has a colorful Spanish-type mural that looks like it's telling a story of some kind, although I don't have a clue what it might be. Inside, the large lobby seems dark at first. People are sitting in the waiting area to the left and there's a line of people in front of the semicircular security desk. Cooper flashes his gold, jerks a thumb back at Brendan and me, we go through, no color-coded ID cards here. Interesting contrast between our lobbies though: NYPD headquarters lobby features an old wooden police wagon, vintage 1880, that had been horse-drawn, and it's one of the few touches of character in the whole place; here, to the right of the security desk, mirrored ceiling lights play on a long row of glass cases and stands holding sports trophies galore, all sizes and shapes, gleaming in gold pride. Question of values here. Case to be made for both sides.

Walking to the elevators, we pass a door marked *Media Relations*. Now, here's a more practical example of what I'm talking about: Modern versus traditional. Grady's department is still called Press Relations, has been for as long back as I is still called Press Relations, has been for as long back as I can remember. Still technically correct, I suppose, but definitely dated. "Media" covers the whole nine yards, Marino to Duper, Don Shula's modern aerial circus. "Press" has the subtle connotation of print media only, takes you back to the days before television took over our lives. I make a mental note to tell Vadney about this. Lay you odds he'll change the name soon as the old stationery runs out. Maybe sooner. Last thing in the world he wants is to be dated. At his age.

Take the elevator up, Cooper tells us more about the place, the helicopter pad, the modern gym, shooting range, cafeteria, even has a modern jail. We get off at the top floor, turn left, another left down a softly lighted red-orange carpeted hallway. Chief Haynes has the southwest corner office, best view in the building. Waiting room just outside doesn't have classchic decor a la Doris, of course, but it's impressive enough. Attractive young female secretary asks us to take a seat, Chief's in conference, shouldn't be long. View of the downtown skyline is nothing short of spectacular and now we get a good look at that new elevated subway system. It's called Metrorail, Cooper tells us, opened May 1984, cost over a billion dollars. Must say, trains look sleek and *clean* shooting along in the late afternoon sun, not even a hint of graffiti. Can't help staring. Haven't seen clean cars like this since my last trip to Disney World.

Take our seats, Cooper asks the secretary for the latest computer readout of the department's personnel statistics. Comes over, hands me five pages, emphasizes these stats are only for the city police, not for Metro Dade (county) or Miami Beach. Brendan and I glance at the first page.

PERSONNEL BY RACE/SEX
POLICE PERSONNEL

	MALE	FEMALE	TOTAL		MALE	FEMALE	TOTAL
WHITE	384	56	440	WHITE	36.9%	5.3%	42.3%
BLACK	130	44	174	BLACK	12.5%	4.2%	16.7%
SPANISH	408	16	424	SPANISH	39.2%	1.5%	40.7%
OTHERS	2		2	OTHERS	0.1%	0.0%	0.1%
TOTALS	924	116	1040	TOTALS	88.8%	11.1%	100.0%

MALE MINORITY REPRESENTATION	51.9%
FEMALE REPRESENTATION	11.1%
TOTAL MINORITY REPRESENTATION	63.0%

CIVILIAN PERSONNEL

	MALE	FEMALE	TOTAL		MALE	FEMALE	TOTAL
WHITE	35	57	92	WHITE	8.9%	14.5%	23.5%
BLACK	19	148	167	BLACK	4.8%	37.8%	42.7%
SPANISH	53	77	130	SPANISH	13.5%	19.6%	33.2%
OTHERS		2	2	OTHERS	0.0%	0.5%	0.5%
TOTALS	107	284	391	TOTALS	27.3%	72.6%	100.0%

MALE MINORITY REPRESENTATION	18.4%
FEMALE REPRESENTATION	72.6%
TOTAL MINORITY REPRESENTATION	91.0%

Bottom line, of the 1,431 departmental personnel, police plus civilian employees, the total minority representation comes to 70.7 percent. Interesting stat. Overreaction? Never had access to NYPD computer readouts like this, can't help wondering how we'd compare.

Page 4 gives a breakdown of police by rank, among other

factors, and I'm surprised to discover there's no chief of detectives; Haynes is actually chief of police, head of the whole shooting match. Under him are 5 assistant chiefs, no deputy chief (although budgeted), 11 colonels, 16 majors, 10 captains, 35 lieutenants, 141 sergeants, 792 police officers (357 are Hispanic), and 29 recruits, for a total of 1,040. Seems small to me, but again I have to remind myself that it's just for the city itself. I ask Cooper the present population of Miami. He says the 1980 census listed just under 347,000, but he's sure it's increased dramatically over the past five years. Okay, even granting that it's increased to 500,000, which is probably realistic, that 1,040 figure seems even smaller to me. Tell you why: Same 1980 census listed the population of New York City (all five boroughs) at 7.1 million; that year, NYPD had a total force of exactly 18,195, considered very inadequate (in 1972 it was about 31,000). Last few years it's leveled off at around 20,000.

What I'm trying to bring out here is simple. If you round out the figures and say New York City has a 1985 population of 7 million and a police force of 20,000, that's one cop for every 350 residents, right? Now, if you say Miami has a 1985 population of 500,000 and a police force of 1,000, that's one cop for every 500 residents. Inadequate, in my judgment, at least on the face of it. Of course, there may be mitigating factors that I don't know about. Have to ask Chief Haynes about that, if I can squeeze it in diplomatically.

We get in to see him about 4:45. Don't know what I expected, but somebody should've warned me, because this guy's appearance really sneaks up on you. Late fifties, medium height and build, dark suit and tie, but as he walks around his desk to greet us and I get a close look, I'm hit with this totally weird sensation: Haynes is absolutely, positively the identical twin brother of John Forsythe. Yeah! Playing Blake Carrington in "Dynasty," spitting image of that character, right down to the pure white hair, thin lips, and cold riveting eyes. Looks

like him, moves like him, smiles like him, even sounds like
him. I don't know, maybe I'm going bananas in the tropics
here, but I'm telling you straight, this guy is John Forsythe
City. Me, I'm shaking his hand, my mouth's hanging open, I
don't know to squirt or howl at the moon here, I'm looking
around for Linda Evans.

Formalities are over now, I'm glad to sit down, I feel a little
dizzy. Thought occurs to me that maybe I'm hallucinating
again. Haven't done that in years. Take a deep breath, blink
rapidly, look out the window, then casually back at him. John
Forsythe. No question. Exchange a quick glance with Brendan, he's picked up on it too, he's got this quizzical expression
like maybe somebody's looking to play a joke on us. Cooper
lowers his large frame into a chair, breaks into a half-smile,
eyeing both of us, enjoying the show.

Haynes knows what's happening, of course, he's obviously
used to this; decides to toy with Brendan a bit. "Detective
Thomas, you seem perplexed. Anything wrong?"

"Wrong? No, sir, nothing's wrong."

Runs a hand through his thick white hair, gives Brendan a
thin, icy Forsythe smile. "I suppose you expected a much
younger man in this job, is that it?"

"Oh, no, sir, not at all." Smiles, shrugs. "It's just—ah, I
guess you must have people telling you this all the time, Chief,
about the resemblance and all."

Lets him twist a little. Then: "What resemblance?"

Brendan looks to me for help, gets an icy Forsythe stare,
grins, squirms in his seat, clears his throat. "Well, beggin' your
pardon, sir, it's nothing, really. It just struck me that there's
a slight resemblance between you and that guy on 'Dynasty'
—can't think of his name."

Haynes arches an eyebrow. "Oh? 'Dynasty,' the TV series?"

"Yeah. You know the guy I mean, the white-haired old
guy?"

"White-haired *old* guy?"

"No, I mean—not old, he's just—very distinguished look-ing."

Magnanimously, I come to his rescue: "John Forsythe."

"No, no," Brendan says. "No, John, I'm talking about that big star on 'Dynasty.' Name's on the tip of my tongue."

"Blake Carrington," Cooper says.

Brendan snaps his fingers. "*That's* it. That's the guy."

Haynes laughs out loud, drops the game now. "Detective Thomas, forgive me, I was putting you on. You're right about the resemblance, of course. Just to set the record straight, the actor John Forsythe plays the role of Blake Carrington on 'Dynasty.' Unfortunately, I bear quite a strong resemblance to the man. I say 'unfortunately' because, frankly, it's gotten to a point now, after two or three years, where it's not even remotely funny anymore, it's a fuckin' pain in the ass. Except at times like this. I mean, on a day-to-day basis, it's not at all unusual for people to stop me on the street, in stores, even in restaurants, and ask me for an autograph. I'm so God damn sick of it, of politely explaining they're mistaken, of sometimes actually having to argue with them because they won't believe me, of going through the whole routine, that I could throw up."

Brendan's smile vanishes. "Ah, Jesus, I'm sorry, sir."

"Not at all," he says, softer now, almost philosophically. "My wife's sick of the whole thing too. My whole family's sick to death of it. My daughter keeps telling me to get my hair dyed, to get it done professionally. She's convinced that would put a stop to it. I tell her the same thing I tell everybody else who has a suggestion: Why the hell should I have to change my appearance because of a God damn TV show? For better or worse, I'm stuck with this face. The irony is—here's the real irony, in my opinion. This job involves a relatively high degree of visibility in this community. People see my picture in the papers fairly frequently, they see me interviewed on television, at least occasionally, they should know my face by now. But they don't. Not the mass public anyway. Why? Because they're not interested in police officers, they're interested in celebrities, in actors, in entertainers. And I'm not singling out Miami, it's the same in every city. Police officers just aren't glamorous enough—'Miami Vice' to the contrary notwithstanding. Police officers don't intrigue people, don't hold their attention. Well, with the possible exception of Chief Vadney. I read this morning's *News,* we subscribe to it here at the office. How's he reacting to the Rambo Bambo thing?"

I shrug. "He's holding his own."

Haynes smiles, gives me this look. "I'll bet he is."

"Didn't mean it that way," I tell him, "but, yeah, I guess it could apply."

"Rambo Bambo," he says, shaking his head. "I didn't mention it when he called this morning, I know how he feels about Vinnie Casandra. I suppose the worst part is, he can't do anything about it. Although, in my opinion, this cartoon thing comes precariously close to defamation of character. What's the libel law in New York?"

"Probably the same as here," I tell him. "Actually, we looked it up back in nineteen eighty-one when Casandra started with the cartoons. Law defines libel as defamation by written or printed words, pictures, or in any form other than spoken words or gestures. Key word 'defamation' is vaguely defined as false or unjustified injury to the good name or reputation of another. Very tricky thing to prove."

"And Casandra's no fool," he says. "I noticed he didn't mention names in the cartoon, plus the talk balloons are carefully worded. But the thing is, the reason I mention libel, it looks exactly like him, it looks like Walt. And, of course, Mayor Koch, everybody knows his face, but he loves this kind of cartoon shit, he's in 'em all the time. Tell me this, Rawlings, Thomas, tell me the truth now. You think most New Yorkers know Vadney's face? I mean, if they saw him on the street or in a restaurant or something, would they know who he is?"

"Most New Yorkers?" Brendan asks. "I'd seriously doubt it. Today—maybe today, sure, with his picture on the front page and the cartoon and all." Glances at me. "Right? But tomorrow, next week, next month, no. I mean he doesn't get that much publicity on a day-to-day basis. Big cases like this, yeah, but only because Casandra's out to make him look like an asshole."

"But consider this," I tell them. "The *News* has a daily paid circulation of one and a half million, the *Post* is up around eight hundred thousand, I believe. Last two days, his picture's been on the front page of both of 'em. So, at the very least, he's gotten exposure to over two million people in two days. To say nothing of television. If I know Vadney, he's got a major press conference scheduled for this afternoon to make all the early evening TV news shows. What's more, he'll pack 'em in. You kidding? Biggest cash robbery in history?"

Gets a chuckle out of Haynes. "And I think *this* job has visibility. I'm in the wrong—by the way, Walt briefed me on why you're here to question the building contractor, what's his name?"

"Mustafa," Brendan says.

"Mustafa. If you need anything, if Cooper can't get it for you, just pick up the phone. I'm in the wrong city if I want visibility like Walt gets. He gets the biggies, we get the druggies."

"Oh, you're not doing too badly," I say smiling. "Impressive national title Miami got this summer: Murder Capital of the Nation. Official FBI stats too."

Closes his eyes to erase the image. "Yes, they went ahead and released those stats, but they left out the most important factor of all. The overwhelming majority of those murders were drug-related hits. Every time a big drug deal goes sour, our hot-blooded friends go out and stage a bloodbath. Strictly private wars, they don't touch anybody else, but the gentle folks in middle America read those stats, they think this is a frontier town."

"Long as we're on the subject," I say, "like to ask you something about the department."

"Certainly."

"When we were waiting outside, Mort showed Brendan and me your latest personnel stats from the computer. You got a force of only one thousand and forty for a city of roughly half a million. That's like one police officer for every five hundred residents. Why so small a ratio? I mean, compared to New York?"

Haynes sits forward, flashes the thin grin. "First of all, your population stats are inaccurate. As of November of this year, the population of Miami itself—a relatively small area compared to New York—was three hundred eighty-five thousand, one hundred forty-two. Divide that by one thousand forty and you get one police officer for every three-hundred-seventy-point-three residents. That ratio is only slightly higher than New York City's at one to approximately three hundred fifty. Now, of course, the figures are constantly changing. According to the Census Bureau, New York City actually lost ten-point-four percent of its population from nineteen seventy to nineteen eighty, while Miami gained three-point-six percent over the same ten-year period. Therefore, based on those percentages, by the year nineteen ninety, New York's population should be down to six-point-three million, while Miami's should be up to one-point-four million."

Can't help but be impressed by this guy's head. I mean, he doesn't refer to a single note, it just gushes out of him like oil from the Denver-Carrington wells.

"Chief," Brendan says. "Let me get this straight. Are you saying New York's losing over ten percent of its population every ten years?"

Haynes shrugs. "I'm not saying it, the Census Bureau is.

But that's nothing compared to most of the big northern cities. For example, over the same ten-year span, St. Louis lost twenty-seven-point-two percent of its population, Cleveland lost twenty-three-point-six percent, Buffalo lost twenty-two-point-seven percent, Pittsburgh lost an even eighteen percent, the list goes on and on, every major northern city you can name, most lost well over ten percent. On the other hand, surprisingly, San Jose, California, gained a whopping thirty-eight-point-four percent, Austin gained thirty-six-point-three, Albuquerque gained thirty-five-point-seven, El Paso was up thirty-two even, Phoenix thirty-point-nine, on and on, Houston, Tucson, San Diego, all over twenty-five percent. You name a major Sun Belt city, it's growing very rapidly."

"How come you know all these stats?" Brendan asks.

"Because he's our resident genius," Cooper says.

"Far from it," Haynes tell us. "I'm just another stat freak, always have been. Numbers just stick in my memory. From what I hear, it's not all that unusual these days."

"Tell you what surprises me," I say. "That Miami only increased by such a small percentage—what was it?"

"Three-point-six," he says. "Two major factors for that. One, we're talking about a small geographical area. The city itself has a total land area of only thirty-four-point-three square miles; New York City has almost nine times as much land area. Two, the most significant factor, most new families moving here don't live within the actual city limits. The real boom is west, north, and south of the city, where there's been an absolutely unbelievable growth in new residential and commercial developments. For example, Dade County's population right now is one-point-seven million; Broward County's now up to one-point-one million. So, for all practical purposes, we're talking about a 'Greater Miami' population of two-point-eight million and growing. Growing at an accelerating rate. Growing at a far faster rate than the city itself ever will, because there's simply not enough space left in the city. In point of fact, to answer your question another way, according to the Census Bureau, the population of Greater Miami actually increased by a huge twenty-eight-point-three percent from nineteen seventy to nineteen eighty. That's the bottom-line figure to remember. Twenty-eight percent and accelerating every year. Which, to be honest, is a little frightening. When you think of the future."

Goes on like that. Now, I'm not a stat buff, never have been, with the possible exception of baseball. But we're in Haynes office only about ten minutes total, I come out with very strong impressions. Here's a guy who's a dead ringer for John Forsythe, talks like somebody from the Silicon Valley, acts like somebody from the Greater Miami Chamber of Commerce, and pulls it all off with the panache of William F. Buckley Jr. on a downhill drag. Hell, this guy could upstage Walter Fosdick Vadney, Times Square, New Year's Eve.

Leaves me with more questions than answers, but at least I learned something in those ten minutes. If Greater New York's losing over ten percent of its population every ten years and Greater Miami's increasing its population by over twenty-eight percent every ten years, then, as the saying goes, I've seen the future. And I don't know if it'll work. Look at it this way: All those millions of New Yorkers who just pick up and migrate to the Sun Belt, somehow I just can't see 'em moving to places like San Jose or Austin or Albuquerque or El Paso. No way. I mean, I don't care what you say, there's just no way in the world that real New Yorkers would ever move to nice, clean, quiet little cities like that. Know who moves to cities like that? My opinion, people from St. Louis and Cleveland and Buffalo and Pittsburgh move to nice, clean, quiet little cities like that. Not New Yorkers. So, next question, here it comes, ready or not, fasten your seat belt: Where, oh, where will all those millions of New Yorkers migrate to? Think about it. Sends a chill up your ass, right?

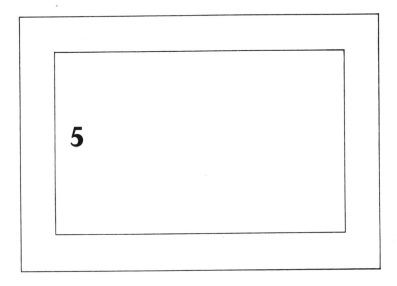

5

FONTAINEBLEAU HILTON has a fascinating little history, Cooper tells us some highlights on the drive over there. Seems it was built atop the remains of a famous 1920s Miami Beach landmark, the Harvey Firestone mansion, fifteen-bedroom winter home purchased by Firestone in 1923 for the then-astronomical tab of $250,000. Mort says the population of Miami Beach back then was about 6,000; today it's around 97,000, with a police force of only 250, give or take a few, but tons of private security guards for the hotels. Anyhow, in 1952, a guy by the name of Ben Novack, principal builder of the hotel, bought the estate from the Firestone heirs for a reported $2.3 million. Horseshoe-shaped Fontainebleau opened to great fanfare in 1954 with 550 rooms and 230 yards of beach-front, nobody'd seen anything quite like it. Story goes, for about twelve years it was considered the top resort hotel in Florida and one of the finest in the country. Then, in the late 1960s, air fares dropped, resorts in the Bahamas and the Carib-bean gained in popularity, and the hotel began to lose ground as a prime destination. In 1970, the construction outfit that was building the third addition to the hotel went bankrupt in the middle of construction. Fontainebleau lost more than $3 million, went into bankruptcy itself, and gradually fell into disrepair throughout most of the 1970s. Last time I saw it was 1976; we didn't stay there, much too expensive for us, we just went in one day to gawk. Looked very, very luxurious to me, but what do I know? Turns out something historic was going on in there (if "historic" is the word) right at the time we saw it, but few people knew about it.

During 1976 and 1977, according to Cooper, drug smuggling into South Florida was at an all-time high and the DEA had identified and selected one big gang as its major target. Later nicknamed the "Black Tuna Gang" by the media, it included at least thirty-eight people; twelve were ultimately named in the indictment. During the two years in question, the organization smuggled vast amounts of cocaine and pot into the Miami area from Colombia, with a street value in excess of $300 million, using some of the most sophisticated techniques ever encountered by the DEA, FBI, Customs, or Coast Guard. To give you an idea of how wild this thing was, the two leaders of the gang were operating the organization from a $300-a-day duplex penthouse in the Fontainebleau. That was their *office*. Suite 16-A in the Tower, Mort says they had a pool table, grand piano, circular staircase, panoramic view of the ocean, you name it. They'd been in business since at least 1974 and the amounts of money were just staggering. The thing is, they were so well insulated, the DEA couldn't hit them with anything really substantive. They had legitimate fronts, plus some of the most expensive accountants and attorneys you could buy. But they were also an excellent target because they had a structured organization and the DEA had been watching them for years. The bigger the outfit, the higher probability you have of finding weak links. And that's exactly what the DEA did. Totally bizarre trial, Mort says, lasted four months, talk of the town. Twelve who were indicted were all convicted, sentenced to very long prison terms. So much for the Black Tuna Gang.

But to get back to the Fontainebleau itself, here's what finally happened: In 1978, Miami Beach developer Stephen Muss bought the hotel and persuaded Hilton Hotels Corporation to manage it. Story goes, Muss spent more than $40 million in renovating the entire hotel and grounds. Amazing what you can do with $40 million and Hilton expertise, Cooper tells us. Now they got 1,223 rooms in three buildings, seven main dining rooms and six lounges, two outdoor pools with three whirlpool baths, seven lighted tennis counts on two levels, and six fully automatic bowling lanes.

"That all they got for forty million?" I ask.

Mort smiles, glances at his watch. "After you question this clown, I'm gonna show you guys a bar that'll knock your socks off. They got this bar called the Lagoon Saloon, you won't believe this shit. It's in a cave under this man-made mountain at one end of the big pool, the rock-grotto swimming pool. You sit there, you drink, you watch the girls in the pool through a waterfall. Fantastic. You nibble on shrimp and oysters, you drink, you look around, there's more bikinis prancing around that little bar than the rational mind can stand. Prancing around, dancing, reaching past you for drinks. Wild, wild women."

"Drive you crazy," Brendan says.

"Drive you insane," I add.

"Me," he says, "I'm just a poe ole country boy, I can't stand much of that shit. Try to follow the bouncing tits in there, you come out with a broken neck."

"Not to mention a broken hard," Brendan says.

Goes like that, Mort's giggling away, we're getting to know the guy, glad to see he's got a sense of humor. Turns off the Julia Tuttle Causeway into Arthur Godfrey Road, then left into Collins Avenue, around the horn at Forty-fourth Street, and up the semicircular drive of the Fontainebleau Hilton. Uniformed car-parkers are having a busy time, place is splendiferous with new Mercedes, Rolls Royces, Jaguars, Ferraris, Porsches, long Caddy and Lincoln limos. Up pulls Mort with his old but clean Chevy Nova. Wish you could see the consternation on the face of the guy who opens the door: Ey, wimp, this ain't no service entrance. Now Mort ambles out, shoots to his full six-ten, holds out the key in a mitt that looks like a ham. Guy's face changes instantly: Ey, buddy, always loved these old Novas, built to last, right?

In we go through the tall glass doors, lobby's completely changed, looks at least twice as spacious, decor is ultramodern, lively, breezy, tropical. Three of the largest, most elaborately tiered chandeliers I've ever seen blaze high above an enormous circular hole in the white marble floor where escalators move gangs of monied sophisticates. Not old money, mind you. One look around, you get the impression that Hilton's target market here is decidedly Yuppie. Don't get me wrong, I'm not knocking Yuppies. Happen to think they're absolutely delightful people. Delightful. Hell, some of my best Yuppies are friends. Follow Mort left toward the reception area and elevators, past stores and statues and flowers and plants. So many exotic tropical monster plants in this joint, it's like a high-class jungle, Stallone would love this crap, he could hide out in here for years. Mort picks up a house phone, calls Mustafa, tells him we've arrived. Come right up, Penthouse A, Chateau building, which is the one we're in.

Big crowd by the bank of elevators. We can't get in the first one and barely manage to squeeze into the second before the doors start to close. And in that instant, I look out and see the man. Only a glimpse, just a split second before the doors click together, but there's the face moving along in the crowd, the profile at least, and it strikes a quick, vague, haunting spark somewhere back in my mind. It's a face you can't easily forget: Rawboned, weatherbeaten, deeply wrinkled, lean, tanned.

Tired maybe, that was it, tired, exhausted even, the face of a man in his mid-fifties who was working himself sick, the face of a heavy drinker who, if he didn't have that deep bronze color that made you look like a million bucks, might have the telltale red and purple blotches at the end of the nose and across the cheeks, and hangdog circles under eyes that were beaten and admitted it. The doors close. My mind gropes for just a moment, names and places and years spinning. But the face draws a blank.

We get off on the top floor, fifteen, follow the signs, we got a long walk. Penthouse A turns out to be the suite at the very end of the horseshoe wing to the north, across from the Tower building. Mort knows this hotel inside out, tells us that during the season, December 1 through April 30, this type penthouse (two bedrooms and a parlor) goes for $570 a day. Off season, it's a steal at only $425.

R.T. Mustafa greets us at the door himself, a short, stocky guy, late-fifties, bald pate, face dark tan. Modern gold-framed glasses, heavy eyelids, half drawn, gives him an almost compassionate expression. Mouth is large and turned down at the corners in deep lines to the jaw; ears seem a bit oversized, sticking out as if held there by the roll of gray-white hair at the temples. Wears a spotless white suit, pale blue shirt, solid yellow tie. Looks distinguished.

Mort shows his gold, introduces us, we walk into a long living room that's exquisitely furnished, the wallpaper, carpets, and curtains in bright pastels, flowers and plants on glass-topped tables all over. Mustafa shows us to a sitting area near the terrace doors where we sit on pale pink couches facing a white marble gas fireplace.

"Let me ask you a question," Mustafa begins. "Did you gentlemen make the trip down here just to talk with me?"

"Yes, sir," I tell him.

He nods, pushes at the nosepiece of his glasses. "I'm sorry to cause you the inconvenience. Let me bring you up to date.

This morning, I called John Holland, the owner of the building, and explained the situation as candidly as I could. I fully expect Mr. Holland and his insurance company to start litigation against me. I told him that I discussed the facts at length with my attorneys last night and they advised me to enter a plea of nolo contendere. That's really all I'm permitted to say at this point."

Brendan jots a few lines on his pad, glances at me before asking his question. "Mr. Mustafa, respecting what you just said, sir, I wonder if you could tell us the names of individuals in your firm or in the subcontracting firms who had specific knowledge about the condition of the roof?"

He thinks about it, turning a ring on his finger. "On the advice of my attorneys, no, I'm afraid I can't comment on that."

"Mr. Mustafa," I say, "that question relates to the criminal aspects of the case, not to the litigation aspects."

"Detective Rawlings," he says, "I'm merely following the advice of counsel. I'm sure you understand that. I know you gentlemen have a job to do, I know you're following orders, I know you came all the way down here for the sole purpose of questioning me. I'm genuinely sorry you were inconvenienced, but I want you to understand my side of it. Obviously, I didn't know you were coming down here. When I talked with Miss Orloski last night she told me to expect a telephone call from you this morning."

In the silence that follows, I hear music from one of the bedrooms, a familiar, lilting, dreamlike overture, followed by lyrics that I remember now from some long-ago movie I saw when I was a kid, lyrics that haunted me so much I memorized them:

> *Where do I come from?*
> *Nobody knows.*
> *Where am I going?*

Everybody goes.
The wind blows.
The sea flows.
Nobody knows.

Mustafa listens, stares straight ahead at the gilt clock on the
mantel of the fireplace. "I honestly wish I could be of more
help. I want to cooperate as much as possible within the
guidelines suggested." He twists the gold wedding band on his
finger, looks at it. "So let me say this. Orloski told me your
people have already questioned employees at the architectural
firm and the structural engineering firm, so you have those
names and you can follow up on them. They have the specific
knowledge you referred to concerning the condition of the
roof. That would qualify them as possible suspects in a criminal investigation."

Where do I come from?
Nobody knows.
Where am I going?
Everybody goes.

He sits back, blinks at the ceiling, still twisting the ring. "Now,
as for my own employees, I can tell you this much. The
specific knowledge you referred to. That was classified intelligence within my company."

The wind blows.
The sea flows.
Nobody knows.

Now he glances at the sliding glass door of the terrace, narrows his eyes. "To the best of my knowledge—this was four,
five years ago—only three people in my firm had access to that
information. One, me, of course. Two, Orloski. Three, Samír

Hassan, our general manager. That's all—to my knowledge. Now, you can run a background check on us, of course."

"Would you spell the man's name?" Brendan asks.

"Surely. First name, Samír, S-a-m-i-r, pronounced Sa-meer. Hassan, H-a-s-s-a-n. He's our general manager. Susan Orloski's been with us for—let's see. This is her tenth year. That's right. Susan joined us in September, nineteen seventy-five, several months after receiving her MBA from Harvard. I trust the woman implicitly. Same with Samír, he's been with us—I think it's sixteen years now. Naturally, I conducted a comprehensive background investigation on both of them. Now, you're more than welcome to see those files if you want to."

"We'd appreciate it," I tell him.

"Fine. I'll call our personnel director, Mr. Fitzgerald. I'll tell him to loan you the original files."

Music continues as a young lady walks toward us from the bedroom area, wearing a white tennis outfit that accentuates a dark tan, holding a racket and a can of balls. First impression from a distance, this kid is a positive knockout, about five-seven, maybe 115, long jet-black hair held by a white band across her high forehead. Walks with a confident spring in her step.

Mustafa stands, smiles for the first time, introduces her with obvious pride. "Gentlemen, I'd like you to meet my daughter Laila."

We stand, he gives our names as we shake her hand. I'm last, I take a careful look, she's even better close up: Dark arched brows, thick lashes framing deep-set dark brown eyes, pronounced cheekbones, full lips, strong chin. Got a nice open smile, too. Looks to be around twenty-three, twenty-four, somewhere in there.

"Laila's on holiday from graduate school," he tells us proudly. "Cairo University. She's earned a master's degree in archaeology, now she's working for her doctorate. She just arrived last night."

"Archaeology?" Brendan asks. "Going on any digs?"

She smiles. "Yes. Right now we're working at Luxor, near the ancient site of Thebes."

Brendan nods. "Where's that?"

"Upper Egypt, on the west bank of the Nile. It's sometimes called the Valley of the Kings."

"Isn't that where Tutankhamen's tomb was discovered?" I ask.

She looks surprised. (A New York *cop* knows that?) "Yes, that's right, in nineteen twenty-two, by Lord Carnarvon." Turns to her father. "We've booked a court for six o'clock. I want to get down there early and loosen up."

"Go ahead." He kisses her on the cheek. "See you later."

"Mother's almost ready. Where're you going?"

"Joe's Stone Crab."

"Have fun." She smiles at us. "It's been a pleasure."

So it shouldn't be a total loss, Mort insists we have a drink in his fantasy bar, the Lagoon Saloon, down near the pool. It's dark outside now, all kinds of activities getting under way, a calypso band is playing somewhere, you can smell the ocean. We pass the seven well-lighted tennis courts, all occupied, take a path through all this lush jungle foliage, suddenly here's this huge man-made mountain of rock slabs, must weigh hundreds of tons, jutting out into a big free-form swimming pool. Follow Mort through a hole in the mountain, walk down a tunnel, here's this gigantic lighted aquarium in the wall to our left, filled with weird tropical fish. Now we go in the bar, Brendan and I can't believe this shit, it's a dark cave overlooking the lighted pool. You see the pool through cascading waterfalls coming from the top of the mountain. Bar itself is a series of thick stone slabs, you sit on real sawed-off tree trunks. Not too crowded yet, from what we can see in the candlelight, have to wait for our eyes to adjust.

We're sitting there talking, drinking, I'm smoking a cigar, for some reason I can't seem to concentrate. I should be having a good time, but I'm not. Mort and Brendan pick up on my mood, they finally ignore me, get off on a conversation of their own. I'm looking at the pool through one of the waterfalls, I don't know if this Beefeater martini's just gone straight to my head or what, I'm a thousand miles away.

You know how you sometimes associate certain people and places and times with certain music or tastes or smells or just plain emotions? Happens to me with some degree of regularity. I hear a certain ballad I haven't heard in years, I automatically think of the girl I loved when I was very young. This sort of thing. Music often does this to me, brings back memories, usually pleasant ones, people I knew, places I lived, things I did. I can't control those memories, they just come. Well, okay, tonight I experience two triggers, one visual, one musical, and they're not exactly pleasant associations. Bear with me on this, it's important, but it's difficult to explain in terms of logic because I'm into something abstract here and I'm definitely not the type guy who kills himself with abstractions.

First, that face in the crowd outside the elevators. There's no question in my mind that I've seen this guy's face before, possibly more than once. When I think about it now, looking through the waterfall, I experience the same sick feeling in my stomach and visualize the same strange image that the face triggered before: Image of a man's face in an oil painting we have in our living room at home. We bought this particular painting on our one and only trip to Rio, one-week vacation in the late 1960s. Found it in a little art shop in the Copacabana area, artist by the name of Alfredo Bichels, fairly well known in Brazil. Had the canvas rolled, brought it back, had it mounted and framed in New York. It's relatively large and the mood is quite somber: Slender figure of a Brazilian street cleaner pushing trash with a long-handled brush, all dimly seen in the orange-yellow glow of a streetlight. Man appears to wear light-blue work clothes, maybe denim, and heavy boots or shoes. Curb of the narrow sidewalk is high red brick. House behind him has a low, narrow doorway and a narrow blue-green window. Almost invisible—I didn't see it for years—is the outline of a person standing in the doorway; I think it's a woman, but I'm not at all sure. In the dark-brown shadows to the left is the man's old wooden-wheeled trash wagon and, beyond that, the bare branches and trunk of a small tree. It's possible the street cleaner might be wearing a skullcap of some kind, it's hard to tell, but one thing is for certain: The man has no face. Not in the conventional sense. His head appears to be wrapped tightly in slender rolls of brown cloth painted in intricate detail.

Second trigger is musical: Dreamlike overture and lyrics that came from Laila's bedroom before she appeared. Don't know anything about the song, don't even remember the title of the old movie I heard it in, but I know I was just a kid at the time, probably the mid-1940s, somewhere in there. Must say, the song moved me for some reason, haunted me enough to memorize the lyrics. Why? Probably had something to do with the fact that I was raised as a good Catholic boy in a good Catholic family, went to a good Catholic grammar school, and we just didn't deal with questions and answers like those lyrics posed. What visions do those lines trigger in my poor, funny little brain now? Ready for this? Visions of the sea. Yeah. Why? *I* don't know why. I don't have a *clue* why. What am I, a shrink? I'm talking just plain old everyday glimpses of the open sea here, that's all. That's all I'm saying. Not an open sea with some kind of classy rainbow in the distance, nothing as imaginative as that, this sea doesn't even have boats or seagulls or a big orange sun rising or setting. So, I mean, you can't really read anything *symbolic* into this thing, not that I'd even pick up on stuff like that. No way. No, what we have here is just a simple panorama of a rolling ocean stretching to the horizon, with whitecaps here and there, an obviously deep part of some ocean, far out, and somehow I'm out there on it. No, I don't hear voices calling my name. God, no. Tell you what, that'd really spook the shit out of me if I ever heard that, I'd probably go see a shrink if that happened. Something I've never done, never intend to do. I mean, if I spilled all this weird crap to some shrink, he'd probably tell me what it all *means,* for Christ's sake. And I don't want to *know* what it means.

Well, wait a minute, that's not really true. I'm not being completely honest about that, I admit it. Reason? Real reason? It's embarrassing. I mean, let's face it, guys like me, we're not supposed to be into deep thinking, right? Carry it one step further, we're not supposed to *care* about stuff like that. Spoils the image. We're supposed to be all up-front. Tough guys. What you see is what you get. Just give us the facts, ma'am. Right? Well, okay, I see the logic in that. When you don't step out of character, people tend to trust you. You're predictable. You're dependable. People like those qualities in cops. People want their cops to radiate confidence. Capital C. Understood. But I'll tell you something. I'll tell you the truth. When you've lived and worked with cops as long as me, you understand that cops, the real good ones, very rarely fit the tough-guy image. That's for the phonies and psychos. And, granted, every police force has its share of them. When you've been around a while, you develop a shell, sure, because you need it to survive. I won't deny that. But inside that shell, most good cops, most veteran cops, ask themselves questions. Because, on a day-to-day basis, they're exposed to dark sides of human nature that few civilians normally see, much less try to understand.

Anyhow, that's what goes through my mind in the Lagoon Saloon, looking through the waterfall. Over very quickly, as usual. After that I join Brendan and Mort in conversation, we have another drink, but one image keeps coming to mind:

Laila. For some reason I can't seem to get her out of my thoughts. I honestly don't know what it is about the kid, something in her eyes, her voice, her manner, but my radar keeps telling me to follow up on her, and I trust my radar. Her father? My gut reaction is no, but we'll check him out anyway, routine stuff.

Since we have reservations on the 9:05 morning flight back to New York, Mort suggests we stay at the Sheraton River House, closest hotel to the airport. As he's driving us there, I ask him to do us a favor: Let's stop at the terminal, go to Pan Am, Eastern, Air Florida, TWA, identify ourselves, ask to speak to the manager on duty, find out if their PNL (Passenger Name List) computers include the name of Laila Mustafa on any New York–Miami flights for Monday, December 16. Long shot, but I always play them. No Laila Mustafa on the PNLs at Pan Am, TWA, or Air Florida. Eastern PNL shows an R.T. Mustafa was aboard its 9:15 P.M. flight Monday. R.T. Mustafa? Ask the Eastern manager to punch up the PNR (Passenger Name Record). R.T. Mustafa's reservation was made via telephone Saturday, December 14; passenger's telephone number—(212)628-5578. Now I dial the Manhattan Information Operator, ask for the home number of Mr. R.T. Mustafa. Long shot again, he's probably got an unlisted number, man in his position, right? Only one R.T. Mustafa listed, 1030 Fifth Avenue: 628-5578.

Soon as we get to the Sheraton River House, around 8:15, Mort calls the Fontainebleau's chief of security at home, old buddy of his by the name of Charley Walsh, asks him to ring the hotel, find out when R.T. Mustafa checked in. Walsh doesn't have to call, he already knows. Mr. and Mrs. Mustafa have been regulars at the hotel since 1979, they book Penthouse A every year like clockwork, December 1 through January 31, they're known to virtually all the hotel's management employees. Now Mort asks him if he remembers Mustafa being out of town last weekend, returning Monday night.

Walsh says he doesn't know that, but he'll make a couple of calls, see if he can find out.

We're on expenses, of course, so we ask the room clerk for a minimum-rate twin-bedded room. How much is that, please? "Ninety-seven, sir." No, not the room number, we want the room rate. "Yes, sir, ninety-seven dollars." Minimum? "Minimum. We're in season now, sir." Oh, that's right, forgot that. I sign the card fast, I figure it must be the cheapest room in town, Vadney should be proud of us. Where's our luggage? No luggage. Guy gives me a look. Have to pay in advance, ha-ha. Fine and dandy. Use Brendan's American Express card, don't happen to have mine on me. Guy rings for the bellhop. No, that's okay, just give us the key, we can't afford a tip, didn't make any drug deals today. Go to the drugstore, make a note of what we're buying here: One Gillette Trac II razor, one economy-size can of Gillette Foamy Lemon-Lime, one tiny tube of of mint-flavored Tartar Control Formula Crest, two Oral-B toothbrushes, one small black Ace comb. Won't tell you how much they took us for. Double numbers. We keep the cash receipt so Vadney won't think we're padding. Now we drop the stuff in the room, freshen up, invite Mort to dinner. I call the hotel operator, tell her we'll be in the dining room, ask her to page Mort Cooper if he gets a call.

We're sitting at the bar in the dining room, about 8:45, when Mort's paged. He asks the bartender for a phone, gets one. Conversation on his end: "Uh-huh. Uh-huh. Yeah? Uh-huh." Sounds to that effect. Thanks him, hangs up, smiles. "Terrific guy, Charley, we go back a long way. He checked room service first. Mustafa ordered and signed for breakfast—breakfast for two—Saturday and Sunday. He had them check the man's signature against the one on file. Valid. Also signed for lunch —again for two—at the Beach Broiler early Saturday afternoon. Signature checks. Also signed a bar tab in the Poodle Lounge late Monday evening. Valid signature there too."

"Bingo," Brendan says.

"Got to be Laila," Mort says.

"Not necessarily," I tell them. "Who else is in the family? Another thing, it's a two-bedroom suite, right? They wouldn't have that, year after year, just for the two of them. I mean, he's a businessman, he wouldn't waste money like that."

Mort picks up the phone, asks the operator to charge our room for a local call, gets an outside line, dials Charley Walsh. Asks who else is in the Mustafa family. Answer: Laila's an only child, Charley's certain of that, he's known Mustafa for seven years. But they often have guests—relatives, close friends, business associates, some stay as long as a week or more, they even register so the operators will have their names. He recalls one regular, Susan Orloski, who usually stays a week in January. Reason he remembers her, he says, she's a real looker. Also, Laila stays with them every December about this time on her two-week vacation from college.

So, logic seems to indicate that Laila was on that flight from New York. But why the hell was she coming from New York? Simple answer: Probably no nonstop flights from Cairo to Miami. Too simple. I light up a cigar, sip my drink, think about it.

"Mort," I say. "Any nonstop or direct flights between here and Cairo?"

"I'd have to check it out."

"How about nonstops from London, Paris, Rome, like that?"

Gives me this indignant look. "John, what the fuck you think we got here, some little jerkwater town in the back of beyond? I mean, New York we ain't, but we got daily nonstop flights coming in here from all over the world."

I nod. "But not from Cairo."

Smiles, sips his drink, picks up the phone, goes through the billing routine with the operator, asks for Pan Am's number. Dials it, asks the question. No, sir, Pan Am doesn't serve

Cairo anymore, may we suggest that you try TWA? Thank
you, hangs up, goes through the bit with the operator again,
asks for TWA's number. Dials it, asks the question. Yes, sir,
TWA offers direct service between Miami and Cairo with one
stop in Lisbon. May I take your reservation? Not today.

That's enough for me, at least for the time being. I pick up
the phone now, ask the operator to bill our room for the
long-distance call I'm about to make, then dial Chief Vadney
at home. It's not quite nine o'clock, not too bad. Wife Samantha answers, tells me to make it fast, "Moonlighting" comes
on at nine. Sure thing. Chief gets on the line, sounds like he's
had a few drinks. I give him a quick rundown on Laila and
her father, he loves it, best news he's had all day. Seems the
JRTF and Bronx Robbery Unit are still playing pocket pool.

"Now, listen up, buddy," he tells me. "Who you working
with down there, who's your contact?"

"Detective by the name of Cooper, Mort Cooper."

"Has he got Chief Haynes's home number?"

Turn to Mort. "Got Haynes's home number?"

"Yeah."

"Yeah, Chief."

"All right, ask him to call Haynes, tell him I requested that
this kid be placed under round-the-clock surveillance, effective immediately. What's the kid's name again—Lolita?"

"Laila. Pronounced Lay-la."

"Laila Mustafa, huh? What're they, A-rabs?"

"I think so."

"How old's the kid?"

"Twenty-three, maybe twenty-four."

"A looker?"

"Believe it."

"You sure get the tough assignments, Little John."

"Well, y'know, we just stumble around."

"Down there in sunny, balmy Miami, hobnobbing with

rich, sultry young Arab broads. What's the temperature down there?"

"Cool night tonight, Chief. Low seventies."

"Jesus H. Christ. Know what we got here, right this minute in Manhattan? Thirty-eight degrees and freezing rain, buddy-boy."

Samantha's voice: *"Walt, the credits are on!"*

"Gotta get off, Little John, now listen up. You and Brendan stay put, join the surveillance teams, report to me on a daily basis. What hotel you at?"

"Sheraton River House. Room four-twenty-seven."

"Wait a minute, wait'll I get a pencil and paper, I'm in the kitchen." *Clunk.* Slams the receiver down on a counter or something.

"Wait, will ya quit gassin' out there!?"

I can hear the "Moonlighting" theme reach crescendo, then the announcer's voice: " 'Moonlighting.' Brought to you by . . ." Thought occurs to me that Samantha must be slightly deaf. Nice on the neighbors.

"Okay, Little John, say it again."

"Sheraton River House. Room four-twenty-seven."

Pause. "Cheapest room they got, right?"

"Believe it."

"All right, Little John, I gotta go. I think you're definitely on to something, I'm counting on you guys to come through. Now, I want you and those Miami teams to bust ass on this kid. Stick to this kid like stink on shit. Y'read me, buddy?"

"You got it, Chief. Stink on shit. Speaking of which, we only got the clothes on our backs down here, we didn't pack. We'll need to buy some—"

"Rawlings, you mean to tell me you guys went all the way to Miami and didn't even *pack?*"

"Begging your pardon, sir, but you told us not to. We had to catch the next flight, remember?"

"God *damn.*"

"So we'll need to buy some—"

"Yeah, sure, jeans and sneakers, go ahead. T-shirts, whatever you think. Within reason, of course."

"Chief, we're talking the Fontainebleau Hilton here. Real posh spot, y'know?"

"Better yet, here's another idea. Here's a—here's a fantastic idea, Little John, listen up. You ever impersonate a woman?"

"A woman?"

"A *woman,* buddy!"

"Chief, come on, huh?"

"I mean, this kid's *seen* you, right? The kid and her old man? Y'got no *cover,* buddy-boy, they'd spot you in one second flat. And if they did, that's it, the ball game's over, our one and only lead is shot in the ass. We just can't *afford* that, buddy."

"Chief. Gimmie a break, huh?"

"Think of the *mobility* it'd give you. Fantastic mobility."

"Mobility? In high heels?"

"Walter, ya missin' some juicy shit here!"

"Sam, I'm talkin' business here!"

"Chief?"

"Yeah, sorry, go ahead."

"If you want my honest opinion—"

"I mean, think about the possibilities here, buddy. You could move around freely, go to bars, restaurants, discos, observe this kid up close, first-hand surveillance."

"Chief, come on, will ya? I'd never get away with that."

"How long you been a cop, Little John?"

"How long? Thirty years this year. And I never—"

"Thirty years on the force. Ever consider the possibility you might be getting stale, buddy?"

"Stale?"

"Stale. I mean, look around. These new guys just getting their gold, these young bucks, thcy're a whole new *breed,* buddy. They're trained to use their imaginations, they're becoming masters of disguise now, they even got a course on it at the Academy. That's *today,* John. That's law enforcement today. *Creative* law enforcement. Whatever it takes to get the job done, they turn the problem on its head, they find a way, they do it. Why? I'll tell you why. They're not *inhibited,* that's why. Y'ask 'em to play a broad, they play a broad. Bing-bing. No sweat, no problem. Not only that, these young guys, they're into *method.* That's right. *Method* acting. Works. Works wonders, I've seen it first-hand. Whatever the role is, they get into it deep, they psych themselves into that character: Executives, clerks, secretaries, drunks, pimps, dopers, dealers, whatever it happens to be. Y'ask 'em to play a broad, they do research on it. I'm talking *serious* research. They think about it, they rap with their wives and girl friends, they study wigs, makeup, clothes, jewelry, they learn how to walk like a broad, move like a broad, talk like a broad, laugh like a broad, cry like a broad, react to any given circumstance. Hell, some of 'em even get to *think* like a broad."

"Chief . . ."

"I mean, let's face some facts here, Little John. Brendan can't do it, he's just too fuckin' *big.* That leaves you. You're short, you're thin, you're bright, you learn fast. You're the only one who can possibly pull it off. Right?"

"Oh, shit."

"Now, listen up, buddy-boy. First thing tomorrow morning, I want Chief Haynes to assign a top woman detective to you, best makeup specialist he's got. Tell your contact there, Mort what's-his-name, tell him to tell Haynes to set it up."

"Chief, if you want my honest opinion, I don't think it'll work. I really don't."

"Why not?"

"Well, I don't know, I just don't look like a woman."

"You *will,* buddy, you *will.* Take my word for it. I'm telling you, this state-of-the-art makeup shit they got today—they call it a 'makeover'—you won't even recognize yourself. Nobody will. I mean, you get a load of yourself in the mirror, it'll knock your—it'll knock your stockings off."

"Chief, look. Listen."

"That's a direct order, buddy-boy. I mean, we're talking the biggest cash robbery in history here, this is just too major a case to let stale, old-fashioned inhibitions get in the way. Y'gotta get *with* it, Little John. Y'gotta get into *today's* techniques. Y'gotta get into *method* acting. That's it, no more nice guy, I'm not asking you, I'm telling you: Play a broad!"

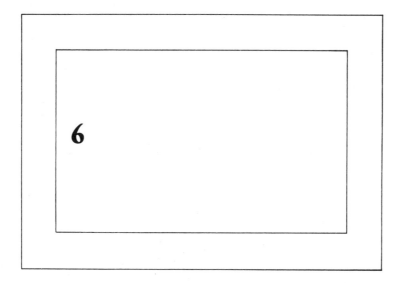

6

EIGHT O'CLOCK NEXT MORNING, Wednesday, December 18, Mort picks us up at the hotel, drives us to headquarters. First thing, we check with Chief Haynes on the surveillance progress reports. Two-man team began the first eight-hour shift at the Fontainebleau 9:30 last night with a detailed description of Laila provided by Mort and us. Didn't spot her around the lobby, bars, or restaurants all night. Starting midnight, one of the men staked out the front entrance full-time on the logical assumption that maybe she'd been out on the town. By the time his shift ended at 5:30, she still hadn't shown. Three possible alternatives: (1) Both men missed her, which wouldn't be that unusual in a booked-to-capacity hotel with 1,224 rooms and at least 2,500 guests; (2) she didn't leave Penthouse A after 9:30 last night; (3) she went out before 9:30 and still hasn't returned. Second shift called Haynes at 8:05 this morning (his hours are eight to four) and reported negative progress. We're guessing she stayed in the suite all night. After all, she only arrived the previous night, Monday, she probably hadn't seen her parents in months, so it seems natural they'd want to spend a few quiet evenings together. We know her parents were about to leave for dinner at Joe's Stone Crab before six o'clock last night because Mr. Mustafa said so in our presence. They could easily have returned before 9:30 and joined Laila in the suite. In any event, the second-shift team is now concentrating on the lobby, the breakfast rooms, the tennis courts, the swimming pool area, the cabanas, and the beach.

Meantime, Haynes has arranged for me to spend the morning with one of the top women detectives in the department, Judith Sever, who's also the best disguise expert he's got. She's been briefed, she knows a makeover has been ordered by Vadney. Mort and Brendan accompany me to her office, grinning broadly, they wouldn't miss this show for the world. Entertainment This Morning.

Going down on the elevator, Mort fills us in on Sever's background, well known around the building: Native Floridian, about thirty-two, single, Police Science degree from the University of Miami, eleven years on the force, seven commendations, generally considered one of the brightest and most innovative undercover cops in the city. I don't know, for some reason I visualize this big, strong, Amazonian type, voice like Joan Rivers on a bummer, face and figure like Bella Abzug on a binge. We walk in her fourth-floor squadroom cubicle, here's this beautiful kid talking on the telephone, voice like Vivien Leigh in *Streetcar,* face and figure like Goldie Hawn on a diet. Motions for us to sit, crosses her legs, looks me up and down, over, under, around, and through as she calmly finishes her conversation, uninhibited as they come. I figure, what the hell, I'll do the same: About five-four, maybe 119 or less, relatively short blond hair worn in an attractive curly-frizz, brown eyes with thick lashes and light mascara, very clear complexion. Wears a fashionably oversized blue V-neck T-shirt pulled up and knotted at the left side of a slim waist, tight Guess jeans with zippers at the trim ankles, white Reeboks. Tell you what, before this kid gets off the phone and says a word to us, I'm quickly starting to lose my stale, old-fashioned inhibitions about playing a broad. Hell, I might even get into method with a teacher like this, what do I know?

Before she hangs up, I glance around her cubicle. Fairly large, as they go. It's against an outside wall where she's mounted a steel bookcase filled with hardcovers, mostly, I can read some titles from where I sit. Lots of reference books, Spanish-English and German-English dictionaries and encyclopedias, various telephone directories, Florida city guides, books on ballistics and forensic jurisprudence next to volumes on cosmetology, fashion, and etiquette. Two black file cabinets flank the bookcase, labels on all drawers carefully typed. Her desk is a standard steel job flush against a wall of the cubicle and she has seven 9 × 12 wooden boxes along the far edge, each box labeled, filled with memos, reports, letters, legal documents, and so on, each box relating to a specific case she's working. Steel table to the left of her desk holds a black IBM Correcting Selectric II typewriter with a single-spaced memo about half finished, strict margins. Small black high-intensity lamp on her desk throws a bright white cone of light on the memo.

Now she hangs up, we stand, Mort does the introductions, we shake hands. Up close, this kid doesn't look anywhere near thirty-two. No lines to speak of, could be the makeup, but somehow I doubt it. Warm smile reveals very white teeth and there's a nice sparkle of mischief in her eyes.

"Please sit down." Her accent is southern, but not heavy. "Chief Haynes briefed me on the surveillance situation. Detective Rawlings, have you ever had a makeover before?"

"No."

Looks me up and down again. "I'd say about five-ten, one-thirty-five, right?"

"Close enough."

"Fourteen and a half collar, thirty-two sleeves?"

"Uh-huh."

"Let's see. Thirty waist, maybe thirty-one length?"

"Just about, yeah."

"What's your shoe size?"

"Nine and a half B."

"You'll be easy." Glances at her small gold watch. "What kind of time are we talking about?"

Mort checks his watch. "Okay, well, the third shift starts at one-thirty, but he doesn't necessarily have to be on it."

"Do you want to be?" she asks me.

I think about it, shrug. "Depends."

"Depends on what?"

"On whether or not I think I'm ready."

"Let me put it to you straight," she says. "We have less than four hours, if you want to work the third shift. I can have you ready physically in that time, but you have a lot of adjustments to make, and that always depends on the individual. Frankly, if you have the time, I'd rather not rush it. Ideally, I'd like to spend the morning on the physical makeover—cosmetics and clothes—to make it as convincing as possible. Then we should really spend—at the very least—we should spend the entire afternoon in getting you started on the more difficult things—movement, psychology, a variety of subtle nuances that require concentration and practice."

"Fine with me."

"Okay? Also, I'd rather not have you start out in daylight."

Mort stands up quickly, buttons his blazer, gives the impression he doesn't want to stay for the show after all. "Okay, Brendan and me, we'll head over to the Fontainebleau, keep out of sight, see what we can do to help the guys out."

Brendan stands, shoves his hands in his pockets. "All right, then. John, you'll be coming over there after—? I mean, I guess you want to play it by ear at first, see how it goes, huh?"

"Yeah, I think so. At this point, I just don't know."

"Another thing," Sever says. "Normally, when I'm working with our own officers, I usually stay with the guy for the
first few shifts. It's just much easier that way, it reduces a lot
of potential problems. I'll recommend it to the chief in this
case. In fact, I'll strongly recommend it, since Detective Rawlings has no previous experience in this kind of duty. We'll see
how it goes, but we could—it's possible we could take the
nine-thirty to five-thirty shift tonight."

"Excellent idea," Mort says. "I mean, if you don't mind the
overtime, Judith. Makes a hell of a long day for you."

"I don't mind. Not at all—in fact, I could use the money
this time of year. Here it is, the eighteenth, I haven't done any
Christmas shopping yet."

"Tell me about it," Brendan mutters.

"Oh, shit," Mort says. "Is today the eighteenth already?"

"You better believe it," she says. "One week to go, one week
from *today.*" Stands up now. "Okay, you guys, we've got a lot
of ground to cover."

Before we get into the heavy stuff, Sever and I go down to the
third-floor cafeteria for a cup of coffee. Glad she suggested it,
because, to be honest, I need the time to psych myself into this
thing. There's no question in my mind this kid knows exactly
what she's doing, she's obviously a real pro, handles herself
real good. But I have a lot of questions before we start. Also,
I think it's a good idea that we get to know each other a little,
since we'll probably be working together for the next few
nights.

She uses a plastic security card to make the elevator stop at
floor three; keeps civilians out of the cafeteria. We step off,
turn left down a short hall, then right, into the counter area.
I grab a tray, two cups and saucers, spoons, creamers, nap-
kins, draw two coffees, pay the cashier. Cafeteria is large and
pleasant, noise level kept low by thick orange carpeting and
a cork ceiling. L-shaped room, white walls with pastel-colored

vertical panels, recessed ceiling lights, dark orange tables, black plastic chairs. Sever leads the way to a table against the far right wall, away from occupied tables, takes a chair with her back to the windows. Waves to someone across the room as she sits, takes her cup from the tray, pours some cream, smiles at me as she stirs.

"Chief Haynes told me basics about the case," she says, "but he didn't tell me anything about Rawlings."

"Call me John, please. Not much to tell, really. Been a cop for thirty years, robbery duty mostly, love my job. Married, one son, we live on Long Island. Mort tells us you kind of specialize in undercover work."

"Right. And please call me Judith." Opens her purse, takes out a pack of Benson & Hedges 100's, lights one quickly. "Well, we have at least one thing in common, John, I love my work too."

"Dangerous work, undercover."

She inhales deeply, blows smoke toward the ceiling, then smiles. "You sound like my boyfriend. If he had his way, John, I'd have a desk job around here. The truth is, I've wanted to be a cop, a detective, since I was a teenager. And not just *any* detective, okay? I wanted to be the best at what I did. Whatever it was, whatever they gave me. And I still feel that way, I still work that way. I can't stand sloppiness or indifference in police work. There's no excuse for it, particularly in under-cover duty, because the risk factor is maximized."

"My sentiments exactly."

"Okay? I admit that I'm a perfectionist, I'm almost compul-sive about it, but that's the way I work. Some of the people around here think I'm a pain in the ass. Fine. That's their problem, not mine. When I'm working undercover, my pri-mary responsibility is to cover my butt upside-down and back-wards and provide the same protection for my partner. That's not to say I don't have a sense of humor about the job. I do. I have to. I get as much kick out of this job as anybody else.

I'm sure you do, too, or you wouldn't have hung around for thirty years, right?"

"Absolutely."

She nods, sips her coffee, tamps her cigarette.

"Keep talking, Judith. I'm interested."

"Okay, let's get into it, let me give you a fast rundown on what's involved in the makeover routine. I do these fairly frequently for Vice when we don't want to place female officers at unnecessary risk. First off, the physical part, the overall appearance. Probably the single most important element is the hairpiece. We have the best on the market, John, I've insisted on that. Real hair, very expensive hair, in a good assortment of colors and styles. This can get complicated, but the basic idea is to match the hair to the eyebrows as closely as possible, then select a hairstyle that conforms to the shape of the face and the head." She narrows her eyes to my brows. "In your case, light brunette, full, medium long. You have slightly bushy brows, John, not really heavy, but I'll have to pluck around the edges, shape and smooth the general lines."

"Pluck?"

"Yes. Problem with that?"

I take out a cigar, hold it up. "Mind?"

"No."

I remove the cellophane slowly. "Okay, cards on the table. This is the kind of thing I was a little apprehensive about."

"Why? Specifically."

"As I understand it, when you pluck eyebrows, it's a permanent thing. They don't grow back."

Gets a smile out of her. "John, you've been watching nineteen-twenties movies, right?"

I shrug, bite off the end of the cigar, drop it in the ashtray. "I've seen older women who—apparently, they had their eyebrows plucked, maybe in the twenties or thirties, yeah. When it was the style. And they never grew back. I mean I've seen 'em. So now they have to use eyebrow pencil. Looks—to me, it looks horrible."

"Okay. That was the result of continual plucking and even shaving the brows on a daily basis for years. So the roots were finally destroyed. The truth is, eyebrows grow back, but at a slower rate than other hairs—your beard, for example. It's not permanent, I assure you."

"All right. Understood."

"In any event, I'm talking about minimal plucking. Actually, you need it anyway, John."

"Think so?"

"Definitely. And you have some white hairs in there that'll have to go. Okay, next, lashes. You'll have false lashes, that's no problem at all. We have a variety of sizes, shapes, they cover your natural lashes, there's an adhesive on the back. I'll trim them, make them as comfortable as possible. Then maybe some light coloring on the eyelids, we'll see. Now, makeup. You don't have an especially heavy beard, but you'll have to shave very closely before I put it on. I'll apply a relatively heavy pancake makeup foundation. It washes off very easily, just soap and water. Lipstick, I'm not crazy about lipstick, I don't really think you'll need it. Maybe just a trace to give definition. Applied with a brush, we'll try it and see. Then earrings, gold earrings, fairly long to show under the medium-long hair."

"Don't have to get my ears pierced, I hope."

"It'd help, to be honest. With long earrings."

"I was kidding."

"I know, but we've had problems with this. The fact is, long, dangling earrings are hard to keep on. Without pierced ears."

"Uh-huh."

She smiles at my expression. "It's not that big a deal, John, it only takes a couple of seconds. The hole doesn't show and it heals up fast as soon as you stop wearing them."

"I think I'll pass."

"Okay, but if they start falling off, you're gonna get pissed. I'm just warning you in advance. I've seen it happen all too often."

"Do I really need earrings?"

"In my opinion, yes. Definitely. If you want to do this thing right."

I look at my unlit cigar, think about it. Can't help remembering Vadney's words, accusing me of being stale, old-fashioned, inhibited. Have to admit, that got to me. Really got to me. Stung my ass good. Thing is, I know it's not true. I know for a fact it's not true. Now all I have to do is prove it to myself. Easier said than done. Go on, prove it. I look at Judith and nod. "Pierce 'em."

"Okay, good. That takes care of the face."

"Is that the hardest?"

"Well, yes and no, it depends on the individual. Ordinarily, I'd say yes, if the guy has a reasonably small frame. If not, clothes are hardest, because you've got to camouflage his shape, which is often very difficult. Fortunately, something's happened in fashion lately that helps a great deal. It's the 'baggy' look. Have you noticed?"

"Yeah, I have."

"Like this shirt I'm wearing. Purposely oversized, they're cut that way. This sort of thing is all the rage now, just a baggy V-neck T-shirt, stuff like this. It hangs low on the hips, you can pull it around, tie it at either side. Very comfortable too. Also, jumpsuits are very much in style this year, baggy jumpsuits. As soon as I saw you, I thought, 'Here's a jumpsuit type.' Because, I mean, it covers a multitude of problems in a makeover. And I'll tell you something, John, the officers who've worn 'em, the guys with the right build, they really liked 'em."

"Kind of a neuter type outfit?"

"No, not neuter, it's quite feminine in appearance, the cut,

the colors and all. But it gives 'em the kind of physical free-
dom and flexibility they're used to in men's clothes. I mean,
it's the same type zipper front that workmen's jumpsuits have,
except it's cut and styled differently. And you don't have to
go through the whole routine of dresses or skirts, which means
you don't have to shave your legs."

"Sounds good to me."

"Okay? I mean, baggy jumpsuits are perfect for some guys.
You don't have to worry so much about arms, breasts, hips,
and legs. Of course, at night, in fashionable places like the
Fontainebleau, you really have to wear heels to make it convincing. Which means you have to shave your ankles and wear
stockings or pantyhose, because the ankles are seen, especially
when you sit down. But low heels are fine, they're perfectly
acceptable."

"Uh-huh. How low?"

"Oh, just an inch. Which really isn't much at all. I know
all the problems guys have with heels, I understand, but don't
sweat it. We'll have plenty of time to practice, you'll get the
hang of it. Now, where was I before we got off on this?"

"The face. You were finished with that."

"Right. Okay, with a long-sleeved jumpsuit, the only parts
of your body that actually show are your face, neck, wrists,
hands, and ankles. The neck is simple, you'll have makeup, of
course, then a heavy gold chain necklace looped around twice.
Wrists, you'll have a slender gold watch, one gold bracelet, a
couple of rings. Ankles, a thin gold ankle bracelet, right ankle.
So the only major thing left is the nails, you need false nails,
and that's a little time-consuming."

"How long's it usually take?"

"At least an hour, sometimes a lot longer, to do it right, but
it's worth the time. It makes a big difference." She looks at my
hands. "You have fairly thin fingers and good nails, so it
shouldn't be hard. What it entails, basically, is using an emery
board to roughen the tops of your nails, filing and shaping the

edge of the false nail that goes against your cuticle, so there's no bump there, then applying glue and attaching the false nails. They come unpainted and they're long. When the glue hardens, I trim and shape each nail. And I'll make them reasonably short. Next, I apply the polish, which is time-consuming, of course, three coats. I'll select a color to coordinate with the jumpsuit. The nails can be removed with simple nail polish remover."

"So I can take them off after a shift and they'd glue back on again easily?"

"Not easily, there's a lot more to it than that, but yes, you can do that. With touch-ups and all, you can use them for some time."

I nod, start to light my cigar, then hesitate.

She smiles, offers me a cigarette. "Better try these, John."

Make a long story short, Judith takes me to a locked and unmarked fifth-floor office, originally used for storage of miscellaneous equipment, that she's converted into a classy wardrobe and makeover room, almost looks like a little boutique. Two walls of racks with padded-hanger designer-brand seasonal selections for m'lady from Palm Beach to Key West, we're talking Courrèges and Gucci to Bloomies and Saks here, with a sprinkling of Lily Pulitzer, literally hundreds of outfits for day and evening, protected by clear plastic covers, all carefully labeled and arranged by size. Above, wraparound two-tiered shelves of big round boxes for the hairpieces, also labeled, plus smaller boxes for purses, belts, scarves, and accessories. On the floor, double-decked shoe racks with labeled boxes, choices here include Capezio, Bandolino, Givenchy, Pandiani, Bernardo, Pappagallo, to name just a few. Dressing table against the third wall, to the right, resembles some I've seen in Broadway theaters, circular mirror peppered with Polaroids, ablaze with individual bulbs, drawers with every type of cosmetic, perfume, and deodorant known to man or beast.

Locked file cabinet nearby contains jewelry, small-caliber weapons in custom holsters, boxes of ammo, an assortment of drug paraphernalia, but no drugs. Full-length mirror behind the door, plenty of walking space, here's where you strut your stuff. Small steps, please, don't break a leg opening night. Tell you what, any transvestite short of Boy George would have an instant blue-veiner at all this crap.

Judith starts with what she calls "coloring." Tosses swatches of different colored cloth across my shoulders, glances at my steel-blue killer eyes, tries to decide which colors play up the eyes, seem most natural. Finally concludes I'm a "winter person," chooses my wardrobe accordingly: Royal blue St. Laurent jumpsuit, closely matching Dior handbag with shoulder strap, closely matching Givenchy snakeskin shoes with one-inch heels. Of course, December nights in Miami tend to be on the cool side, so she selects a Blass jacket with vertical stripes in beige and navy, just about long enough to hide my hips—or, I should say, lack of same. Bra with average-sized foam-rubber cups to give at least a suggestion of bazooms, conservative panties, dark blue knee-high stockings with elastic tops. That's my basic outfit, providing it all fits. Must say, the kid's got excellent taste.

Now she puts the clothing aside, asks me to remove my blazer, tie, and shirt, sits me down at the dressing table, pins a barber's cloth around my neck, trains a high-intensity lamp on my face. Here we go. Selects a tweezer, starts on the eyebrows. Pluck-pluck-pluck. Smooth, fast, practiced movements, nothing to it, only hurts when I laugh. Five, ten minutes later, when my eyes stop watering, she hands me a mirror. Bushy, craggy, rugged, rough, Neanderthal brows are transformed into smooth, full, sophisticated, slightly arched and tapered facsimiles of those worn by—yeah, Don Johnson. I mean, I'm talking sex symbol brows here. Above my very eyes. I'm impressed, I admit it. How long has this been going on? Where was I, in a drawer someplace? Can't resist a few quick, devilish arches before she grabs the mirror back with feigned disdain.

Makeup's next, so she gives me a safety razor, can of shaving cream, towel, sends me off to the men's room down the hall. Not only do I have to shave my puss for the second time this morning, now I have to shave my hands, wrists, and ankles, yet. I'm walking down the hall in my two-day-old grubby T-shirt and aching arching eyebrows, I'm wondering how I'm going to pull this off with at least some degree of dignity, standing there at a sink in full view of every officer who comes in to take a leak, shaving my hands, wrists, and *ankles,* for Christ's sake. I mean, what the hell am I supposed to say? "Oh, hi, there, fellas, forgot to shave my ankles this morning, ha-ha." Me? No way. Have to come up with another solution.

As luck would have it, I walk in the men's room, here are these two clowns having a long, drawn-out conversation in heavy accents, y'all, leaning against the sinks, smoking stogies. Big, strong, rawboned, two-fisted, foulmouthed, fearless all-Americans, as it were. I need this, I haven't got enough problems already. Me, I look like an anemic midget standing next to these guys in my pee-you T-shirt. Both of 'em do a fast double-take: Hot *damn,* Joe-Bob, another one of them de-viated *pre* verts! Thoughts to that effect. Now they watch bug-eyed as I peel off my T-shirt, hold it limp-wristed, drop it gingerly in the sink next to them. Idea hits me out of the blue, here's a way to get rid of these dudes fast. I turn to them, blink shyly, touch a little finger to my tapered brows, speak just above a whisper:

"Excuse me, gentlemen, but I feel a moral and medical duty to alert you to the potential danger of exposure to my vital bodily fluids."

Both step back quickly, eyes wide, cigars dancing.

"What yew say, boy?" older one asks.

My left brow jumps to an outrageous A-frame. "Well, I

mean, you *know*. One can't be too careful these days, can one? Unnecessary exposure to sweat, saliva, urine, even to inert *feces,* for heaven's sakes."

"Now, hold on there, boy," younger one says. "Yew—are yew sayin' yew got—?" Just can't bring himself to say it.

"To put it delicately," I say, "it rhymes with raids."

Older dude chomps clear through his stogie, sweeps his arm back to protect his younger buddy. *"Hole-* lee humped-up *Geezus!"*

Out they scuffle-shuffle in a confusion of cordovans. I figure as how word-of-mouth should quarantine this here can in nothin' flat, if y'all'll excuse the expression, y'honor, suh.

Well, okay, hot water, aerosol lather, I shave my face carefully, try to make it as close as possible, particularly the neck, without nicks. Used to nick my Adam's apple regularly when I was a rookie cop, then it'd drip, it'd run down and leave a big red blot on my collar because I didn't want to wear a Band-Aid. I mean, who wants to wear a Band-Aid on his Adam's apple all day, right? Doesn't look good, especially when the blot turns brown and all. Then I wised up. Discovered a secret. Last twenty-five years or so, I'm walking around with a no-nick neck. Secret solution to the problem, did a lot of research. I mean, if I could patent and market the sucker, I'd be a millionaire. Story of my life. Share it with you, what the hell, I feel magnanimous. Easy directions: While grasping the handle of the safety (or straight) razor firmly in the fingers of the right (or left) hand, gently probe the middle (or lower) front region of the neck with the fingers of the left (or right) hand to locate and identify the exact position of the thyroid cartilage (Adam's apple) under the protective layer of lubricating shave cream (or gel); place the tip of the index finger of the left (or right) hand over the tip of the thyroid cartilage, thereby effectively shielding the protuberant from the proposed upward and/or downward vertical route of the razor (a direction perpendicular to the plane of the horizon), then proceed to shave unwanted hair from the neck with the right-hand-held (or left-hand-held) razor in the accustomed manner, exercising caution to immediately interrupt the upward and/or downward passage of the blade(s) at the instant when probable or actual physical contact is anticipated or made with the tip of the finger and/or fingernail of the left (or right) index finger protecting the tip of the thyroid cartilage.

Nothing to it. Of course, when I'm in a hurry, I nick the shit out of my index finger, but no system is perfect.

Now I have to face the inevitable, my first overt identification with the trappings of transvestism: Shaving sections of my exposed extremities. I look around, check the door, turn, walk over to peek in the swinging doors of each of the seven empty stalls, then come up with a compromise solution. I mean, maybe it's stale, old-fashioned, and inhibited, but, quarantine or no, I just got to do this kind of shaving in a stall. Sitting on the can in a stall. A locked stall. And that's what I do. Select the stall against the far wall, go in, lock the door, hang up my T-shirt, take a seat. Graffiti scratched into the paint on the door: "He who writes on shithouse walls/Should roll his shit in little balls." Below that, some good ole boy has penned: "He who reads these lines of wit/Should eat them little balls of shit." Strictly cerebral-type cops at the headquarters level, Vadney would love it. Makes me homesick.

Shave the backs of my hands and wrists in complete comfort and privacy. Comes to my ankles, gets a little complicated. Question of logistics. Have no real alternative but to roll up my trousers, place my Guccis and knee-highs on the floor, brace my feet against the door, and go to it. Use the water in the toilet, no sweat at all, excellent fluorescent lighting overhead. Halfway through, hear the big outside door open and bang shut. I freeze. Some guy with squeaky cordovans ambles over to the row of urinals opposite the stalls. Easy to tell he's heavy, I figure about 220–240, somewhere in there. Now I sit there like a statue, razor poised over my left ankle, listening.

Zzz-zzz-zzz, unzips his fly. Goes, "Uuuhhh," as he pulls out
Big Peter. Long pause. Can't get it started, needs a pump-
primer. Tries the old trick, breaks the silence with a low
whistle. Fine with me, I've done it myself many times, really
works. Don't ask me why, probably some age-old orangutan
instinct, what do I know? Thing is, this sucker can't leave it
alone with a simple couple of notes, now he's into a tune, yet.
Not only that, he's whistling it through his teeth. I can't
believe this tub of lard, he's whistling "Dixie." Yeah! This is
no shit, this clown's standing there holding his brains in his
hands and whistling "Dixie" through his teeth. I'm visualizing
him, I'm getting this almost irresistible urge to laugh. I'm
telling you, I can't hold it in, it's welling up in me deep down,
I'm starting to shake. I shut my eyes, clench my teeth, hold
my breath, try to think of something sad. Can't do it. Listen
to this yokel, he's whistling all-out now, he must be ready to
open Niagara Falls here.

Finally, I do it, I burst out laughing. I mean, it just gushes
out of me, a good healthy "Haaaaa!—ha-ha—hahahahaha!"
Instantly, lardass quits whistling. I clamp my hands over my
mouth, stifle all the rest. Silence. Five seconds. Ten. I figure
his bladder and bowels are suddenly frozen tight: Gol-*lee,*
somebody's watchin' me *exposin'* myself! "Uuuhhh," he
pushes poor limp Big Peter back in. Zzz-zzz-zzz, zips his fly
back up. Squeak-squeak, squeak-squeak, turns around, faces
my stall. Silence. Of course, there's a big space between the
stall walls and door and the floor, so he can't miss seeing my
shoes and socks sitting there next to the aerosol can of shaving
cream. Must look weird. Must stun the imagining mind. What
in Sam Hill could a guy be *doin'* in there?

Deep, macho, graveled voice: "Somebody in the stall
there?"

Imitation of his voice: "Nobody but us chickens, yew piss
ant."

Pause. Squeak-squeak. "What yew say, boy?"

"Nobody but us piss ants, yew chicken fucker."

Pause. Squeak-squeak. "What the hell yew doin' in there, boy?"

"Jes pullin' m'pud, yew horny-toad Peepin'-Tom scrote, yew."

Squeak. Pause. "Gawd a-mighty," he says, more to himself than to me. "I ain't never seen nothin' like this."

Slowly, slowly, I reach up, take my T-shirt from its hook, roll it into a ball, then quickly lob it over the stall in the direction of his voice. Must've hit him or come damn close, because he lets loose with this startled *"Ahhheee!"* Squeak-a-squeak-a-squeak, he's running for the door.

"Stick around, cornball!" I yell. "Yew ain't seen nothin' yet!"

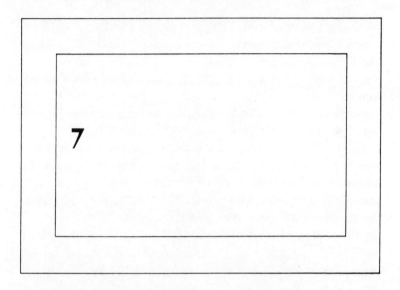

7

JUDITH SEVER IS AN ARTIST. That's the only word
for her. In three hours of nonstop concentration, this classy
kid transforms me from a short, thin, undistinguished middle-
aged man into—dare I say it?—into a tall, slim, stunningly
attractive young broad. No exaggeration, this is straight, this
is what happens. Remember what Chief Vadney said about
state-of-the-art makeovers today, about how I'd glance in the
mirror and not even recognize myself? Man was right. Hate
to admit it, but he was right on the money. Got to hand it to
Judith, she's a perfectionist all the way, so she's real flexible
in the early stages, doesn't lock into anything final until she
sees it in perspective, compares it, plays around with alternatives and combinations. Like, last minute, she changes her
mind about basic makeup. Decides against a relatively heavy
pancake foundation and all that goes with it, switches to the
most expensive stuff she's got, all Chanel products: Moistur-
izer, light liquid foundation and blush-on, mascara, eye
shadow, powder, lipstick, nail polish, the whole shot, topped

off by Chanel No. 5 perfume, no less. Combine all this with a $1,795 dark brunette hairpiece, the real thing, medium-long and full, custom-tailored lashes and nails, a sprinkling of expensive but conservative jewelry, the royal-blue St. Laurent jumpsuit, matching Dior handbag with shoulder strap, matching Givenchy snakeskins with one-inch heels, now you're talking class.

It's just 12:45 now, I'm standing in front of the full-length mirror on the back of the makeover room door, I can't believe what I'm seeing here, gives me a strange feeling: Slim, tanned, sexy brunette gazes back at me, definitely a Liz Taylor type, maybe mid-thirties, thick hair has a windblown look over the forehead, dark eyes and lashes dominate an oval face, flawless complexion, well-defined lips. Long gold earrings dangle from pierced lobes that still sting a little, but Judith's right, they feel secure and the subtle feminine effect is more than worth it. She's into the nitpicking stage of the overall physical appearance now, adjusting the two-strand gold necklace, pushing up the breasts, inspecting the pale pink polish on the superbly manicured nails, checking to see if the thin gold watch and two bracelets show enough under the long sleeves, asking if the ankle bracelet feels too tight. Kid takes nothing for granted. Like her style.

Turns me around slowly, narrows her eyes, steps back. Now she smiles, finally, first all-out smile in three hours. "Well, John, you sure as hell *look* like a lady. How do you feel?"

"Strange. Real strange."

"You'll get used to it. The important thing at this point is that you *look* absolutely convincing. And you do. If you want the truth, your physical characteristics—height, weight, build—happen to be ideal, they make my job relatively easy. Physically, you're one of the most convincing makeovers I've done. Question: Do you *feel* convincing?"

I glance in the mirror, put my hands on my hips, make a couple of moves.

"Be honest, John."

"Okay. Okay, I *look* convincing, no question about it. But, no, I don't—I don't really feel it. Not really."

"Do you understand why?"

"Probably because I feel like a man and move like a man." She nods. "Good. Very good. I wanted *you* to say it. We'll send out for lunch, then we'll spend the afternoon on the really difficult parts—movement, mannerisms, psychology. How to walk, how to stand, how to sit. Gestures, what to do with your hands, plus a lot of subtle stuff. You'll catch on fast, I know you will. The critical thing is, you've got to *feel* feminine. I know that sounds like a big order, but it's not, most guys can pick it up quickly with the right training. You'd be surprised. Even the most masculine guys can get into it, at least the basic feelings, once you get past the barriers, the defensive mechanisms. You've got to *feel* like an attractive female, you've got to convince yourself before you can convince anybody else. You're tight now, I can see it, I can sense it. Which is only natural, John, it's perfectly normal, natural, and predictable. Every guy I've done a makeover on has been uptight at the beginning. Every one of 'em. You kidding? They get on the makeup, they get on the clothes, they look at themselves in the mirror—*pow!* Blows their minds at first, most of 'em. Absolutely floors 'em. I mean, here's this—this *girl,* this *woman* standing there looking out at you. Interesting thing is, interesting from a purely psychological standpoint, the guys who laugh the loudest, who clown around, they're usually trying to send a message to me, a transparent message, I might add, that it's the very first time in their whole lives they've ever seen themselves in any form of drag."

I wait for her to continue. She doesn't.

"Well, what? It's not true?"

She walks to the dressing table, sits down, lights a cigarette. "John, you've been watching nineteen-twenties movies again, right?"

"No, I'm curious. It's not true?"

She inhales deeply, blows smoke toward the ceiling. "They're all fighting a very deep-rooted sociological taboo that's been drummed into their heads, consciously and subconsciously, since they were small children. All of us went through the same kind of conditioning, whether we realize it or not: You're a boy, boys don't wear that, they wear this. You're a girl, girls don't do that, they do this. In our society, at least in the recent past, the lines were clearly drawn. They still are, with notable exceptions. For example, rock groups, some of the wilder rock groups, are flaunting transvestism and exerting some influence on kids. One obvious example, over the past fifteen, twenty years, unisex clothes and hairstyles became perfectly acceptable here and in Europe."

"But you're not really answering the question you posed. About drag. About the guys who laugh the loudest."

"Sending me a message, yes. Trying to. This doesn't seem to embarrass you, that's good."

"Oh, it embarrasses me, all right. But I want to know what you think about the subject."

"It's not what I think, John, it's a matter of long-term scientific research. I have books in my office right now that you're welcome to borrow if you're interested, the most recent studies about human sexual behavior. Complete with statistics compiled over years, involving thousands of subjects. The fact is—let's stick to this country. The fact is, during a ten-year study completed in nineteen eighty-two on more than sixteen hundred college students, aged seventeen to twenty-two, male and female equally divided, exactly seventy-nine-point-four percent reported having at least four voluntary and secretive transvestite experiences at some time in their lives, most frequently after the age of thirteen. And eighty-three-point-one percent cited 'curiosity' as the principal reason."

"Curiosity?"

"Sure. Curiosity about how they'd look and feel in clothing

clearly associated with the opposite sex. So the question is: What's the big deal? Curiosity about the opposite sex isn't exactly deviant behavior in this country, right? And the fact that they're curious enough to try on clothes clearly associated with the opposite sex certainly doesn't make them transvestites. But I'll tell you what the big deal really is, in my opinion: That we've been conditioned to believe there's something inherently immoral about it, something dirty. Something we're expected to feel embarrassed about, the way you're embarrassed now. That's the big deal, the way we've been brainwashed, the way we've had guilt trips laid on us since childhood about any departure from archaic and essentially arbitrary definitions of sexual identification. Do me a favor on this job, John, do yourself a favor. Try to wipe at least some of that defensive nonsense out of your mind. It's a job, you're following orders, so get into the role and study it. Ask questions. Take constructive criticism from me in stride, try to learn by it. My job is to make you look, feel, and act as convincing as possible by the time we take the nine-thirty shift tonight. And I'm out to do just that. By the time I get through with you, you're going to feel like a female. Not only that, we're both going to have some fun getting you there."

And we do. For some reason, after listening to this kid, I start to lose my inhibitions in a hurry. Must say, she's as good a teacher as she is a cosmetician. After lunch, for the next eight hours straight, I not only learn movement, mannerisms, and psychology, I start to get feedback from real people out there in the real world. About 5:15, Judith decides I'm ready for some dry-run action, a dress rehearsal, if you will. We go down to the garage, west side of the building, jump in her car. What kind of car? Ready for this? Kid's got a 1984 Nissan 300-ZX Turbo. White. Two-seater. Loaded. Power? Awesome. First time she gooses this beauty, turbo boost actually sounds like a siren. No, this is no shit, ask anybody who's been

in one of these suckers, engine goes, *Whhheeeee!* Me, I'm
looking behind us, I really believe some cop's on our tail.
Judith gets a laugh out of it, obviously I'm not the only clown
who's been conned by this. She's changed to an evening outfit,
of course, loose-fitting pink Metropole jumpsuit with buttons
from high neck to waist, wide matching cloth belt, almost-
matching Pandianis, white Cardin jacket with pink stripes. On
her advice, I'm wearing the Blass jacket; when the sun sets just
after 5:30, the temperature drops rapidly. Don't want frigid
falsies.

Heavy traffic across the Julia Tuttle Causeway, lots of sail-
boats on Biscayne Bay, straight ahead is the panorama of
condos and hotels on Miami Beach, clean and white in the
sun. I've had worse duty. Where to? Judith's got it all planned:
Eden Roc Hotel for final exams in the Fortune Cookie bar,
then next door to the Fontainebleau for graduation cocktails
in the Garden Lobby. Dinner in one of those seven restaurants
there, we'll check them out, after which we start our eight-
hour shift. How do I feel? More like a female than any guy
has a right to expect, first time out. All I can tell you, if some
neat-looking young gigolos don't try to hit on me in these bars,
I'll just die of mortification, y'know? After all this work? Not
that I'd solicit any attention, mind you, I'm just not like that.
Still, I know exactly what I'm going to do when one of these
lovely young animals approaches me. *When,* not if—note the
confidence? I mean, this is my own personal Enchanted Evening here, I can see it all now: Soft lights, piano playing "As
Time Goes By," this tall dark wet dream in a tight white suit
slinks his slim tight ass onto the stool next to mine, flashes his
$6,000 perfect white caps, says, "What're y'all drinkin',
honey?" Me, I've always depended on the kindness of stran-
gers, right? I blush, cross my legs, show some ankle, blink my
Liz lashes, arch my brow, cradle my chin in my hand, immac-
ulate pale-pink nails against my silky smooth cheek, and whis-

per, "Blow it out your teeth." Can't wait to see the Hurt Expression in the slimebag's eyes, sadistic bitch that I am. Caveat emptor, as they say.

Whhheeeee, Judith turbos up the wide semicircular drive of the posh Eden Roc, slams to a dignified skid under the long red-and-white striped canopy. Young attendants in red uniforms open our doors quickly, we step out, these boys give us the kind of hard-on glances we fully expect and richly deserve. Adrenaline starts pumping, I'm on a roll now, in we go, short steps, balance is no problem for me in these one-inch heels, you kidding? Bring on the spikes, get serious. Luxury lobby's alive with trendy tanned tourists, holiday hype galore, Happy Hanukkah, Merry Christmas, pay your money, take your choice. White marble floor glitters like water, rushing over black inlaid designs, under modern blue furniture, falling smoothly into split-level areas bordered by cool columns of black marble. We turn right, clickety-click, toward the Fortune Cookie, I play the eye game with almost all of the passing gentlemen, shameless hussy that I am.

Enter honorable Fortune Cookie Restaurant, make way to bar. Fu Manchu barkeep not have happy thoughts about unescorted fortune cookies at bar. Judith show glint of gold. Ah-oh. Please sit. Bong. Authentic Chinese decor, soft lights, bar's relatively crowded, it's 5:45, Happy Hour's in full swing. Although Judith showed her shield very discreetly, I suspect any ass-men around probably picked up on it. Any rate, we're given a wide birth now. Pity. She orders a vodka on the rocks, I order a very dry Beefeater martini on the rocks. When Fu Manchu brings the drinks, he includes a fortune cookie for each of us. We clink glasses, take a swallow. She cracks her cookie first, takes out the slip of paper. Utters a low, devilish laugh, passes it to me: *The cautious seldom err.* I crack my cookie in a ladylike way, pull out the paper: *We would often be sorry if our wishes were gratified.* Roll my eyes, pass it to her. She laughs out loud.

Half an hour later, about 6:20, she leaves the bar to use the pay phone, calls Mort Cooper at home, gets an update on surveillance. Two-man team that started at 1:30 concentrated on the lobby and pool areas. Bingo: Laila Mustafa shows up at the pool around 2:10, takes a swim, joins her parents in their private cabana, has a snack, makes a couple of phone calls. Short time later, our man in the lobby speaks with the Fontainebleau's chief of security, who goes to the switchboard, gets the telephone numbers dialed from the cabana and billed to Mustafa, Penthouse A. One call is long distance to Islamorada, Florida, the other is local. Mort checks both numbers through Southern Bell Security. Islamorada call is to the Howard Johnson's Motor Lodge on Windley Key; local call is to the Bancara International, N.A., 8506 N.E. Second Avenue. He knows nothing about the Howard Johnson's in Islamorada, but says the bank is one of many in the area suspected of laundering large amounts of drug-related money. Judith tells him where we expect to be before our shift begins, along with approximate times, and asks for the names of the two men we'll be replacing; she knows them both. Before we leave, I call Brendan at the Sheraton River House, bring him up to date, ask him to call Vadney at home, brief him on what's happening.

About 7:25, we're finishing drinks in the Fontainebleau's big Garden Lobby Bar, almost ready to go to dinner, when Judith's name is paged for a phone call. Gets up, goes to the phone, she's gone at least five minutes. Comes back in a hurry. Mort just got a report from the surveillance team, they're in downtown Miami, first chance they've had to call: Laila Mustafa left the hotel at 6:56, picked up out front by a light blue 1985 Chevy van, New York license YZY 971. Team followed the van across the Thirty-sixth Street Causeway, then south on N.E. Second Avenue to N.W. Fifth Street, where it turned into an alley leading to the parking lot of the Bancaro International. One of the officers followed on foot, observed the van

enter a small garage in the rear of the bank before the overhead door rolled shut. Subjects have not left the bank as yet.

Sign the bill fast, off we go. Judith says it's about a twenty-
minute drive in normal traffic. Across the causeway, due south
on N.E. Second Avenue, Judith's in radio contact with the
surveillance car, officers Canizares and Infante. When we pass
N.W. Fourteenth Street, Canizares radios that the van just left
the alley, they're following it south on N.E. Second again.
Judith tells him our location, we're only nine blocks behind
now. Less than three minutes later, she spots the surveillance
car and the van (two cars ahead), both turning into South
Dixie Highway, heading south. She tells Canizares that we'll
take over now, says much obliged. It's now 8:10, we're starting
our shift almost an hour and a half early. Me, I'm happy for
the action. Reach in my handbag, check my S&W .38 Chief's
Special, best friend a girl's got in this town.

Judith explains that South Dixie Highway here happens to
be the famous US-1 route that extends all the way from Maine
to Key West. Heavy traffic both ways even at this hour and
as we follow the van, trying to stay at least two cars behind,
we talk about what might have happened. Stress *might* have.
Obviously, we're into wild guesses at this point. If most, or at
least part, of the $8 million robbery money had been in that
van, driven down from New York, and if a carefully prearranged transaction had been quickly consummated in the
bank, viz., the currency exchanged for another country's currency (and/or gold, negotiable bonds, whatever), then the
burden of proving that such a transaction took place, beyond
a reasonable doubt, is virtually impossible. Why? Simple. All
of the $8 million had been in used, untraceable bills. All of it.
We don't even have one serial number. Bancaro International,
like many banks, routinely stores large amounts of currency
in its vault. No law against that. And, since we can't even
begin to prove some of it may be stolen (or drug-related), we
have no legal grounds to request an audit.

Of course, if we lucked into a solid legal reason to search the van and found some kind of obviously incriminating evidence like drugs, stolen property, anything that would hold up in a court of law, that might alter the whole situation. But the occupants of the van haven't broken any laws—yet. In fact, they're driving well under the speed limit. And we can't get a make on the New York plate until the DMV opens tomorrow morning.

One mile south of Florida City on US-1, the "mile markers" begin on the right shoulder of the road, small green signs with white numbers that can be seen clearly in our headlights. They begin with number 126 and, according to Judith, continue in descending order each mile of the way to Key West, ending in zero. Originally, white stone markers were installed in 1912, when the Florida East Coast Railroad was completed, connecting Miami with Key West, a journey of eleven hours. Much of the railroad was destroyed by a hurricane in 1935 and the line was closed. Today, the railbed lies deep under the asphalt of US-1. By the time we drive through Everglades National Park and reach mile marker 107 just north of Key Largo, where the keys begin and US-1 is called the Overseas Highway, Judith's convinced these clowns must be headed for Islamorada, probably plan to spend the night at Howard Johnson's.

Turns out she's right.

Continue on, not too much traffic, can't get lost because it's the only road. Van stops for gas south of the shopping center in Key Largo; we pass it, fill up our tank five miles down the highway. Wait at the station, van speeds past, we see Laila in the passenger seat, off we go again. At 9:35, van slows just past mile marker 84 on Windley Key, turns left into the Howard Johnson's Motor Lodge on the Atlantic side of the road. Judith passes the Lodge, turns left into the large parking lot of the Holiday Isle Resort & Marina. A gas station separates the two motels by about fifty yards, but from where we park we can see the Chevy van parked directly in front of the brightly lighted lobby entrance now. Motor's off, headlights are out, so we're guessing both Laila and the driver went inside to register. We kill our engine and lights. Judith tells me to open the glove compartment and use her binoculars. I'm expecting these big, heavy, high-powered things, but I find a little black plastic case, maybe 4 × 5 inches. Unzip it, pull out a genuine state-of-the-art surveillance tool: Nikon binoculars so powerful for their size I can't believe it. Focus on the New York license plate, looks like a billboard.

Next thing that happens really spooks me. I'm focused on the lobby door, framed in colored Christmas lights, white wreath in the center, when it opens and here comes Laila, long jet-black hair, deep-set dark eyes, high cheekbones, she's wearing a blue windbreaker, jeans, thong sandals, walks out with a spring in her step. Followed by a figure who sends a quick chill from my neck to my ass: Man I saw from the elevator of the Fontainebleau yesterday afternoon. Face strikes the same haunting spark of recognition somewhere back in my mind: Rawboned, weatherbeaten, deeply wrinkled, lean, tanned. Doesn't look so exhausted now, doesn't look that tired, doesn't seem to have those pronounced circles under the eyes. Wears a yellow turtleneck, jeans, boots. Opens the passenger door for Laila, she jumps in. Walks around the back of the van. Momentary sick feeling in my stomach. *Slender figure of a Brazilian street cleaner* Opens the door, climbs in, starts the motor, turns on the lights, *pushing trash with a long-handled brush,* drives straight ahead, then takes a right turn, *all dimly seen in the orange-yellow glow of a streetlight* and disappears behind a wing of the motel. I lower the binoculars, frown, press the bridge of my nose. Names and places and years spin. But the face draws a blank.

"You all right, John?"

"Yeah."

"You know the man?"

"No. But his face looks familiar."

She takes out a pack of Benson & Hedges, offers me one.

"No, thanks."

"Sure you feel okay?"

"Yeah."

She lights her own, looks out the windshield. "Well, obviously, they've checked in, so we'll have to spend the night."

"Yeah. You want a separate room?"

"Sure, then you can watch nineteen-twenties movies, right?"

"Right. *Cagney and Lacey in the Keys.*"

Gets a smile out of her. "Don't flatter yourself. I suggest a twin-bedded room as close to theirs as possible."

"How're you going to manage that?"

"Watch me." She starts the engine, flicks the lights, drives through the gas station into the Howard Johnson's area, pulls up at the entrance to the lobby. We both go inside. Short steps, clickety-click.

Small lobby, nicely decorated Christmas tree on the large desk. Young female room clerk smiles at us, doesn't give me a second glance.

"May I help you?"

"I sure hope so," Judith says, smiling. "Our friends just registered—the couple just before us?—they had reservations."

"Yes."

"They called for reservations this afternoon, but I'm afraid we just plum forgot to."

"No problem, we have a few vacancies."

"Oh, thank God! It was real stupid of us."

Clerk pushes a registration card toward her. "Twin beds?"

"Yes, please."

"Will you be using a credit card?"

"Yes." She reaches in her purse, takes out her wallet. "Is American Express okay?"

"Certainly."

Judith hands her the credit card, starts to fill out the registration. "I don't suppose you have a room close to theirs."

Clerk checks her board. "Let's see. Mr. and Mrs. Todesfall are in two-twenty . . ."

Todesfall, Todesfall, Todesfall. Man appears to wear light-blue work clothes, maybe denim, and heavy boots or shoes. Curb of the narrow sidewalk is high red brick. House behind him has a low, narrow doorway and a narrow blue-green window.

"I'm afraid not," the clerk says. "But I can put you—they're in two-twenty, on the corner, they're facing the parking lot. Best I can do, I can put you on the same floor, two-thirty-eight."

"Oh, that's super, thank you. What's the room rate?"

"Ninety-seven, double occupancy."

"Fine." Judith completes the registration card, signs it.

"How many nights do you expect to be with us?"

"Just tonight, as far as we know."

Clerk zaps the American Express card on her machine, hands it back, takes the registration card, writes the in-and-out dates, turns, takes the key from the mailbox of Room 238. Hands it to Judith with a warm smile that includes me. "All right, Miss Sever, Miss Rawlings, just drive straight ahead, then take the first right turn into the guest parking lot. There's a sign, you can't miss it. Two-thirty-eight is at the far left end as you drive in. Top floor. Checkout time is twelve noon. If your plans change and you want to stay another night, please check with the desk as early as possible."

"Thanks so much."

I nod, smile, mutter a soft "Thanks."

"Have a pleasant stay."

Out we go into the balmy evening, breathe in the fresh salt air, slide into her sleek white 300-ZX Turbo, even the door-slams sound classy.

"Congratulations," I tell her.

"Nothing to it, Miss Rawlings."

"What'd you put for my first name?"

She laughs, starts the engine. "Johnnie, with an i-e."

"You rotten bitch. Now she'll think we're lessies."

"That was the whole idea, doll. Kid looked like she needed a nice juicy fantasy to get her through the lonely night."

Off we go in a flash of white, thundering hoofbeats of the great horse Silver. There's the sign, hang a right, lighted parking lot is almost full. We slow down, spot the light-blue Chevy right away, far right end against the building, near the stairs. I press the button to roll down my window, glance up at the top-floor room on the right corner. Small terrace is empty, curtain is drawn across the glass door and window, lights are on. Judith selects a parking spot halfway down the lot, facing the building, gives us a good but distant view of their room. I roll up my window before she turns off the motor.

She kills the headlights. "Did the name Todesfall mean anything to you?"

"Not really. Vaguely familiar."

"Do you know any German?"

"No. Just a few words."

We hear a car engine starting just across the lot to our left. Late-model Cadillac backs out carefully, turns, drives past us slowly. Reflection of the headlights move across Judith's face.

"Do you know what the name means?" she asks softly.

"Todesfall? No."

"In German, *Todesfall* means 'death.' "

"Are you serious?"

"Absolutely. Would I lie—"

"No, I'm serious, Judith."

"German is one of my languages. I used to speak it fluently in college. *Todesfall* and *Tod* are both nouns, masculine gender, initial caps, translated literally as 'death.' "

"What're you, some kind of language freak?"

"I seem to have an affinity for languages, yes. *Hablo es-
pañol?*"

"*Nein.*"

"*Français?*"

"*Sí.*"

Goes like so. We decide to stay in the car for at least half
an hour, following the logic that they haven't had dinner yet,
it's now 9:50, so chances are good they'll go out to a restaurant. Naturally, we'd love to get a peek inside the van, but it's
too risky at this point. As we're talking, Judith brings up an
interesting question: Since there are at least half a dozen posh
and exclusive resorts in and around Islamorada, including the
Cheeca Lodge only two miles ahead and the Holiday Isle
Resort & Marina just next door, why in hell would they
choose Howard Johnson's for their romantic rendezvous, if
that's what it is? One possibility, it's December 18, high season,
holidays, maybe the chichi resorts are all booked, but Judith
doubts it. Besides, Laila tried only one motel from the cabana,
Howard Johnson's.

Our hunch about dinner was right. About 10:05, out they
come, holding hands as they trot down the outside stairs
between the wings, wearing the same clothes. Todesfall unlocks the passenger-side door, opens it for her, gentleman all
the way. He walks around, gets in, revs the motor, flicks the
lights, backs out cautiously, heads for the front. Judith starts
her engine, waits until they make the left turn before she hits
her lights and starts slowly after them.

Van makes a left turn into the still-crowded US-1, drives
south at a moderate speed, we stay a comfortable three cars
behind. Continues for a couple of miles, then his left-turn
indicator starts flashing just beyond mile marker 82. He turns,
shoots across the highway into the parking lot of a restaurant.
We pass him, Judith flicks her left-turn indicator, slows, hangs
a sharp left across the road into the semicircular drive of

another restaurant, swings around, counterclockwise, stops before the end. Traffic seems heavier on this side.

She laughs. "Well, they have good taste in restaurants, anyway."

"Yeah?"

"The Green Turtle. Just happens to be the most popular in the upper Keys. Arguably the most famous in all the Keys. Not counting *the* Sloppy Joe's in Key West."

"Hemingway's hangout?"

"Yeah. Strictly a tourist trap."

She turns right, turbos ahead, hits her right-turn indicator, and I can see the place clearly, front jammed with cars. Long, one-story, clean white building, floodlighted, low railing along the roof, green awning with white fringe above wide picture windows holding outside flower boxes. Big sign above the entrance, lighted figure of a green turtle with yellow letters on its back:

Sid&Roxie's

GREEN
TURTLE
INN

As we drive in, we catch a quick glimpse of our lovebirds going in the front door, followed by another couple. Judith pulls into the lighted parking lot to the left of the building, looks for the van, spots it, then selects a parking place about ten cars away. Before getting out, she presses the steel button under the dash to activate the Chapman security system. I know this Chapman system, I have it on my own car. Unlike the new gee-whiz electronic junk on the market, this system has real teeth in it. I mean, let's face it, all car alarm systems have a siren, some of them are triggered if you so much as rap your knuckles on the window; that's why you hear so many false alarms going off all over New York City, any time of the day or night. They're a nuisance. They stink. Fact is, today, professional car thieves simply ignore sirens. That's right. Ask any cop on the street, ask any insurance investigator. Pros routinely steal cars with the siren blasting. Two big differences with the Chapman. First, the ignition suppressor electronically overrides the ignition; there's just no way you can start the thing, I know, I've tried. Second, there's a deadbolt that locks your hood shut and it operates independently of any electrical power source. Of course, the Chapman system has all the other high-tech stuff—detect module, motion detector, light flasher, polytonic siren of over 100 decibels—but crooks hate it primarily because of the ignition override and the deadbolt hood lock. All right, okay, I hear you, any vehicle can be stolen, there's no totally foolproof system. All I'm saying, this one makes it much harder than most. My philosophy, if somebody wants to steal my car, fine and dandy, but he's in for some hard manual labor.

Judith gives my hair, makeup, and getup a practiced critical appraisal in the parking lot. Says I look lovely—in soft light. Says I could pass for Liz Taylor's twin brother. Little green monster in all of us, I guess, competitive bitches that we are. There's a closed-in porch with a prominent sign to the right of the inside door, bold black letters against pristine white: SHIRTS with SLEEVES and SHOES REQUIRED. Must be difficult to find a shirt with sleeves and shoes. Still, it keeps out those packs of riffraff with bare arms. Relatively dark inside, graceful strings of colored Christmas lights and decorations all over. Nice relaxed atmosphere, strictly informal, long wooden bar to the left, rows of wooden tables with glass tops and paper place settings spaced out economically. Walls are covered with hundreds (maybe thousands) of snapshots of guests, protected by sheets of plastic. Female maître d' comes over smiling: Jes the tew a yew? Yes. Stayin' fer dinner? Yes. They's a fiftaine-minute wait. Oh. Y'all care to have a drink at the bar? Yes. Escorts us to two empty stools (high captain's chairs) at the far left end of the bar near the wall, hands us menus. Ah'll come getchall.

We both glance around, can't spot our subjects right away, but the place is packed. Unusual thing about the bar, dozens of U.S. dollar bills and foreign currency hang from the ceiling, all colors and sizes—francs, pasos, yen, deutsche marks, pounds sterling—you name it, apparently donated by foreign guests. One stands out because of its size, a U.S. $100 bill, very old but in excellent condition, it's about three times as big as today's currency, looks like Ben Franklin's face on it, but I can't be sure. We order drinks, light cigarettes, sit back, cross our legs, let the happy ambience of the joint wash over us. Can't help wondering if some geek will try to hit on me in here.

When we still can't seem to find Todesfall and Laila after our drinks are served, we reason that they, too, had to wait for a table and are probably at the other end of the bar, the far right end we can't see. There's a big open door near that end with the inscription "MA-'n'-PA" over it, opening to a hallway. Judith decides to go to the ladies' room so she can check out that end of the bar. Off she goes, maneuvering her way through the crowded tables and bar stools. Comes back a few minutes later with a worried expression. They're not at that end of the bar and they're not in the back room off to the right. She checked the ladies' room too and Laila's not there. Where the hell could they be?

Judith calls the bartender over. "Are there any private dining rooms in here?"

"Not really, ma'am. Just—we use the back room in there for private parties, birthday parties, stuff like that. You have to reserve it a couple of days in advance."

I tell Judith to wait, get up, grab my purse, walk out the

front door. As I'm crossing the closed-in porch, away from the noise of the crowded room, I hear the distant sound of a siren, police or ambulance, seems to be coming from US-1. But as soon as I open the porch door and head for the parking lot, I realize it's a car alarm, high-pitched and multi-toned, coming from somewhere back in the crowded lot. Spotlights from the roof of the restaurant frame the big shade tree in a yellow haze and spill bright ribbons on the glossy tops of cars.

The Chevy van is gone.

I run in the direction of the siren. Sound is all too familiar to me now. Grab my gun from the purse as I run, adrenaline's pumping like crazy when I get close to Judith's car. Suddenly, the siren stops. I crouch quickly, move closer, try to catch my breath. Only two reasons why that siren would've stopped: Somebody turned it off from inside with the key, which is improbable, or it shut off automatically. Chapman system is programmed to sound the alarm for exactly three minutes, then shut off and reset. I'm crouched by the rear wheel near the driver's door. I hold the revolver in the straight-armed two-handed position and yell: *"Police! Come out!"* Nothing happens. *"Police! Open the door!"* Silence. Five seconds. Ten. Fifteen. Now I hold the revolver in my right hand, shuffle ahead slightly, slide the fingers of my left hand under the recessed door latch, take a deep breath, open the door fast and swing it wide. It catches and stops in the full-open position. All I can see is a fraction of the steering wheel, part of the dash, and the small stainless-steel button that must be pushed in to arm the security system. The button is still depressed, meaning the siren shut off automatically. When I'm more or less convinced that nobody's inside, I stand, flatten my body against the car, lean cautiously to my left, and take a quick look.

I'm wrong.

Laila Mustafa is sitting upright in the driver's seat, hands in her lap, palms up. Her deep-set dark eyes stare blankly

ahead. Her full lips are parted, as if in surprise. Blood is
pumping from her left temple, pouring down her cheek in a
single thick stream, branching off into narrow rivulets down
the front of her blue windbreaker.

> *Where do I come from?*
> *Nobody knows.*
> *Where am I going?*
> *Everybody goes.*
> *The wind blows.*
> *The sea flows.*
> *Nobody knows.*

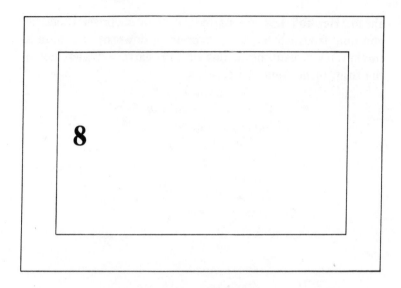

8

ISLAMORADA hasn't seen a homicide like this in years, so word spreads like wildfire. Within half an hour, it's total chaos around here, big parking lot of the Green Turtle is jammed out to the highway with state and local police vehicles (I counted eleven), ambulances from two hospitals (don't ask me why), plus private cars, trucks, vans, RVs, and even motorcycles from miles around. Place is teeming with people, throbbing with emergency lights, crackling with police radios. Turns out it's the tip of the iceberg. Right after notifying the local police, Judith calls Chief Haynes at home, he decides to get on the horn and pull all stops for a very sound reason: When word leaks to the media—as it undoubtedly will—that Todesfall's not only wanted for murder but is now the prime suspect in the biggest cash robbery in U.S. history, it'll be politically judicious to have one's ass covered from as many angles as possible, particularly if he escapes. Consequently, an immediate statewide APB is put out on the Chevy van and New York plates, together with a description of Todesfall and the warning that he's armed and considered extremely dangerous; large and small airports, bus and train stations are alerted throughout South Florida; they even set up roadblocks at Key Largo, Marathon, and Key West, where troopers from the Florida Highway Patrol will stop vehicles in either direction until 6:30 A.M.

Couple of things are obvious early on. Laila was not shot in Judith's car. Monroe County Medical Examiner Dr. David Westlake, who arrived only ten minutes after the first squad car, made a preliminary determination that she was killed instantly with a single high-caliber slug, probably a .38, .45, or 9 mm, but not a .357 magnum. It entered her left temple at point-blank range, leaving severe powder burns, and exited just above her right ear, blowing away a section of her skull about the size of a quarter. However, Judith's car was undamaged, inside and out, with the exception of bloodstains on the driver's seat.

We're debriefed for almost an hour by Monroe County Sheriff Harold Kominski, a tall, heavyset, deeply tanned man in his mid-fifties, casually dressed (he came directly from his home), who wears a baseball cap with the insignia of the National Rifle Association, and speaks with a heavy but pleasant southern accent. Only thing about this guy, he just can't seem to adjust to the fact that I'm not a broad, despite my explanation, despite my voice, despite my gold shield and ID. Granted, it's late in the evening, he's obviously had a few belts at home, which is perfectly okay, but while he's asking questions and his young deputy's taking notes, he keeps calling me ma'am. Very politely, no sarcasm at all, he just calls us both ma'am, that's it, grace under pressure.

Throughout the debriefing, which takes place in the sheriff's car, I have this sinking feeling in my stomach because of a mistake I made, a bad one, a dumb one that may very well have cost Laila Mustafa her life. I've made my share over the years, most of us do, but this one makes me feel really frustrated and depressed because I liked the kid, you couldn't help but like her, no matter how deeply involved she was. I made the mistake of seriously underestimating the criminal intelligence, experience, and acute paranoia of Todesfall. And maybe of Laila too, although I doubt it. She was just a kid, she wouldn't have had the experience I'm talking about, and she didn't seem to be the paranoid type when I met her. Based on logical intuition, I suspect Todesfall first picked up on Judith's car when he turned off US-1 into Howard Johnson's and observed us making the turn into the Holiday Isle Resort parking lot, with only that gas station in between. It's always possible he could've picked up on us sooner, but I think the probability is almost negligible because US-1 is, after all, the only road to the Keys and we usually stayed three cars back. Also, in the unlikely event that he suspected a tail, I don't think he would've turned into Howard Johnson's, where he had a reservation, in the first place. No, I think he was experienced enough to understand that if anyone was in fact following him and saw him turn left into the motel, they'd pass, and then probably turn left at the next opportunity to reduce the risk of losing him. A logical assumption, if you were dealing with relatively young and/or average undercover cops who didn't have the experience necessary to anticipate you or your degree of paranoia. *Anticipate.* That's the word. That's what I didn't do. After thirty years as a cop, I should've known better, I should've warned Judith to continue up the highway until we were completely out of his sight. Why didn't I? I mean, something should've clicked long before that happened, I should've reasoned that if there was even a remote possibility of this guy being associated with the biggest cash heist in history, then it's axiomatic that you anticipate a high degree of intelligence, experience, and probable paranoia— whether you believe it or not. Why didn't I? What the hell was wrong with me?

Still, I doubt that Todesfall was convinced by that one

event. He needed to be positive. So he placed real bait in the trap. He went in the office with Laila, registered, took plenty of time, came out, looked relaxed, never even glanced in our direction as I studied him with the binoculars. Then, when they were up in their room, he waited for us to make the mistake that would convince him. We did. I swear to God, in retrospect, I can't believe my own stupidity. I can't believe I'd be that dumb. When Judith drove into the motel parking lot, I actually rolled down my window to glance up at Room 220. In that instant, undoubtedly watching me from one side of the closed curtain, Todesfall knew. Knew that we'd either registered and conned the young clerk into revealing his name and room, or identified ourselves to the clerk as cops and obtained the same information.

And, in my judgment, he also knew something else.

He knew what he'd have to do.

Sitting there in the back of Sheriff Kominski's car, listening to Judith answer questions, I'm looking out at the white 300-ZX with both its doors open, where a cop is photographing Laila's body from a variety of angles, and I'm trying desperately now to remember where or when I saw Todesfall before. Or, at this point, to be absolutely honest with myself, *if* I actually saw him before that quick glimpse from the elevator at the Fontainebleau yesterday afternoon. If. Jesus, could the whole thing have been my imagination, some sort of bizarre mental aberration, a fragment from a dream that somehow triggers that momentary sick feeling and the image of the Brazilian street cleaner in the oil painting? Thought occurs to me, maybe I'm losing my grip here, two days of strange surroundings and unfamiliar people. Todesfall, Todesfall, Todesfall. Who, what, where, when? How did he open the locked door of Judith's car that fast? Why did he place Laila's body in the driver's seat? To show us how bright he is? To show us how dumb we are? To shock us? To scare us? To warn us? Maybe all of the above, maybe none. Wonder what kind of specific mental disorder would drive a person to do something that ghoulish? Chronic paranoia has a whole wide range of symptoms, but in modern psychiatry it's typically characterized by systematized delusions of persecution or of grandeur and the projection of highly personal conflicts that are blamed on the supposed hostility of others. With considerable variations on that theme.

What if I turn the question around and ask: Where or when has Todesfall seen *me* before? Could this possibly be some nut I sent up long ago? Very doubtful for a number of reasons: When I saw him from those closing elevator doors at the Fontainebleau, it was just his profile moving along in the crowd; I doubt that he saw me beforehand, getting out of Mort's car, entering the hotel, standing near the house phones, walking to the elevators, but it's just a gut feeling, of course, I can't be positive. That same evening, I was in the hotel's Lagoon Saloon with Mort and Brendan, and I suppose he could've seen me in there or elsewhere, walking through the lobby on our way to and from the bar, getting in Mort's car out front. There are a number of possibilities, even the time we spent in the bar of the Sheraton River House, but they become remote to the point of being illogical, in my opinion, after I was in drag. Illogical but not entirely improbable, given Todesfall's sharp eye and experience. I can't really believe he picked up on me in the bar of the Eden Roc's Fortune Cookie, the Fontainebleau's Garden Lobby Bar, or even when he saw my face in the opened window of Judith's car from his room in the motel. I mean, I couldn't even recognize myself when I looked in the mirror that first time in the makeover room at headquarters.

Still, if he saw me up real close, that's another story. One of the intriguing questions that remains to be answered is exactly how Laila and Todesfall exited the Green Turtle. We saw them go in; there's no doubt they went in. Aside from the outside door to the closed-in porch, there are three other doors: Inside front, into the main room and bar; delivery entrance out back off the kitchen; and a fire exit off the back dining room. Of the two most logical possibilities, fire exit and inside front, I'm persuaded, despite my instincts, it was the inside front. Tell you why. After Judith called the local police and was on the phone with Chief Haynes, I questioned the female maître d' who seated us at the bar. When I described the subjects in detail, she couldn't remember them specifically, but she recalled that around 10:15 all the tables in the front and back rooms were occupied and there was a fifteen- to twenty-minute wait. She routinely took the names of those who wanted to wait, together with the time they arrived, seated them at the bar, then escorted them to tables as they became available. When she checked her waiting list for me, the name Todesfall was not on it. Couples who didn't want to wait always left via the front door. As I remember, when Judith and I entered, I automatically opened the porch door and inside door for her. The room was dimly lighted and, judging by the noise level, very crowded, including the area just inside the door. I have absolutely no recollection of closing that door. Lighted bar was the only focal point I recall clearly as I waited for my eyes to adjust. Naturally, the very last thing I expected was to have Laila and Todesfall standing behind the door. If they were, as I strongly suspect, they got a fast but close look at our right profiles before passing behind us to leave. On the other hand, if they'd used the fire exit, they would've had to maneuver all the way back through two jammed rooms, which would have required a knowledge of the layout, in my opinion. Of course, it's always possible they had that knowledge. Point I'm trying to make, given what I know about the way Todesfall operates, I just have to believe he'd select the option involving more risk, the one we wouldn't anticipate. When I say *more* risk, I'm talking about more risk according to the so-called rules of logic that most of us would probably use in a similar situation. But there's an important distinction here, I think, critical to understanding this guy. In the mind of a man like Todesfall, choosing this option involved *less* risk, because it had the element of unpredictability, something almost farcical, something you'd smile at in a film, but never try yourself because it was illogical, things simply didn't work that way in the real world.

Well, maybe that depends on how you define the real world. Apparently, this guy just doesn't play by the rules of logic that most of us associate with our definitions of the real world. So how do you deal with a mind like that? Simple and complicated. Once you have a handle on at least some of his rules, you play by them.

One thing I know for certain, I've got to get my act together here. Ever since Brendan and I arrived, I've felt that I was taking a break of some kind, a vacation, it's just been a strange combination of circumstances—warm climate, Christmas season, playing a broad for the first time in my career. Tough duty. Opening the door of Judith's car tonight was a healthy shock. Party's over. Time to go to work.

Debriefing ends about 11:35. By then they've finally removed Laila's body from the car, placed it on a gurney, covered it, transferred it to one of the two ambulances, and taken it to the office of the Monroe County Medical Examiner, where Dr. Westlake will perform the autopsy tonight. Sheriff Kominski will have to notify Mr. and Mrs. Mustafa as soon as possible, of course, and he wants to get back to his office to get his paperwork started before the Miami media descend on him, but Judith and I persuade him to accompany us to the Howard Johnson's Motor Lodge, just to cover himself by personally checking the registration card and the room itself for his report, and also to identify us to the security guard and the room clerk, to clear the jurisdictional authority.

Sheriff's deputies are still dusting Judith's car for fingerprints, concentrating on the exterior of the driver's door, the window, and the glass T-top on that side, so Kominski drives us back to Howard Johnson's himself, opposite direction from his office in Marathon, but it's just a couple of miles. After the introductions, both the security guard and the room clerk are very cooperative, they've heard about the homicide, of course, their friends have been calling for more than an hour now. First thing we study is the registration card for Room 220. Todesfall circled *Mr. & Mrs.,* then printed very carefully:

Abbild von Todesfall
Mittwoch Abend, 18-12
Grün Schildkröte

He paid for the room in cash, so there's no credit-card information, but he listed the correct New York license number, YZY 971, and correctly identified the vehicle as a 1985 Chevy van.

Sheriff Kominski copies the information on his pad, then tilts back his baseball cap with the NRA insignia, turns to me. "Any idea where that city is in Germany?"

"Haven't got a clue. Judith?"

She takes the card, blinks as she reads it, then frowns.

"What?" I ask.

She hesitates, speaks just above a whisper. "This guy is something else."

"What's it say?" I ask.

She frowns at the card again. "In eleven years, I've never seen anything like this guy."

"What does it say?" Kominski asks.

"In German, the first—this is an exact translation now. The first line reads: 'Image of Death.' The second line reads: 'Wednesday evening, eighteen December.' Last line reads: 'Green Turtle.' "

In the silence that follows, I feel a cold shock. I've underestimated him again. My whole theory about when he made the decision—and why he made it—was wrong. It was wrong because I was still making the mistake of following sequential rules of logic. Todesfall (obviously that's not his name) knew precisely what he was going to do long before he was positive of our presence. Apparently, it didn't make any difference to him one way or another. Laila was as good as dead anyway; Judith and I simply became minor irritants—or maybe minor stimulants, for all I know. Again, I'm theorizing, but at least I have more solid information now. I still can't believe he could've been certain beyond any doubt that we were following him until he went up in the room and observed us driving into the guest parking lot. And when we did, and I looked directly up at his room, I'm sure he realized only too well that we could have identified ourselves to the clerk as cops and read his registration card. Of course, the probability that one of us would speak German was virtually zero, so the irony of his message would have been all the more delicious to him, I suppose, given what we know about him so far. In retrospect, of course, if we'd done exactly that, identified ourselves to the clerk as cops and simply asked to see his registration card, at least we would've been alert to the fact that he planned to pull something strange. But I'm not sure, at that point, we would've picked up on the meaning, *"Image* of Death." In fact, I'm still not sure I understand what he meant by it. By "Image of Todesfall," could he have been referring to an image of himself? Is the man insane enough to believe that he's a personification of Death?

Judith hands me the card. "This guy is—I mean, John, this guy is frightening."

I hand the card back to the room clerk. "Can we take a look at the room now?"

Security guard, stocky young guy by the name of Bob Laramie, casually dressed, escorts the three of us up to Room 220. It's 11:55 now, very quiet, and the long, well-lighted hallway is empty. Although there's not a chance in hell anybody's in the room, all of us take routine precautions, under the sheriff's direction, draw our weapons, get up against the wall, both sides of the door. Kominski takes over now, knocks hard, five times. Silence. Tries it again, harder. Nothing. Now he uses Laramie's passkey, unlocks the door, turns the knob, steps aside fast as he shoves it open wide. Waits a few seconds, listens, then calls: "Police! Come out!" Waits, listens, finally reaches in and turns on a wall switch. Waits another few seconds, walks in cautiously, revolver pointing up, checks the bathroom immediately. Calls: "All clear." In we go. Room looks untouched. Queen-size bedspread doesn't have so much as a wrinkle, virtually nothing's been disturbed, not even a bar of soap or a towel. No personal belongings of any kind. Floor-to-ceiling curtain is drawn across the glass wall and sliding glass door to the terrace. I walk to the far left of the curtain, look out through the quarter-inch vertical space between the curtain and the glass. Excellent view of the lighted guest parking lot. At least I was right about that.

Driving back to Miami, Judith has a green plastic tarpaulin covering her seat, supplied by Sheriff Kominski. We listen to soft stereo music and don't talk very much. Just inside Key Largo, mile marker 100, troopers of the Florida Highway Patrol have a roadblock, stopping vehicles in both directions, two squad cars parked on both sides of the highway, emergency lights flashing, plus bright red-orange flares in the center of the road. It's about 12:45 A.M., not much traffic on US-1 now, but we have to wait in line, five cars and a pickup truck in front of us. For the first time tonight, while we're waiting, I try to concentrate on the logistics and probabilities of Todesfall (call him that for now) getting off the Keys. If he headed back to Miami immediately after the murder, the roadblock here at Key Largo would be his only big obstacle—if it was set up soon enough. Green Turtle's located at mile marker 82, so he'd have to cover eighteen miles to get here. Say he could average about sixty miles per hour at that time of night; if so, he could've made it here in eighteen minutes. Okay, I know I discovered Laila's body at exactly 10:17, because I checked my watch automatically. I also know she'd been dead in the car for at least three and one-half minutes, because the Chapman alarm is programmed to sound for exactly three minutes, then shut off and reset, and I opened the door about twenty-five or thirty seconds after it stopped. So, for round numbers, give Todesfall a four-minute start at that point. Judith called the Monroe County Sheriff's office at 10:19, then called Chief Haynes at home immediately. Now, after Judith's conversation with him, which included detailed descriptions of Todesfall and the van, I'll assume Haynes started making his calls no later than 10:22, and the first was probably to the Florida Highway Patrol. I'll also assume that the three FHP roadblocks (Key West, Marathon, Key Largo) were in operation no later than 10:35. I may be off a little, I don't know how fast the FHP responds to emergency situations, but I think 10:35 is probably a realistic assumption.

So, counting the four-minute lead Todesfall had, let's say he left the Green Turtle parking lot at about 10:13. Now add the eighteen minutes required to drive those eighteen miles at an average speed of sixty. According to that scenario, he would've arrived at mile marker 100 at 10:31, four full minutes before the roadblock was in operation. Only one true way to test this theory, we'll ask one of the FHP troopers exactly when this roadblock was set up.

Five or six minutes later, it's finally our turn. Tall, heavyset, smartly uniformed trooper motions us ahead, indicates where we should stop. Judith rolls down her window, we both take out our badges and ID.

He comes over, tips his wide-brimmed hat. "Good evening, sorry to inconvenience you, ladies."

"Good evening." Judith hands him our badges and ID.

He inspects the photographs closely with his flashlight,

frowns, glances in at me. "Are you Detective—*John* Rawlings?"

"Yes, sir."

"New York City Police?"

"Yes, sir."

"He's working undercover with me," Judith says.

Flashing red and blue emergency lights pulsate on his face as he tries to get a better look at me. "Detective Rawlings, would you mind switching on the overhead light in there?"

I switch it on quickly. "Disguise is necessary on this job."

"Uh-huh, okay, thank you." Hands back our badges and ID. "We have to check out everybody. Sorry for the inconvenience. We're looking for a man suspected of homicide. We just don't know what to expect."

"I understand," I tell him. "Officer, one question: Do you know exactly what time you set up this roadblock?"

"Yes, sir, I do. We stopped our first vehicle northbound at ten-twenty-seven P.M. Two units were in the area when we got the call. Two other units got here within seven minutes."

"Much obliged."

"Yes, sir. Drive carefully now."

As we pull away and I switch off the overhead light, my first thought is: Obviously, he didn't head for Miami. Then I think: Wait a minute, hold on. He didn't head for Miami—in a motor vehicle. There are, of course, three ways to get from Islamorada to mainland Florida—land, sea, and air. Most logical way, particularly at night, is by land, via motor vehicle, right? Especially if you already happen to be in a motor vehicle, right? Rules of logic in the real world. Precisely the logic Todesfall would *not* follow.

"Where's the closest airport?" I ask.

"There's one right in Key Largo for small non-jet aircraft."

"How about Islamorada?"

"No. Next closest airport is in Marathon."

It's seventy-six miles from Islamorada to Miami, so we

figure we'll reach headquarters in about an hour and a half, maybe sooner in light traffic. Now, as the mile markers drift slowly past on this long dark highway, I sit back, I listen to the stereo music, I try to put myself in Todesfall's place for a change. I try to anticipate this guy. Intelligent and experienced pros like this always operate according to carefully researched, sophisticated plans, I've never known a successful one who didn't. And sophisticated doesn't necessarily mean logical. In fact, the more complicated the plan, the more illogical it often appears. Master plans always have contingency plans, often quite a few. That's a constant I've noticed, almost nothing is left to chance.

Okay, me in his place, here I go. After many months, maybe years, I finally research, plan, and execute the big one of my career, eight million in used, untraceable currency—with at least one accomplice. Then, cool as you please, I drive the cash from New York to Miami. Next, in a carefully prearranged transaction at Bancaro International, N.A., in Miami, I have the cash converted into a foreign currency and deposited in a corporate account I've maintained in another country. Officers at Bancaro International, experienced in the business of laundering drug money, routinely deduct their standard commission of 30 percent ($2.4 million) and deposit—by computer —the remainder ($5.6 million), converted into the currency of my choice, at the current exchange rate. Within seconds of the computer transaction, my corporate account in some foreign bank is starting to earn interest of such a magnitude that I could live luxuriously on the interest alone for the rest of my life. Of course, I'd probably invest heavy chunks of it in blue-chip stocks, gold, real estate, whatever.

So I'm home free. Maybe I'll even think about retirement in that foreign country, I'm no spring chicken. I could travel, see the world, live like a king, join the supersonic set, what the hell. Except for one potential problem. My accomplice. Laila Mustafa was obviously the key, or at least one of them, she was absolutely necessary, I couldn't have pulled it without her. But she's young, she's inexperienced, she's emotional, and the combination could be dangerous. She could be the weak link that I dread so much. Solution? We're talking cold, clinical professionalism here, nothing left to chance, that's how clowns like this stay out of prison, they don't tolerate loose ends. Solution? Get rid of her. How? Don't fool around with murder-mystery stunts. Blow her away. Clean and simple. When? Just as soon as possible. Where? Anywhere we won't be recognized. Fine and dandy. Now I'm into the home stretch, following my plan to the letter, what happens? I pick up on the fact that two female undercover cops are doing surveillance on me, undoubtedly lured by Laila's presence. They're obvious, they're no challenge, it's no contest. But could they delay my plan? No way. I'll not only make the hit on schedule, I'll rub their snot noses in it, I'll show them up for what they are, I'll scare the piss out of 'em. Why risk that kind of indulgence? I've got my reasons. Besides, my escape is prearranged clockwork just like everything else. Nothing left to chance.

Prearranged clockwork. Of course. It had to be. Now it dawns on me why he selected Howard Johnson's over the posh Holiday Isle Resort & Marina. More anonymity, few questions asked, and, most important, he wouldn't run the risk of being recognized as a Holiday Isle guest when he arrived for the sophisticated finish of his evening's work. He pulls into the Holiday Isle parking lot at 10:15 that night and removes whatever belongings he has in the van. Walks calmly past the crowded outdoor restaurants and bars to get out to the marina. Where he boards the small but luxurious yacht he'd chartered and paid for weeks, maybe months, in advance. Quietly departs for Miami at the precise appointed time, probably 10:20. Engine of the sleek white Chris-Craft purrs, windows of the cabin throw gold patterns across the water. Uniformed captain has a pitcher of martinis ready for him, chilled to perfection, and a frosted glass. Gourmet dinner already sizzling in the galley. Pardon me, sir, but do you happen to have some Grey Poupon? But of course.

First order of business when we get back to headquarters around 1:45, Judith calls the FHP dispatch, asks to have a unit go to the Holiday Isle Resort in Islamorada and check the parking lot for the light-blue 1985 Chevy van, New York license YZY 971. Leaves her call-back number.

Off we go to the makeover room now, these one-inch heels are killing me after all. Basic transformation back to a recognizable male requires less than fifteen minutes. Liz Taylor mid-thirties sex-symbol mystique dissolves before my wondering eyes to John Rawlings early-fifties tight-ass menopause. Grab a towel, take the elevator down to the empty men's locker room, leave my clothes on a bench, take a long, hot, soothing shower, followed by a short, cold, tingling one. I'm me again. Happy to be back. Earlobes still sting a bit, but that's the price you pay for being a modern cop.

About 2:15, I'm back in Judith's cubicle, fully dressed now, helping her write the surveillance report. She's changed back to her blue V-neck T-shirt, Guess jeans, Reeboks, looks a little tired. We're sipping coffee, trying to remember details, when she gets a call from the FHP. Listens, raises her brows, takes a few notes, asks a number of sharp questions. Thanks the man, hangs up.

"Chalk one up for our side," she says.

"Holiday Isle?"

"Parking lot, yeah. Big as life. They opened it, searched it, came up empty. When the dockmaster gets there later this morning, they'll check with him about the charter boat. Frankly, I think we'll draw a blank there, but it's worth a try. I know that marina, they've got all kinds of boats coming and going, day and night, especially now, in season. And it's relatively informal. You don't have to rent a slip just to pick

somebody up. So the boat could've been from almost anywhere. But they'll check it out anyway."

"What're they doing with the van?"

"It'll be towed to the FHP substation in Marathon. Then
the Monroe County Sheriff's office will dust the inside for
prints sometime this morning."

Must admit, it gives me a good feeling to know that I
guessed right for a change. All right, granted, it was an educated guess based on experience and narrowed alternatives,
but a guess all the same. This guy's not unfathomable by any
means, but he's about as bright as they come. Cocky as they
come too. Real arrogant. Could be an important flaw. Every
super-bright criminal I've tracked in my career had at least
one major flaw in his or her personality or method of operation. At least one weakness. Me, I like to do what pros do in
most competitive sports: Identify the weakness, understand it,
and then play to it with everything you've got. Our man is
cocky because he knows he's good, real good. Mistakes are
made that way.

For example, this question keeps coming to mind, and
maybe it's significant: Why did he elect to kill Laila right out
in an open parking lot and then leave her body where we
couldn't possibly miss it? Somehow, that just doesn't make
any sense to me, although we're back to the question of logic
again. I mean, in a professional hit (unless it's an execution),
it's much easier to kill in private and just dispose of the body
without a trace, if that can be arranged. In the eyes of the law,
the victim becomes a missing person, officially, just another
statistic to add to the many thousands of missing persons
reported in this country every year, and remains classified as
such until the body is recovered and the cause of death is
determined, or until the mandatory seven-year period has
elapsed, after which a missing person may be declared legally
dead. So why didn't he kill her in private and dispose of the
body? What did he have to gain by going public, by making

it so crystal clear who did it, by ghoulishly flaunting it?
I keep visualizing that registration card:

Abbild von Todesfall
Mittwoch Abend, 18-12
Grün Schildkröte

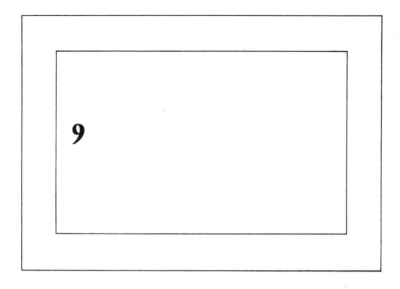

9

WHEN I CALL VADNEY at 9:05 A.M., he starts to get real excited fast. I lay it out for him point by point, chronologically, often reading verbatim from the surveillance report, and I can hear him slurping his coffee in rapid sucks, going "Ahhh" after each gulp, then making these rhythmic lip-smacks and teeth-grinds and hum-like sounds deep in his throat as he devours his cheese Danish. Early on, he gets Doris Banks to call Department of Motor Vehicles Security, highest-priority request, for the registration on New York license YZY 971, which, at this point, is actually the only scrap of information that might possibly lead to Todesfall's real identity. After five minutes or so, when I get to the part about the murder, I can sense that he's getting super-excited. Tell you how I know that. I can always tell when Vadney's verging on super-excitement on the phone because, number one, he stops interrupting altogether and shuts up like a clam; number two, he starts breathing real heavy like those pud-pulling geeks in obscene phone calls; number three, his breath starts coming faster and faster, like he's in the home stretch of an orgasm. When I get to the part about the Howard Johnson's registration and translate it for him, he sounds like he's on the brink of hyperventilation. I mean, I'm starting to get short of breath just listening to this guy. As I'm finishing up on the charter-boat theory and the eventual discovery of the van in the Holiday Isle parking lot, Doris interrupts on the intercom, says she's got the information from DMV Security. Chief asks her to come in fast.

"Hold on," he tells me.

"Will do."

Click.

I'm sitting up in bed in our luxury room at the Sheraton River House, wearing my T-shirt and jocky shorts; managed to grab about five hours' sleep. I take a sip of the coffee Brendan brought me from the coffee shop. He's had breakfast already, he's sitting on the other bed now, reading the *Miami Herald.* Sun's streaming in the window, I can see blue skies and some fluffy white clouds.

"What's the weather report?" I ask.

He checks the index on the front page, turns to page two, clears his throat, reads it in a cheerful weatherman's voice: " 'Today is expected to be partly sunny. Highs in the low to mid-seventies; lows in the upper fifties. Winds, east, ten miles per hour.' "

"What's it in New York?"

Runs his finger down a column. "New York. Yesterday—high, thirty-one; low, eighteen. Today—high, thirty; low, twenty-one. Tell Vadney we need to stay down here at least a couple more days, we got some important—"

Click. "Rawlings?"

"Yes, sir."

"Got a pencil and paper?"

"Wait a minute. Okay, shoot."

"Okay. According to the DMV records, that Chevy van is

registered to Morningside Motors, an outfit that leases vehicles, located up on Amsterdam in Manhattan. That's all they had. Doris called Morningside, identified herself, left the callback number. They just got back to her. The van's leased to —take this down now—van's leased to Ismat Farah. Spelled I-s-m-a-t, then the last name F-a-r-a-h. Address, Five-twenty-six West One Hundred Fourteenth Street, Manhattan. Age, forty-three; height, five-eleven; weight, one-fifty-four. Naturalized—"

"Chief?"

"—American citizen. Okay, I'll slow down. Naturalized American citizen. Occupation, associate professor—"

"Chief?"

"—of radiology, Columbia University. Okay, okay, slower. Occupation, associate professor of radiology, Columbia University. Office, Six-twenty-two West One Hundred Sixty-eighth Street, Manhattan. Got it?"

"Got it. Chief, that's not—"

"Now, listen up, Little John, here's what I'm gonna do. Effective immediately, I'll get the boys from JRTF to dig up everything possible on this guy. Also, I'll call Chief Haynes this morning, tell him what a fantastic job his clowns are doing, see if he can get any poop on that Bancaro International bank there. Also, I'll see if he can get the Coast Guard down there to nose around on that charter boat. Meantime, you guys stay put, y'read me?"

"Loud and clear. Chief, one thing. That physical description of Ismat Farah? It doesn't fit our suspect. The man we want—"

"*What?*"

"That's not our man, Chief."

"Oh, shit."

"Not even close. The man we want is tall, about six-foot-three, one-seventy-five, mid-fifties to maybe sixty."

"Oh, shit."

"Gray-white hair worn short. Deeply lined face, strictly Aryan features, probably German."

Pause. Then: "Shit. There goes our only lead."

"Not necessarily."

"Rawlings, come on. It's obviously a stolen vehicle."

"Not necessarily. Frankly, I don't think our man would drive a stolen vehicle down here. Not with eight million dollars in cash in the back. Much too risky. He'd never do that. I know he wouldn't."

"Yeah, maybe you got a point there, Little John."

"My opinion, it'd have to be legit all the way. He'd have to have this guy Ismat Farah's New York license, his lease registration—no. No, he wouldn't do it that way."

"What?"

"It's a long story, but the bottom line is, he wouldn't be that predictable. He'd do something we wouldn't expect."

"Like what?"

"I don't know yet. But a thought just occurred to me. Chief, may I make a suggestion?"

"Absolutely."

"Call the Radiology Department at Columbia, ask to speak with Farah. I doubt he'll be there, but maybe you can find out where he's supposed to be. Next, get a search warrant, send Telfian and Thalheimer up to Farah's apartment. I doubt he'll be there, either, but the super can let them in."

"You think Farah's involved?"

"I think he's either involved or he's dead."

"In his apartment?"

"It's possible, yeah."

"Okay, we'll check it out. You guys stay put, Little John, I'll get back to you before noon."

Brendan's deep in an article in the *Herald* (there's no story about the murder yet, it's too soon), so I sit back, sip my coffee, light a cigar, look out the window, and try to put myself in Todesfall's place again; I'll continue to call him that. Now, I don't have a clue what connection an associate professor of radiology might have with this man, but *if* Ismat Farah was involved with the robbery and I was Todesfall, the mastermind, how would I use him? Okay, me in his place, here I go again. Since I'd want to keep as low a profile as possible, my plan would call for the actual robbery to be accomplished by Laila and Ismat. Laila? Yeah, Laila, that makes sense to me. Tell you why. Remember, when I was in the money room, I wondered why the four large convex mirrors for the closed-circuit TV cameras had all been turned up to face the ceiling, despite the fact that the two robbers wore ski masks? The reason could be that one of them was a female, whose mannerisms would be recognized on the videotape. In any event, my next move in the plan, I'd have Ismat drive his own van from New York to Miami with the fifteen to seventeen moneybags, while Laila and I flew down—separately. I mean, I'd keep as far away from that money as I could, until the actual prearranged time for my transaction at Bancaro International.

So, in this scenario, what becomes of Ismat? Would the plan target him as a potential problem that had to be resolved quickly like Laila? If so, the man's undoubtedly dead now. But for some reason my intuition tells me Todesfall's not finished with him yet, that he still has some useful function in the design of the master plan, and I think his occupation leads me to that conclusion. Of course, there's the unexpected problem of the van's license plate now. But keep this important fact in mind: Todesfall knew exactly what we knew, that we couldn't trace the license through the DMV in New York until nine o'clock this morning. By then, it wouldn't make any difference anyway, he'd be long gone. Following his plan to the letter, he'd have first-class airline reservations from somewhere to somewhere, booked months in advance, and he'd be out of the

country by now. With Ismat? No, I think they'd travel separately, but to the same eventual destination. From where, to
where? Excellent questions.

All right, first things first. What city would we logically
expect him to depart from? Again, we know that he knew
exactly what we knew, that a statewide APB would be more
or less standard procedure in a case like this. Therefore, if the
original plan called for him to leave from, say, Miami (which
I seriously doubt now), or another major city in Florida, one
of his contingency plans would have selected the next closest
major out-of-state city—Atlanta. Wouldn't take all that long
for a good-sized oceangoing yacht to make it up the coast;
besides, he's in no hurry, as far as we know. So that's what we
might logically expect him to do under the circumstances, just
cruise up to Atlanta. Okay, now I can rule out Atlanta. If he
didn't head north, what's east, west, and south?

I get up, go to the little desk, pick up our colorful in-room
tourist magazine, flip through the exciting destination stories
to the map of Florida, then to the map of the Keys. Go back
to bed, sip my coffee, puff my stogie, study it out. From Key
West, according to this thing, Nassau is ninety-three miles due
east. To the west is a sixty-eight-mile string of islands reached
only by boat or seaplane or helicopter, including the Mar-
quesas Keys, Rebecca Shoal, and the famous Tortugas.
Havana is exactly ninety miles southwest. All within easy
reach of the craft he's on, in my judgment. Well, he wouldn't
go to Key West, he wouldn't go to the islands west of there,
and he certainly wouldn't go to Havana. But I won't rule out
Nassau. He could hop an early morning flight from there to
a number of major cities, including New York and, if I'm not
mistaken, London. What airline? Don't know which ones go
there, but I take an educated guess—British Airways.

Grab the Greater Miami telephone directory, look up British Airways. Here it is, I dial reservations, 377-2051.

"Good morning, British Airways, Barbara speaking."

"Yes, good morning, Barbara. I wonder, do you have nonstop flights from Nassau to London?"

"Nassau-London? One moment, please." Click, click, click-click-click. "Yes, sir, we offer nonstop service, Nassau-London, every Thursday and Sunday."

"Thursday? Could you tell me the departure and arrival times of the Thursday flight? That's today, right?"

"Yes, sir. Flight Two-sixty-two departed Nassau this morning at eight-ten; its scheduled arrival at London-Heathrow is eight-fifty-five this evening, London time."

"I see. And what other cities do you fly to from Nassau?"

"From Nassau? One moment, please." Click, click, click-click-click. "Yes, sir, I'll read the destinations alphabetically. From Nassau, we offer flights to Aberdeen, Belfast, Dublin, Edinburgh, Glasgow, Jersey, Kingston, London, Manchester, Montego Bay, and Newcastle."

"I see. And just one other question, Barbara. How many of those flights are nonstop?"

"Let's see. All of the transatlantic flights stop in London first, where you would have connecting flights. Apart from London, we offer nonstop service from Nassau to Kingston and Montego Bay."

"So if I wanted to fly from Nassau to anywhere in Europe, I'd have to take the flight to London first?"

"That's correct. Would you like to make a reservation?"

"Not today, Barbara. But I appreciate your help."

"Thank you for calling British Airways."

Now I sit back, puff my cigar, look at the map, think about the scenario again. If I remember my nautical numbers, a good-sized oceangoing yacht, say, thirty-five, forty feet, can average eighteen to twenty knots an hour on calm seas. One knot is equal to one nautical mile, or about 1.15 statute miles per hour. Nassau is ninety-three miles due east of Key West.

So, from Islamorada, we'll call it an even ninety miles. That means if Todesfall's craft left the Holiday Isle Marina at 10:20 last night and averaged only fifteen knots in the dark, he would've reached Nassau in about six hours. That's around 4:20 this morning. Let's say five o'clock, what the hell. They'd anchor in the harbor, he wouldn't have to get up until, say, six. Nice leisurely breakfast aboard, maybe a couple of Bloody Marys to start, look at that fantastic sunrise. He's dropped off at the Nassau Immigrations and Customs dock, nothing to declare, probably a garment bag and one carry-on bag. It's now seven o'clock, a taxi takes him to the airport, which can't be that far away on an island of this size. Goes straight to the gate, British Airways' Flight 262 starts boarding about 7:40, he's already got his ticket, purchased weeks, maybe months, in advance, all he needs is his first-class seat number and boarding pass. Off he goes at 8:10, next stop London. If we knew his name, we could find out if he's aboard that flight right now.

But what about Ismat Farah? Could he have been on that yacht last night? Could he be on the flight with Todesfall right this minute? Would he be using his real name? Today, at all major European airports, the immigrations and customs authorities have what's called a "profile" on possible terrorists. And the profile leans heavily on individuals whose physical characteristics and/or names resemble those of Semitic people from the Arabian peninsula and parts of northern Africa. When individuals meeting this profile pass through immigrations and customs at any major European airport, special attention is given to the examination of their passports and luggage. As a result, many forged passports have been discovered since 1983, the bearers arrested, their luggage confiscated, and some of them were undoubtedly terrorists. Ismat Farah, although a naturalized American citizen, and probably holding a valid U.S. passport, would still fit the profile and his passport would be examined carefully. Under such tight airport security precautions, he wouldn't risk a forged passport, he'd travel under his real name. On the other hand, Todesfall obviously doesn't resemble the Arab profile in the slightest. He could risk a forged passport. In my judgment, immigrations officers in London wouldn't give him or his passport a second glance. Knowing what I know about the man so far, it wouldn't surprise me if he had a number of passports under various names, plus backup ID. But would he risk traveling with Ismat? Now I have to remind myself of an important fact: In the eyes of the law, Ismat Farah has not committed a crime. *If* he drove his legally leased van from New York to Miami—and we still have no proof that he did—there's no crime in doing that, right? So far, we have circumstantial evidence that the driver of the van killed Laila Mustafa last night, but we know the driver wasn't Ismat. So, even if he's on the flight, the most we could do is ask the immigration authorities at Heathrow to detain the man for questioning and search his luggage. That's it. Under the law, we don't even have prima facie evidence of any wrongdoing. Technically, Ismat Farah is free to travel anywhere at any time.

Okay, now I call Mort Cooper at headquarters. He's read Judith Sever's surveillance report, so I don't have to brief him on details, and he has some interesting updates for me. Dr. Westlake's autopsy confirmed the probable cause of death, a single .38-caliber slug, but didn't come up with anything else that might be valuable to the investigation. Mr. and Mrs. Mustafa identified their daughter's body in Marathon at 2:15 A.M., submitted to questioning by Sheriff Kominski, but apparently didn't have any knowledge about Todesfall whatsoever or Laila's possible involvement in the robbery; this doesn't surprise me. The sheriff's office was unable to get any clear fingerprints from the exterior of Sever's car, but they got plenty from the interior and exterior of the Chevy van and they're now being scanned and digitized for the new NEC computer at headquarters.

After giving Mort a rundown on what we know about Ismat Farah, I ask him to call British Airways at the airport, identify himself, request the manager on duty, tell him we have some confidential questions, ask him to go through the call-back routine. When he does, we want him to tell us if the PNL (Passenger Name List) computer includes the name of Ismat Farah on Flight 262 this morning, Nassau-London. If so, we want his seat number and the name of the passenger sitting next to him. Also, we want to know if Farah (and/or his seat companion) is booked on a connecting flight in London. If so, we want all available details. Mort says he'll make the call immediately and get back to me soonest.

Less than five minutes later, exactly 9:28, Mort calls back, excited as hell: "Ismat Farah's on that flight, John! He's definitely on that flight! First class seat number five-J."

"Who's sitting next to him?"

"Nobody. Seat's empty."

"He listed for a connecting flight?"

"Bingo! He's got first-class reservations on British Airways' Flight One-fifty-five, nonstop to Cairo, tomorrow afternoon. Leaves three-fifteen, arrives ten o'clock, Cairo time. Hold on, there's more. I had the manager check the PNR. Farah made the whole reservation, Nassau-London-Cairo, on November twenty-six. Tuesday, November twenty-six, by telephone. Passenger's phone number, area code two-one-two, number two-eight-one seven-seven-eight-one. I called the Manhattan Information Operator, asked for the number of Ismat Farah. That's it, he gave his home number. Address, Five-twenty-six West One Hundred Fourteenth Street in Manhattan."

"Mort, you're a genius."

"Nothing to it."

"It's our first solid lead."

"Better get on the horn to Vadney."

And I do, pronto, exactly 9:30. Doris puts me through fast, but before I can start my spiel, Vadney launches into a breathless nonstop discourse on how he personally called Columbia University's Department of Radiology, identified himself, talked to the head honcho there, drew static, pulled rank, muscled the squirt into revealing that "Doctor" Ismat Farah started a sabbatical when the university broke for the Christmas holidays on December 13, that he's now en route to Cairo, Egypt, where he'll be in residence at Cairo University from January through August, doing research on a new book, after which he'll return to Columbia for the fall term. "How's *that* for a lead, Little John? Huh? Tracked the sucker down in one phone call, nailed down his itinerary, times, places, dates, the whole nine yards. Cairo, *Egypt,* buddy-boy! That's where our suspect's gonna be! Cairo University! I even got the telephone number of the place. Know anything about Cairo University?"

"No, sir."

"Doris looked it up in her encyclopedia, she's got a new unabridged deal here, strictly up-to-date. Cairo University, it's one of the great research centers of the *world.* Eleven faculties and higher institutes. Three thousand, three hundred *teachers.* Sixty-two thousand *students.* Imagine that? Sixty-two *thousand!*"

"Wow. Good place to get lost."

"Now, listen up, Little John, we're on a roll here. Telfian and Thalheimer, they got the search warrant for his apartment, they got it all typed up already. They're on their way to Criminal Courts right now to grab a judge, get a signature. They'll be inside that apartment inside of an hour."

"Chief, you're a genius."

"Nothing to it. Seems like we're doing all the work up here, buddy-boy. What're you guys doing, improving your suntans?"

"Naw, just stumbling around. Reason I called, thought you'd like to know that Ismat Farah sailed to Nassau last night with Todesfall."

"Nassau?"

"Nassau. At eight-ten this morning, Farah took off on British Airways' Flight Two-sixty-two, nonstop to London."

"London?"

"London. First-class seat five-J. Nobody in the seat next to him, but my intuition tells me Todesfall's on that flight under another name, maybe his real one, maybe not."

"Intuition again, huh?"

"Intuition. Flight arrives Heathrow eight-fifty-five tonight, London time. Farah's booked tomorrow afternoon on British Airways' Flight One-fifty-five, nonstop to Cairo. My guess, Todesfall's on it too. Departs Heathrow three-fifteen, arrives ten o'clock, Cairo time."

"Excellent work, Little John. Excellent. Okay, we gotta stay on top of these two. Now, what's the name of that— what's the name of that little Arab from the Nineteenth, the guy on your team—Addressy?"

"A-*dree*-see. Nuzhat Idrissi."

"Yeah, right. Now, he's a real Arab, right?"

"Born and bred."

"Now, what's the language in Egypt, they speak Arab or what?"

"Language is Arabic, far as I know."

"Idrissi speak it fluently?"

"Far as I know, yeah."

"He ever live in Cairo?"

"I honestly don't know."

"All right, doesn't matter, long as he speaks the language. Now, listen up. You two stay put. I'll get hold of Idrissi fast, bring him up to speed, tell him to haul his ass over to the Egyptian Embassy, muscle 'em into quick visas for all three of you. You need visas for Egypt, right?"

"Far as I know, yeah."

"Rawlings, do me a favor, huh? Knock off the 'far as I

know' shit, huh? Answers like that get on my nerves, y'read me?"

"Yeah. Sorry, Chief, didn't get much sleep last night."

"I *know* that, Little John, I'm cognizant how hard you guys been working down there. You're the only two guys got anything *solid* for me since the case began. I'm depending on you. That's why, as a reward for such excellence, and as a solid vote of confidence, I'm sending you guys to Cairo, along with Idrissi. Huh? Cairo, Egypt, Little John, how about *that!?* How y'like *them* apples, buddy?"

"Certainly appreciate it, Chief."

"Bet you never been *there,* right?"

"Not even close."

"Well, you deserve it, both of you, you've earned it. Now, make reservations on—wait a minute. Hold on a minute while I get out the *Official Airline Guide* here. All right. Now. Let's see. What time you say that flight from Nassau arrives in London?"

"Eight-fifty-five tonight, London time."

"Something just occured to me, Little John. Just hit me out of the blue. Let me look it up here. Yeah. Yeah, here it is! Yeah, I was right! This thing flies between London and *three* American cities—New York, Washington, and *Miami!"*

"What thing, Chief?"

"Concorde."

"Concorde? The SST?"

"Absolutely, positively, buddy-boy. British Airways' Concorde. Now, listen up, get a load of this. According to the *Guide* here, Concorde leaves Miami at ten-forty-five this morning, makes one stop in Washington, then arrives in London at exactly ten o'clock tonight, London time. Now, London's five hours ahead of us. So that's—let's see. That's exactly four hours' flying time, Washington-London. As opposed to—let's see. As opposed to *eight* hours on a conventional jet. Christ, that's almost unbelievable. Cuts the flying time in half. Yeah, now I remember. Now I remember all this shit, it's all coming back to me. Know anything about Concorde, buddy?"

"Not much. Just that it's supersonic."

"Well, tell you what, Little John. Tell you what. You're gonna learn about it fast. I mean, we got no viable alternative here. What it boils down to at this point, our biggest problem now is *time*. We finally got these fuckers nailed down, we know where they are, we know where they're headed and when, now we gotta pull out all stops. Why? I'll tell you why. Because it might be our only chance. We just gotta face that fact. If we lose 'em now, we've had it. If ever there was a time to spend money on a case—a big case, one of the biggest we've ever had—if ever there was a time when it was absolutely justified, it's now. All right, here's the game plan. Y'got a pencil and paper?"

"Wait a sec. Okay."

"Now, first off, this Concorde deal is just too expensive for you and Brendan both. Sorry to split you up, but it's just way too expensive to justify. Only one of you can go with Idrissi. That's you. I want you on that Concorde flight to Washington this morning. Idrissi will board in Washington. You leave Miami at ten-forty-five, get into Washington at twelve-ten. That gives Idrissi plenty of time to hop the Eastern shuttle and get over to Dulles."

"Chief, we'll need our passports, we'll need—"

"I *know* that, Rawlings, don't get—don't get *nervous* on me, huh? Now's the time for cool heads around here. It's only —right now it's only nine-thirty-six. Huh? Concorde doesn't depart Washington till—let's see. Till one o'clock this afternoon. Huh? Cool heads, Little John. Here's the game plan. I'll have Idrissi call your wife immediately, ask her to meet him at LaGuardia, at the Eastern shuttle there, with your passport, clothes, everything you need, all packed and ready to go. Matter of fact, you can call her yourself, tell her where you're going, what you'll need, the whole shot. All very calm and cool. Nothing to get nervous about."

"I'll call her. Appreciate it, Chief."

"But before you do that, call British Airways, book a seat on that Concorde. Use your American Express card. You got an American Express card?"

"Sure do. What's the fare?"

"Fare? Let's see here. Concorde, Miami to London, one way. Holy shit. Two thousand five hundred ninety-eight dollars."

"Holy shit. One way?"

"One way. Only one class of service on this sucker. That means, let's see here for Idrissi. Concorde, Washington to London, one way. Two thousand four hundred seventy-one bucks. God *damn.* Lemme add that up here. Two-five-nine-eight, two-four-seven-one. That's—nine; sixteen, carry the one; zero, carry the one; five. Jesus. Five thousand and sixty-nine dollars. These Brits don't fool around."

"Catchin' crooks ain't cheap."

"You said it, buddy-boy. Still, it's justified, in my opinion. Probably our last shot at these guys. Can't afford to blow it now. Besides, we're talking killer-crooks now, major-league killer-crooks. Biggest cash robbery in history, just remember that, Little John. I mean, we're talking eight million dollars here. Keep that in mind. We can't afford to swallow a camel and strain at a gnat, know what I mean? Keep reminding yourself what's at stake here, the incredible pressure that's on *me* now. Building. Building by the day. Vinnie Casandra, the sadistic little ratfucker. Y'see the latest 'Rambo Bambo' cartoon in this morning's *News?*"

"Not yet, no."

"Third straight day, usual spot, page three, nobody could

possibly miss it. Somehow the scrote got wind of the fact that we traced these guys to Miami. Highly confidential information, of course, which means we must have a canary at headquarters. Anyhow, he's got Rambo—oh, and today's title is 'Miami Nice.' He's got Rambo Bambo in his usual getup, y'know, this time he's sitting cross-legged on a beach, sipping a tall beer, palm trees and ocean in the background. Sitting next to him, here's Ed Koch, wearing a typical Don Johnson outfit, sipping a martini. Koch's talk cloud says, 'You sure this is where the boys are?' Rambo's talk cloud says, 'Ey, wimp, trust me, will ya?' "

"Man's got no respect, Chief."

"Tell me about it. Poor Ed Koch, he's sitting there in that dipshit outfit, he doesn't even have any socks on."

"Outrageous."

"Anyway, that gives you an idea what I'm up against here, Little John. Every day that passes without anything solid, the pressure mounts. Now, listen up, here's the rest of my game plan, take notes on this. Okay, that flight from Nassau's scheduled to arrive in London at eight-fifty-five tonight; let's call it nine. Now, even flying at twice the speed of sound on Concorde, you and Idrissi won't arrive until ten. But that's almost perfect timing, in my opinion. Why? I'll tell you why. Obviously, you can't arrest this Ismat Farah character for anything, because we got nothing on him, and we don't even know for sure that Todesfall, or whatever you want to call him, is on that particular flight. For all we know, maybe he's not. But here's my psychology on this thing: We know Farah's eventual destination is Cairo, right? And we suspect that Todesfall's eventual destination is Cairo. If they're both on the flight from Nassau, they've got eight hours of flying time ahead of them today, then another—let's see. Seven hours minus one —Cairo's one hour ahead of London. So they got another six hours of flying time tomorrow. In other words, when they get off the plane in London at nine o'clock tonight, London time

—four o'clock their time—they'll be suffering from jet lag. Dehydrated, fatigued, debilitated. They'll try and grab some sleep, probably in an airport hotel, but their physical time-clocks will be screwed up by five hours. Then, tomorrow, they'll stumble back to get on another jet for another six-hour flight that'll make zombies out of 'em. By the time they arrive in Cairo tomorrow night, their bodies will be six hours out of sync and they'll be so dehydrated and exhausted they'll be basket cases. Now, follow my logic here, follow my game-plan psychology: You and Idrissi, you'll be relatively fresh. By comparison. Well rested, bright, sharp, alert. Know why?"

"Concorde?"

"Yeah, but that's only part of it, Little John. Here's the payoff: When you get to London at ten o'clock tonight, London time, it'll be only five o'clock in the afternoon, your time. Just four hours of flying time. No appreciable jet lag. Hell, why do you suppose this Concorde deal is so popular with businessmen, top executives? You step off the plane, you stroll over to—let me look it up here, hold on a minute. Let's see. Here it is—Egypt Air. You stroll over to Egypt Air, where you'll have reservations on their—let's see. Egypt Air, Flight One-oh-six, departs twenty-three-hundred hours, that's eleven o'clock. Where you'll have reservations on their eleven o'clock flight nonstop to Cairo. We'll handle it all from here, natu-rally, round-trip tickets, paid in advance. Six hours later, you're there. At six in the morning, Cairo time, which is—let's see. Midnight, your time. Perfect! Total of ten hours in the air, sure, but now, wait a minute, get a load of *this:* You go directly to your hotel—we'll book the hotel from here and tell Idrissi before he leaves. You go straight to your hotel, buddy-boy, pleasantly tired. Then what? You go to *sleep!* Yeah! Sleep for at least eight hours, right? Get up, what time is it now? Six plus eight, it's two o'clock in the afternoon, Cairo time, but only eight o'clock in the morning, your time. Get up, have a nice leisurely breakfast, you got it made! You guys'll be fresh as daisies! Hour later, off you go to the Cairo police headquarters—we'll handle the preliminaries from here. Off you go to the police, identify yourselves, touch base, clue 'em in, get 'em up to speed on the case, I'm sure they'll cooperate in any way possible. Now what? Take a tour of the city, get your bearings, let Idrissi buy some inconspicuous Arab clothing for you both. Whatever they wear these days, so you melt straight into the crowd. Bottom line, Little John, when these guys arrive at the airport at ten o'clock that night, totally exhausted, you'll be waiting for them. Well rested, bright-eyed, bushy-tailed, dressed like Arabs, ready to start surveillance. That's why it's so critical to have Idrissi with you. He'll know the language, the customs, the currency, all shit like that. We'll make sure he gets a good cash advance for both of you—traveler's checks. Then you guys are on your own. Make sure you work closely with the Cairo police, don't make a move without them. Keep me strictly up-to-date, I don't care what it costs. Okay, that's all I—oh, yeah, you gotta leave your service revolver with Brendan. Can't carry firearms into England or Egypt. Far as getting on that Concorde flight, might be a problem that you don't have your passport right now. I'll call Chief Haynes, ask him to ring the head honcho at British Airways down there, explain that it's an emergency, that you'll get your passport in Washington."

Bang. End of conversation. Have a pleasant trip, Little John, good luck, let's be careful out there. Thanks a million, Chief, we'll do our best.

"John?" Doris stayed on the line, as usual.

"Hey, Doris. Nice to hear a friendly voice."

"Did you buy your wife a Christmas present yet?"

"Yeah, luckily. She knows where it is."

"Don't forget to call her."

"Will do. Thanks, Doris."

"Merry Christmas!"

"Merry Christmas to you, too."
"Oh, and John?"
"Yeah?"
"Don't drink the water."

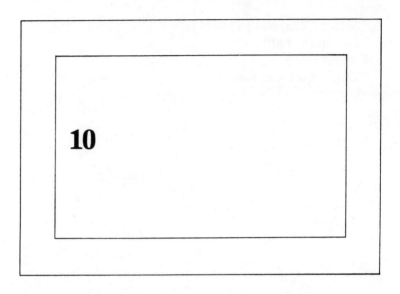

10

SOMETIMES I WONDER where my head's been for the past
ten years. No, I'm serious, this is straight. I mean, here we are
in the middle of the computer revolution, the exciting tidal
wave of the future, and I feel like Rip Van Winkle in a leaky
rowboat. Take this Concorde thing. According to Brendan,
who sees me off at the airport, next month marks the tenth
anniversary of the inaugural flight, January 21, 1976, London
to Bahrain, the dawn of commercial supersonic flight, so to
speak, and I can only dimly remember seeing it on the news.
Oh, I've seen thousands of pictures of it since then, of course,
it's the most famous aircraft in the world. Couple of times I
even saw it from a distance out at Kennedy. But that's it. Still
don't know squat about it. Ten years of the SST passed me by.
Like I slept through it. Must say, gives me a strange feeling.
Stale, old-fashioned feeling. I mean, if Vadney knows all the
facts and figures about this sucker, as I'm sure he does, how
come I draw a blank? Where've I been, in a desk drawer? Only

thing that makes me feel better, Brendan doesn't really know all that much about it either, except the date and route of the inaugural, and he's six years younger than me, he's still a kid.

Airport's only about five minutes from the hotel, so we get there at 10:12, go to the desk and buy the ticket with my American Express card, $2,598, one way. First thing we learn is that British Airways people don't call it "the" Concorde, they simply call it Concorde, with just a hint of the French pronunciation. Not that they're snooty about it, don't get me wrong, that's just the way they say it. Before giving me my boarding pass (window seat 19-A, smoking section), the ticket agent makes a quick phone call, then asks me to please wait a moment, that I'm being met by Mr. Arthur Braunstein, who will escort me to the gate. Obviously, Chief Haynes has cut the red tape about my passport.

Braunstein turns out to be a tall, deeply tanned, good-looking kid in a smart uniform, crisp white short-sleeved shirt with epaulets (three gold stripes against black), plastic ID card clipped to his breast pocket, navy-blue tie and trousers, black shoes. He explains that his boss, Airport Manager Jeff Rhodes, planned to meet me himself, but got called away unexpectedly. Ordinarily, he says, we'd go to the first-class lounge, but it's now 10:17 and the flight's ready to board.

Off we go down the long corridor toward the airport security station, show my ticket to the first guard. Rule is, only passengers are allowed beyond this point, but Braunstein tells the guard it's okay for Brendan to accompany us to the gate; he wants to get a close look at Concorde. I have no luggage to place on the roller for the X-ray machine, so all we have to do is pass through the metal-detector doorframe. Brendan anticipated this, hoping he'd be allowed to go to the gate, so he left both our service revolvers back at the hotel. We pass through squeaky clean. When he flies back to New York this afternoon on Pan Am, he'll follow the same routine with the guns that we did coming down, standard procedure, they're checked in a special Pan Am "personal effects" container and returned upon arrival.

Concorde is at Gate E-9, "Echo Nine," as Braunstein calls it on his walkie-talkie, at the right side of a spacious modern departure lounge. There are wide floor-to-ceiling windows just to the right of the check-in desk and we can see the tail of the aircraft with its distinctive British Airways logo, but that's about all. An extremely long boarding bridge blocks our view of the famous white pencil-slim fuselage and needle-shaped nose. You should see Brendan's face.

Passengers are boarding now and I can't help noticing that this is definitely a dress-up deal here, coats and ties, pricey designer fashions, no jeans and sneakers in sight. Obviously, Concorde doesn't cater to the great unwashed. Doesn't surprise me at these prices. Another thing, there aren't many passengers. Braunstein tells us only 17 are booked on this leg of the trip; most of the 100 seats will be filled in Washington. Very quiet and elegant atmosphere around here, no shouts, no announcements, no signs. Passengers are escorted from the first-class lounge to the gate, greeted with a smile, and that's it. Refreshing British understatement. Like their style.

Well, everybody's aboard, it's time to say good-bye to Brendan now, we shake hands, try to smile, but it's difficult. First time in years we've been split up like this. He's standing there, towering over me in his blue blazer, dark tie, three-day-old blue shirt, but he still looks sharp as ever. Gives me a lonely feeling. I mean, we trust each other with our lives, what can I tell you? And here I am, going off to Cairo without a weapon for an indefinite period of time.

"Hope you get back by Christmas," he says.

"Hope so. What the hell day is this?"

"Thursday, the nineteenth."

"Seems like we've been here for weeks."

"Sorry I didn't get to see you in drag."

"I'm not."

"Merry Christmas, John. Be careful, huh?"

"Will do. Merry Christmas."

Absolutely hate to say good-bye to people at airports. Hate it. Always chokes me up. Always say dumb things. Braunstein and I go to the boarding bridge, I give my pass to the attractive girl there, she smiles, rips off the stub, wishes me a pleasant trip. Once I step inside this bridge, I have a strange sensation, not unpleasant. This thing is very long, no windows, no doors, no people, and every inch of the walls and floor is covered with thick carpeting in the Concorde color theme—"silver," they call it. To me, it looks like very pale gray, but I'll go along, I'll call it silver, what do I know? Anyhow, Braunstein and I walk soundlessly down this long, silver, hall-like boarding bridge, fluorescent lights overhead throw weird vertical stripes down the carpeted walls, and it all has the mood of a Fellini film. Who knows, maybe that's the whole idea, maybe it's deliberate, a subtle altering of the senses to prepare you for the rarefied atmosphere of supersonic travel. End of the hall, turn left, pass a security guard, then it's just a short distance to the door of the aircraft, where two flight attendants are waiting.

Now, here's the deceptive part, here's where I was surprised. When you hang around New York long enough, over the years you're bound to meet people who've actually flown on Concorde, or know people who've flown on it, and I'm no exception, I've heard my share of stories about it. Okay, according to these people (and some of them may be lying through their teeth, they've never set foot on Concorde), the dominant impression is one of narrowness, a narrow-bodied, cramped feeling, compared to conventional wide-body jumbos like the 747 and DC-10. Well, I'm here to tell you, that's just plain bullshit. Granted, I'm only five-ten and 132, I'll give you that argument, no contest, but I still think the "narrow and cramped" rap is bullshit. Tell you why. Okay, first off, when you step through that door and turn right toward the cabin, there *is* a tendency to duck your head, even I did that. Why? Because in that one corridor, from the cockpit through the first galley, before you reach the cabin, the ceiling *does* seem low and the passage *is* quite narrow. But then, when you enter the cabin, it's all different. I'm not saying the single aisle is *wide* and the ceiling is *high,* by wide-body jumbo standards. No way. All I'm saying, it's just not all that claustrophobic as I'd been told. In fact, frankly, I was pleasantly surprised.

Dominant impression? To me, this thing gives the feel of an expensive sports car. Like the interior of a brand-new Jaguar, something like that. Why? Because of the seats, they're built like sports-car seats, two to a side, silver colored, headrests and borders in genuine top-grain cowhide. I can actually smell the leather as I walk down the aisle. White overhead storage compartments sweep up gracefully to a ceiling that's "vaulted," like the ceilings of the new jumbos. Windows are slightly smaller, but not by much. There are two cabin sections, separated by a galley and restrooms, first section has forty seats, second has sixty. Second also has the smoking section, rows seventeen through twenty-five. Me, I chose the smoking section, even though cigars aren't allowed. When I fly, I smoke cigarettes, I'm incorrigible, what can I tell you?

Okay, I'm in my seat now, window seat 19-A, nobody next to me. Very comfortable, lots of legroom, each row has two windows like first class on the jumbos. Pillows are silver, lighter shade than the seats. Reach in the seat pocket ahead of me, here's this classy silver briefcase, soft plastic, Concorde logo embossed at the bottom. Open it up, see what goodies I got. Full-color twelve-page brochure on the aircraft, history, facts and figures, the works, I'll have to read this. Next, "In-flight Entertainment Guide" for December, eight pages covering five channels of stereo selections, full-color photos of the artists. Next, four sheets of heavy, watermarked stationery, embossed with the logo at the bottom, plus two envelopes, same deal. December issue of their in-flight magazine, *Highlife*, 146 pages of travel news, destination stories, route maps, all like that. Plastic packet of silver-colored slipper-socks to match the decor. Finally, here's this watermarked and embossed "Concorde Flight Certificate," signed by the head honchos, attesting to the fact that blank name flew supersonically on blank date between blank city and blank city. Nice touch. Me, I'm going to get this thing filled out and framed. You kidding? One and only chance I'll ever have to fly this sucker, I'm not about to be blasé about it.

Glance around now, Arthur Braunstein's chatting with a crew member in the aisle, I notice the man's got four gold stripes on the epaulets of his short-sleeved white shirt. Must be the captain. I glance at my watch, just 10:29, plenty of time before we leave, hope I get to meet him. Looks a bit shorter than me, maybe five-eight, five-nine, so I like him already. Distinguished-looking guy, lean, well-built, dark thinning hair parted on the right, same as me, gray sideburns, hint of a tan, pleasant smile, bright white teeth tell me he's not a smoker. Seems a tad young to be a Concorde captain, I assume only the very senior officers get a shot at this job, but appearances are deceiving, maybe he just takes care of himself better than most.

Couple of minutes later, Braunstein brings him over, does the introductions. "Detective Rawlings, I'd like you to meet Captain Massie."

He shakes my hand. "John Massie. Happy to meet you."

"John Rawlings. Pleasure to meet you."

"I understand you'll be joined by another detective in Washington."

"Yes. He'll have my passport and luggage."

"I see. Well, I certainly hope you enjoy your flight."

"I'm looking forward to it."

Braunstein glances at his watch. "We're in good shape, everybody's aboard now except that one late arrival."

"Is that the charter jet?" Massie asks.

"From Palm Beach, yes. He's due any minute now."

As it turns out, the lone straggler arrives at 10:41, only four minutes to spare, an elderly man in a wheelchair pushed by a porter. He's been assigned a seat in the first row, behind the bulkhead, so he doesn't have far to go. Everybody's sipping champagne now, including me, watching this guy as he uses a silver-handled cane to maneuver out of the wheelchair and into window seat 1-A. When he's finally all settled in, he tips the porter, who folds up the chair and puts it in the stowage closet nearby.

Door closes punctually at 10:45, about a minute later we're moving slowly backward, away from that long boarding bridge. Brendan was determined to get a good look at this beauty, first from the gate lounge, so I unbuckle my seat belt (know I'm not supposed to), cross the aisle, slide into the window seat on that side. There he is with Braunstein, standing right up against the big windows. Well, I can't resist the temptation, I start waving like crazy. I mean, I've never been accused of being a sophisticate, so what the hell, why start now? Unfortunately, he can't see me, maybe the windows are too small, he just stands there with his hands in his pockets. Now we start moving forward, I go back to my regular seat and buckle up. As we taxi away from the terminal, the champagne glasses are collected and the announcements begin. Nothing out of the ordinary, except the British accent, just the standard safety instructions. Ever notice how nobody ever watches the flight attendants when they show you how to get a life jacket on and inflate it? I mean, it's just not sophisticated to watch that, right? Because, if you did, somebody might see you and get the idea that you're not a frequent traveler, right? Wonder how many frequent travelers really know exactly how to get into those life jackets properly, so they'll stay on, and how to inflate them fast without any guesswork?

Can't wait to look up some facts about this bird, so I open my silver briefcase again, take out the brochure, leaf through it, skip the hype, just want the facts, ma'am. Four Rolls-Royce engines in under-wing nacelles. Thrust, 38,000 pounds times four. "All up" weight, 400,000 pounds. Typical cruising speed, 1,350 mph. Approximate maximum range, 4,500 miles. Here's a picture of what they call the "data display," rectangular glass panels that are built into the four bulkheads in the cabin. They give the airspeed readings, outside air temperature, altitude, and Mach number. Says Mach is the term for the speed of sound, which varies according to the outside temperature, but 1,340 mph is Mach 2 at Concorde's cruising height of 50,000 to 60,000 feet. Didn't know that, didn't even know this thing went faster than Mach 1, shows me how dumb I am, if I needed a reminder. Last page has specifications. Crew of two pilots, one flight engineer, six cabin attendants. Overall length, 204 feet, 1 inch. Height, 37 feet. Goes on and on, of course, whole page of stats, even lists the "tyre" pressures of the main wheels and nosewheels. Here's one I like, wingspan is eighty-three feet, nine inches. Love those graceful, swept-back wings.

Flight attendant comes by, hands me a four-page menu with a photo of pink orchids on the cover, asks if I'd like something to drink after takeoff. Says it with such a delightful smile, I can't bring myself to refuse. Glance at the menu, it has a full page devoted to drinks: Apéritifs, cocktails, spirits, beers, soft drinks, wines, and liqueurs. Should I be adventuresome on such an auspicious occasion? Here's a champagne called Cuvée de René Lalou Millésimé. Description reads: "René Lalou is Mumm's finest cuvée—a blend of the choicest black and white grapes of vintage years only, gathered in the most famous vineyards of the Champagne district. This special

cuvée is a prince amongst champagnes—a privilege to drink
and a rare gift to receive." Can't even begin to pronounce it,
so I tap my finger against the name, thoughtfully, of course,
smile, and say, "I'll have the champagne, please." Words to
that effect. Wonder if anybody ever ordered a beer in this
palace?

Takeoff is fun. We head due west down the runway, then,
very shortly after leaving the ground and retracting the landing gear, we nose up, start to climb and bank south with
smooth but tremendous thrust. I've got my nose against the
window like a kid now, I'm really eating this up. Strange to
look out at the wing, the sharp angle of it, makes me feel like
I'm in a rocket. Continue to bank for about 180 degrees, then
we're out over the Atlantic heading north, still climbing. Can't
see much now, so I sit back, light up a Marlboro, look at the
menu again. Champagne is served, I pull down the tray table
from the seat in front, flight attendant plunks down a silver
napkin, then the elegant champagne glass. I thank her kindly,
toast to absent friends, sip the bubbly. Ahhh. If only Vadney
could get a load of this. A stumble-bum like me, sitting here
in regal splendor, sipping a prince amongst champagnes,
about to experience the ultimate poetry of aeronautical technology—quietly breaking the sound barrier. Not bad for a
street kid from the Lower East Side. Now I study the menu.
This leg of the flight takes only an hour and forty minutes, so
they have a snack deal here in French and English. French in
silver, English in black. Fillets of fresh orange, grapefruit,
pineapple, grapes, and kiwi fruit, with cottage cheese; also,
crescent roll and danish pastry served with butter and orange
marmalade, and a choice of coffee or tea. Turn the page,
glance at the "lunch" from Washington to London, I almost
laugh out loud. Six courses, count 'em. Most incredible menu
I ever saw on an airplane. Tell you about it later. This stuff's
enough to make you salivate like Pavlov's mutt.

Thirty-five minutes into the flight, Captain Massie makes the announcement I've been waiting for in his crisp British accent: "Ladies and gentlemen, we are just approaching the point where this delightful airplane comes into her element, and we are now going to accelerate her through the sound barrier, Mach One, eventually climbing to achieve Mach Two at fifty thousand feet. To achieve this, I shall be reapplying full-climb power from all four engines. We do get an increase in drag on the airframe in the transonic region as the shock wave builds up and, to overcome this, we have to reintroduce our afterburners, a pair at a time, because we need the extra thrust from these to overcome the drag. They do, in fact, increase the overall thrust by twenty percent and, as this extra power comes on, you will notice two very, very slight kicks. Apart from that, the airplane goes through Mach One, the speed of sound, without any worry or fuss, very, very smoothly. If there is any bumpiness, it's nothing aerodynamic, it would be caused by clear-air turbulence that we sometimes get at these altitudes. I'm just applying the climb power now and the afterburners will be coming on in a couple of seconds."

Here comes the moment of truth, I'm automatically gripping the armrests of the seat, my whole body is tensed, I don't know exactly what to expect, but the anticipation is exhilarating. My eyes are wide now, glued to the data display panel on the bulkhead, where the big bright-yellow miles-per-hour numbers are changing: 655 . . . 660 . . . 665 . . . 670 . . . *MACH 1*. What? Wait a minute, I didn't feel anything, must be a defective indicator.

Captain Massie's voice: "There we are, ladies and gentlemen, smoothly through Mach One, the speed of sound, at thirty thousand feet. We are now supersonic."

I'm sitting there, I'm still tensed, I'm frowning now, I'm blinking, I can't believe this. I mean, *this* is the legendary

Mach 1 that all the shouting's about? Come on. *Nothing happened.* What is this, some kind of joke? This has got to be the greatest non-event in aviation history. What the hell am I supposed to tell my son, that I joined the ranks of astronauts and test pilots and didn't even know it? I mean, I'm all for British understatement, but this is ridiculous. Now I can't wait for Mach 2. Drama like this could put you to sleep.

Of course, in fairness, what they're selling on this thing is speed, not drama. Last thing you want on any commercial flight is drama, right? In any event, the trip is uneventful. After breakfast, served on Wedgewood and Royal Doulton china (I gauched out and peeked under the plates), with silver damask table linen, no less, I light up a Marlboro, lean back, put on my silver stereo headset, and check out the five channels, Classical Concert, Slipstream (contemporary), Swingtime, Sky High Country, The World of Concorde, and Good Humour (that's how they spell it). Actually, I liked Good Humour best, they got this British jazz trumpet player named Humphrey Lyttelton who's a very funny guy, plus sketches by Bill Cosby, Woody Allen, and an album called "The Secret Policeman's Other Ball" that makes me laugh out loud.

Before I know it, we're starting our descent into Washington. Smooth landing at Dulles slightly ahead of schedule, 12:20, it's overcast in D.C., temperature's announced as thirty-one degrees. You don't taxi to the gate here, you're transported to and from the aircraft by these big modern "mobile lounges" that look like weird buses. Every passenger aboard Concorde is in transit, of course, and we're not permitted to go to the terminal because it's an international flight. Still, they have to clean the cabin and prepare for the new passengers, so what we do, all seventeen of us, we step off the plane into a mobile lounge, where we're served just about anything we want, within reason, while we wait. Me, I'm simple, I have a Bloody Mary. Hits the spot.

First chance I've had to get a good look at the other sixteen passengers. Primarily middle-aged couples and older, probably retired, a few elderly women traveling together, all expensively dressed, many have good tans. Majority seem British to my eye and ear, aristocratic types, old money, conservative. My guess, they spend winters in places like Palm Beach, Barbados, Nassau, but always go home for the Christmas holidays. On the other hand, the old guy in the wheelchair seems more European, French maybe.

Fifteen minutes later, we file back on board, take our seats, everything's meticulously neat and clean again. At exactly 12:40, the Washington passengers are boarded from another mobile lounge. I'm sitting forward, can't wait to spot Nuzhat, know he'll be full of fun, traveling in such chichi élan. First dozen or so passengers are almost all men, typical gray-haired MBA corporate pricks with "I am the president" written on their worried-hurried pusses, or silver-haired ball-breaker board-chairman types who look like they chewed tacks for breakfast and want second helpings.

Now, here he comes, here comes Nuzhat, trying desperately to keep a straight face, dark Arab eyes sparkling behind his aviator-style glasses, neatly trimmed mustache twitching, heavy build packaged fashionably in a banker's-gray suit, white shirt, solid red tie. Makes his way down the aisle with two attaché cases, one of which I recognize as mine, haven't used it in years. His new Burberry raincoat's slung over his arm.

"Naharak sa'id!" he says.

"Hey, Nuz!"

He smiles, places the attaché cases on the seat, shakes my hand warmly. "Your wife is a delightful lady, John, we had a wonderful chat at the airport. She sends her love along with a very important message."

"Yeah? What's that?"

"She said—and I quote her now—she said, 'Tell him to take his two vitamin C tablets every day and to stay away from the belly dancers.' "

I laugh. "She pack my bag and all?"

"Yes, it's checked with mine." He hands me my attaché case, places his under the seat in front of him, and sits down. "Delightful lady, John, you're a lucky man. When I spoke with her on the phone this morning, I told her to pack a minimum of Western clothing because we will both be wearing the *galabiyya,* the full-length traditional garment worn by Egyptian men, and also the *tarboosh,* the traditional headgear. We will not have to buy these, I have brought along a variety of my own."

Flight attendant comes by, hands him a menu, asks if we'd like some champagne or orange juice before takeoff. Champagne, please.

"I had a long talk with Chief Vadney," he says. "He wants us to change into the Egyptian garments in the men's room at Heathrow."

"What?"

"So that we board our Egypt Air flight as inconspicuously as possible. I explained that wasn't necessary, reminding him that our suspects would not be arriving until the following evening. He said—and I quote him directly—he said, 'You guys gotta look like A-rabs from the outset.' I corrected his pronunciation of Arabs, very politely, of course, and said I had never heard of an Egyptian area called the Outset."

We both chuckle softly. Nuz, he's a real pisser.

"Logic to the contrary notwithstanding," he says, "the man actually ordered us to change at Heathrow. I agreed, of course. His next order was that you must start growing a mustache and/or beard, effective immediately."

"Oh, shit."

"He approves of my mustache, but thinks it should be— well, the word he used was 'scraggier.' I said, 'Scraggier, sir?'

He said, 'Yeah, *scraggier,* Idrissi. That means shaggy, ragged, unkempt.' He said, 'Both you guys gotta melt into the crowds of common, scraggy street Arabs.'"

I sit back and laugh out loud now. Nuz has the accent down cold. We're served our champagne, we clink glasses, sip, and I start laughing again. I can just picture us.

He reaches into his inside breast pocket, takes out my passport, hands it to me. "It was not necessary to obtain visas in advance. I called the embassy. We can get visas upon arrival, no problem. I asked your wife if you had any extra passport photos. For your visa. She found two—they're inside—but she thinks they're about five years old. Still, she thinks you have the same steel-blue killer eyes."

I open the passport, glance at the photos. Always hated these shots, but today they make me smile. Got them taken in that little shop in Grand Central about five, maybe six, years ago. Look like mug shots. Make me look like a hardened criminal. Can't help wondering how I'll look in a scraggy mustache and beard. Might be an improvement.

When the flight attendant asks if we'd like something to drink after takeoff, Nuz clears his throat and starts to order, but I interrupt, as any Concorde frequent traveler and connoisseur of the finer things in life should, as a courtesy to the hoi polloi, and suggest that he might want to depart from the commonplace and partake of the subtle delicacies of vintage René Lalou; I've practiced saying it now, it just rolls off the tongue, know what I mean?

"It's a prince amongst champagnes," I assure him.

He gives me this look. "A prince *amongst—?*"

"Champagnes, yes. Take my word for it."

Now he smiles at the flight attendant, adjusts his glasses. "Young lady, when I glanced at the menu, I noticed a superb red Bordeaux, Château Talbot St. Julien, nineteen seventy-six?"

"Yes, sir, it's excellent."

He turns to me. "I would recommend it highly, John. Soft, rich, and well balanced. In fact, this particular vintage was regarded by Talbot as being *amongst* the finest examples of classic St. Julien, as you undoubtedly know."

I look at the young lady, hold up two fingers.

Door closes at precisely one o'clock, we start to taxi out, the announcements begin. Both sections of the cabin are relatively full now, maybe seventy-five passengers. Take out my pen, make a rough calculation. If we all had round-trip tickets, British Airways would gross $375,000. Not too bad. Nuzhat's got his silver briefcase open, he's going through his goodies, he takes out his Concorde Flight Certificate, feels the paper, holds it up to the light to see the watermark. Now he sees me watching, he puts it back in the briefcase quickly, clears his throat.

"Gonna get it filled out?" I ask.

He raises an eyebrow. "I beg your pardon?"

"Gonna get it filled out and framed?"

Thin smile crosses his lips; he touches his mustache to hide it.

"Captain will sign it for you, Nuz. Make it look official."

"John, *allem sittak tmus el-beid!*"

"Come again?"

"It's an extremely popular Arabic saying," he tells me solemnly. "Especially among members of the *askari,* the police. Literally translated, it means, 'Teach your grandmother to suck eggs!' "

Takeoff is smooth, off we go into the wild gray overcast, through it fast, into the blue, we're climbing on full thrust, won't stop now till we're up around 58,000–60,000 feet, never been that high before, wonder what it looks like? Soon as the seat-belt sign is turned off, drinks are served, then our six-course lunch begins. Canapés are first, get a load of this, I'm reading from the menu now: Foie gras, caviar barquette, and shrimp with seafood mousse. Nuzhat's in Arab heaven now, switches from red Bordeaux to white Burgundy, Meursault 1982, I go along with the gag, it all tastes good to me. Except the caviar. Nuz, he's wolfing down the caviar like it's peanut butter, spreading it on these canapés thick as you please, making purring sounds in his gullet, washing it down with the Burgundy. Me, I've never been partial to caviar for some reason, guess my palate's just not sophisticated enough to enjoy black fish eggs.

"I have some interesting items for you," he says between bites. "It seems that Telfian and Thalheimer telephoned Vadney after conducting a routine search of Ismat Farah's apartment. Apparently, they did not find anything of an incriminating nature, so they asked him what to look for. He told them to conduct a thorough search of the man's papers and books, looking for anything relating to Egypt, Cairo, or Cairo University."

"Good thinking."

"Well, yes, you might say that. You might also say that he was grasping at straws. In any case, he ordered them to turn the apartment inside-out, with emphasis on his desk, searching for material that was even remotely concerned with Egypt. And, as it turned out, they came up with some very interesting items. At least, Vadney thought they were. They're in my attaché, I'll show you after lunch."

"What kind of items?"

"Three business letters addressed to Farah and one book written by him."

"Written by him?"

"Correct." He pops still another cavier-covered canapé into his mouth, goes, "Mmmm," like a cat, sips his wine. "As you know, Farah is an associate professor of radiology at Columbia. Now, in the academic community, there is a cliché that, however hackneyed, is as true today as it ever was. To wit: 'Publish or perish.' Telfian and Thalheimer discovered a total of seven books authored by Ismat Farah over a twelve-year period, all very scholarly works, all published by Columbia University Press. He had many copies of each book, of course. The most recent volume, published in nineteen eighty-three, caught their eye because of the title: *The Riddle of Cheops.* It's subtitled: *Concepts of Theoretical Radiology Within the Great Pyramid.* "

"Can't wait to see the movie."

He laughs softly, finishes his glass of Burgundy. "Ah, it must be fun to be an egghead. Of course, you understand, nobody outside of the specific academic fields of study ever reads these books. Universities all over the world publish thousands of these titles every year, in very limited printings, of course. The thing is, you have to be a certified egghead to understand what another certified egghead is talking about."

"But Vadney expects *me* to understand?"

"Of course. I mean, John, *he'd* read it too, but . . ."

"Yeah, I know. Happens to be a certified *meat* head. What's the story on the three business letters?"

"I just glanced at them, John, I didn't have time to do more than that, they were three or four pages each. The letterheads were easy to remember—IBM, GE, and General Motors. Apparently, Telfian and Thalheimer picked up on them because they were—still are—in a manila folder marked 'Cairo.' I'm curious to read them too. After lunch."

After lunch. Reading this menu, I wonder if we'll be able to *move* after lunch. After the canapés, they serve medallions of fresh lobster with smoked Scottish salmon, garnished with a crown of tomato with mustard and horseradish-flavored mayonnaise. I mean, that's a lunch in itself, you should see this stuff. Before we finish all that, Captain Massie announces that he's about to accelerate through Mach 1, eventually climbing to achieve Mach 2 at 50,000 feet. This time, just before we break the sound barrier, there are two very slight bumps from the rear, seconds apart, as the afterburners are turned on.

I nudge Nuz. "Feel that?"

He keeps eating. "Feel what?"

"Those two little bumps."

"Sorry about that, John, I apologize."

"What?"

"Indigestion."

Captain Massie's voice again: "There we are, ladies and gentlemen, smoothly through Mach One, the speed of sound, at thirty thousand feet. We are now supersonic."

Nuz glances up at the data display panel, where bold yellow capital letters proudly proclaim *MACH 1*. "Son of a gun," he says, and goes back to his Scottish salmon.

Entrées are served nice and hot. I have the prime fillet of beef, medium rare, with green peppercorn and brandy-flavored butter, served with leaf spinach, gratin of turnip, potatoes, baby squash, and cherry tomatoes. Nuz opts for the medallion of fresh turbot, pan fried, dressed with creamy cider sauce, garnished with wild mushrooms, chooses the same vegetables as me. We both have the mixed salad with radicchio lettuce, palm hearts, tomatoes, and anchovy vinaigrette dressing. I'm back to the red Bordeaux now, I figure they'll have to carry me off anyhow, what the hell. Finish all that, now they come around with dessert. Looks positively sinful, but I pass, I'm up to here. Not Nuz. No way. Now he goes for a chocolate cream mousse with mandarin Napoleon brandy. Slurp-slurp, gulp-gulp, it's gone, vanished, I think the man inhaled it. Next, they come around with cheese. My eyelids are drooping now, but I can smell it. Nuz goes easy, selects only the English Stilton, French St. Andre, and Double Gloucester. Munch-munch, phew-phew. Care for coffee and a selection of fine chocolates? No thanks, but we both consult the menu and order the Remy Martin Napoleon Cognac. Wait a minute, hold on here, what's this? Can't believe this. Last item on the menu under "Liqueurs," it says, "Jamaica Macanudo cigars." *Cigars?* I show Nuz, who's a cigar smoker from way back.

His eyes open wide, he blinks, he frowns. "No, no, John. No, it's a gift. To be taken off the aircraft."

"Yeah, huh?"

He nods with great authority. "All cigar smoking was banned from all commercial flights. Years ago."

I motion to a flight attendant, who comes over smiling. "Excuse me, but these Jamaica Macanudo cigars listed here. They can't be smoked on the aircraft, can they?"

"Certainly, sir."

Nuzhat sits bolt upright. "They *can?* My God, we thought —we assumed that cigar smoking was banned on all commercial flights."

"Ah," she says, "but this is Concorde."

Sure is. As a classy finishing touch, all passengers are presented with a little gift, a "memento," as the flight attendant says. We're sitting there, we're smoking our Jamaica Macanudo cigars (we each ordered three, what the hell), sipping our second Napoleon Cognac, feeling absolutely hedonistic (Nuzhat's word, not mine), we thank the young lady kindly as she hands us each a little silver box with the logo we've come to know and love. Open it up, here's a silver velvet bag. Open it up, here's a sterling silver decanter label on a silver chain. My label's engraved BRANDY with a tiny logo below. Nuzhat gets one labeled VODKA. I mean, I don't want to go overboard about this stuff, but I got to admit these people give you a class act.

After we reach cruising altitude, 58,000 feet, where the sky seems more black than blue, and Mach 2, 1,340 mph (no sensation of speed, but it's a kick in the head to know you're going that fast for once in your life), Captain Massie comes out of the cockpit and strolls through the cabin, shaking hands and all, and I watch to see how many people ask him to fill out their Flight Certificates. Ten, fifteen minutes later, he gets all the way through the first section of the cabin and nobody's asked him. Nobody. Well, I mean, these are obviously laid-back members of the supersonic set, right? Chairmen and presidents of multinational conglomerates. Multimillionaire play-people. Money and power up the gazoo. What're they going to do, ask the captain to fill out their goddamn Flight Certificates, for Christ's sake? Embarrassing to even think about it. Not to mention humiliating. Only children, adolescents, out-and-out peons, or common, scraggy street Arabs would even consider doing something of such a degrading nature. Right? Think that stops me? NO WAY! I get out my certificate, get out Nuzhat's (he's not only fast asleep by now, he's snoring), I shake hands with Captain Massie again, tell him how much I'm enjoying the flight, which I am in spades, plunk down my tray table, give him my pen, and tell him how to spell our names. This guy Massie, he's about as far removed from a snob as you can get, he's delighted to do it, fills them out in an easy, practiced manner, signs his name, then stands there and talks with me for a good five minutes, tells me all kinds of things about this bird that you won't find in any brochure. My kind of guy. I thank him kindly.

Okay, I'm wide awake, I'm ready to do some reading now. I reach under the seat in front of Nuz, pull out his attaché case, open it, browse through all the crap he's got crammed in here. Can't find the manila folder with the business letters, but the book's there, so I take it out, close the case, put it back. Turn on the reading light. This thing looks like a textbook, no dust jacket, fairly thick, I flip through it, 388 pages, formal academic format—foreword, glossary, prologue, ten chapters, epilogue, appendices, sources, index, plus a section of charts and diagrams.

Ho-hum, here I go. *The Riddle of Cheops: Concepts of Theoretical Radiology Within the Great Pyramid.*

All I can say, never judge a book by its academic appearance. From the opening page, I'm hooked. Hypnotized. By the time I get to Chapter 5, I know exactly why these people needed eight million dollars.

And what they're going to steal next.

11

WE ARRIVE EARLY, 9:46 P.M., London time, flight took only three hours and forty-five minutes. Plenty of time to make our connection with Egypt Air Flight 106, their redeye special, departing at eleven for Cairo. Of course, we have to clear Immigrations and Customs, but at Heathrow it's a streamlined operation all the way. Only potential hitch, Nuzhat fits the terrorist profile in both name and appearance, so the Immigrations officer examines every page of his passport very carefully, then begins to look up names, passport numbers, and photos of suspected terrorists in several large books. Finally, Nuz decides to show his NYPD shield and ID; acts like he's still half asleep, what can I tell you? Anyway, that does the trick instantly: Oh, sorry, sir, very good then, have a pleasant stay. Customs is a breeze, all we have to do is go down a flight of stairs into the enormous, modern Customs Hall, pick up our two bags from the carousel with the lighted sign *BA188-Concorde,* and walk out under the sign that reads *Nothing to Declare.* But first we have to wait with all the others for our bags to arrive on the carousel. It's still only about ten o'clock, so we're not worried.

While we're waiting by the carousel, something happens that really blows my mind. This smartly dressed, good-looking, middle-aged Englishman comes up to me, smiling, holding his Concorde briefcase.

"I beg your pardon," he says cheerfully, "but is your name John Rawlings?"

"Yes."

"My name is Congdon, Lucky Congdon, I was on the flight with you."

"Oh? Nice to meet you, Mr. Congdon." We shake hands. "This is Nuzhat Idrissi."

"How do you do, Mr. Idrissi." He shakes Nuzhat's hand, laughs a bit self-consciously, turns back to me. "I'm sorry to trouble you, Mr. Rawlings, but I was asked to deliver something to you." Reaches in his briefcase, takes out a large white envelope, hands it to me. "My seat companion pointed you out to me and asked very kindly if I'd give this to you. Delightful old gentleman, he said he was an acquaintance of yours, and made me promise not to give it to you until we were in the Customs Hall. I think it's a surprise of some kind."

I look at the sealed envelope. "What was the man's name?"

"Ah! He begged me not to tell you until you opened the envelope. I think it's all part of the surprise."

I shrug, open the envelope, take out a standard Concorde Flight Certificate:

CONCORDE

Flight Certificate

Presented to
SHABAH al-MAYYIT

who flew supersonically on Concorde between

nur - 'itim

on
al-Khamis, 19-12

Colin M Marshall
Chief Executive.

Captain Brian Walpole
General Manager, Concorde Division.

As soon as I see the carefully printed SHABAH al-MAYYIT, I feel suddenly cold. I'd recognize that printing anywhere. I hand the certificate to Nuzhat. "The fill-in words are in Arabic, right?"

Congdon's still smiling. "Surprised?"

"Where was the man sitting?" I ask.

"Window seat one-A. Right next to me. You do know Mr. Mayyit, don't you?"

"I know who he is, yeah."

Nuzhat's frowning at the certificate, as if confused. "What's it say?" I ask.

"The transliteration is always difficult from Arabic to any language, especially English. 'Shabah al-Mayyit' in a straight, literal translation, means 'look,' 'image,' or 'appearance' of 'death.' Between 'nur-'itim' means, essentially, between 'light' and 'darkness.' And 'al-Khamis, nineteen-twelve' means—it's simply today's date, 'Thursday, nineteen December.' "

Congdon's lost his smile. "How very odd. Is it some sort of private joke?"

"Something like that," I tell him. "Did you get a chance to talk with Mr. Mayyit at any length?"

"As a matter of fact, no, I didn't. He was listening to the stereo and reading a good deal of the time."

"Did he have an Arabic accent?" Nuzhat asks.

"Oh, heavens, no, not in the slightest, the man is British. No question in my mind whatsoever, his accent, his choice of words, all decidedly British."

"When did he point me out?" I ask.

"Actually, it wasn't until you were leaving the aircraft. As you were walking up the aisle towards the door. You see, Mr. Mayyit is handicapped, he had to depart last because he needed a wheelchair, so I stayed aboard with him until the porter arrived from special services."

"Did he fill this out right after he saw me?"

"No, no, the certificate was all filled out and sealed in the envelope by then. He merely pointed you out, very discreetly, told me your name, and asked if I'd be kind enough to give you the envelope. To give it to you in the Customs Hall and not before. That it was a surprise. And that I mustn't give the game away and tell his name until you'd opened it. I must say, the old man was very charming about it, you know? Very charming indeed. I mean, I couldn't very well refuse him his little game, could I?"

"Did you accompany him through Immigrations?" I ask.

"No, I didn't, I took my leave directly after the porter arrived. We shook hands, he thanked me very much indeed, and that was that. I do hope I haven't—I'm sorry if I've caused you any worry about all this, Mr. Rawlings."

"No, not at all."

"You seem a bit upset."

"No, I'm fine."

Truth is, I'm much more than upset. As the cold reality of it sinks in, I'm angry. This whole encounter had to be completely accidental. There's no way in hell he could possibly have known I'd be on that flight, because even I didn't know until about an hour and fifteen minutes before takeoff. So that's out of the question. But then, when he saw me on board, God knows when, why didn't he remain anonymous? He had an absolutely superb disguise, he's obviously a master at it, which is valuable for me to know, but why would he decide to flaunt his presence after the fact, to stick the knife in? What would motivate him to do that? What did he have to gain? At least I can't recriminate myself this time and I have no intention of doing it, but it just floors me, the balls this clown has.

As the carousel begins to turn and the luggage starts to come down the shoot, I feel dizzy. Thirty years as a cop and I've never, ever, come across anybody with the unmitigated arrogance and cunning of this guy. I should've been more alert back in Miami. Right? Not that I'm blaming myself for being so excited about the aircraft, but I knew a chartered jet was coming in from Palm Beach with a late arrival, Massie and Braunstein discussed it right in front of me. If I'd been thinking, if I'd been anticipating the unexpected, I would've picked up on that. I would've taken a long hard look at the man. Something just might've clicked and I might've thought: Wait a minute, put yourself in his place. What's the fastest, most luxurious, and most conspicuous way to get from Miami to London, the most convoluted and imaginative plan that could be conceived by the mind of a super-bright paranoid psycho? What would *I* do to bypass normal minds with tendencies to follow logic? Okay, here I go again, me as him: When my chartered yacht got to Nassau about five o'clock this morning and anchored in the harbor, as my plan called for, it would leave me plenty of time to change into my disguise right on the yacht. Then, when I went ashore and cleared Nassau Immigrations and Customs, I'd have a chartered jet ready and waiting for me at the airport, reserved weeks in advance, with a wheelchair aboard. After a leisurely flight up to Palm Beach, where I'd clear U.S. Immigrations and Customs (and be handled with kid gloves as an elderly handicapped person), I'd hop the same chartered jet to Miami, where I'd be met and rushed through to make my connection with Concorde. Window seat 1-A, of course, reserved far in advance, facing the bulkhead, where no one would be turning around to worry me, an old gentleman who just wants to listen to stereo, read, look out the window, and piss on the establishment. Who could ask for anything more?

Now, watching the carousel go around, something else dawns on me. This is the first time he's proved that he knows my name. So maybe it's not so far-fetched after all that he could be somebody I put away years ago. Or somebody I collared years ago who beat the rap in court; that's happened frequently over the years, thanks to our outdated, inadequate, inefficient, underfunded, understaffed criminal-justice system. The man knows my name and I don't know his. Again, my mind gropes, names and places and years spinning, as I watch the carousel. For just a minute, I experience the weird optical illusion that the rapidly turning carousel is actually stationary and *I'm* moving ahead, the floor's moving. When that happens, I have to brace my foot on the curb of the carousel, but I still feel dizzy.

Mayyit, Mayyit, Mayyit. Man appears to wear light-blue work clothes, maybe denim, and heavy boots or shoes. Curb on the narrow sidewalk is high red brick. House behind him has a low, narrow doorway and a narrow blue-green window.

"John, are you ill?" Nuzhat asks.

"No, I'm—I'll be okay."

"You look—why don't you sit down?"

"No, really, I'll be fine."

"This Shabah Mayyit, he is our man, the one Vadney told me all about, correct?"

"Yeah."

"The one he called Todesfall?"

"One and the same."

"All right, listen to me, we will approach this logically, we have enough time before the flight. We can go back to Immigrations, we can go to the officer who is checking the British passports, we can—"

"No good, Nuz."

"Why?"

"Number one, Mayyit's not his name. Number two, he'd have a forged passport, not necessarily British, with a phony name, undoubtedly the one he used for the airline reservation. Number three, he didn't check any luggage, obviously, so the porter wheeled him straight out of here to the street, to a taxi —or probably a hired limo, if I know this guy. My guess, there's no way in hell he'll be on that flight into Cairo tomorrow night. Ismat Farah might be, he's got nothing to lose, we've got nothing on him. But this guy, no way."

Our two bags finally come down the shoot and move toward

us on the carousel, both medium sized, we grab them, they're relatively light, so we don't need a trolley. Off we go under the *Nothing to Declare* sign, out into the crowded Terminal 3 international arrivals lobby, hundreds of people in heavy winter togs waiting behind the low barricades, wide-eyed, waving, shouting greetings, uniformed chauffeurs holding up signs with names, lighted Christmas decorations all over, public-address announcements booming with crisp British accents. Out the door now, into the bitter-cold night, wind-chill factor must be close to zero here, God *damn,* slaps me in the face like an ice-cold rag. Me, I left my topcoat back in Miami with Brendan, didn't want to lug it around, now the wind's whipping through my blazer like I'm naked. Nuz, he's bundled up in his new Burberry raincoat, clean tan job with the belt and all, collar turned up, looks like Peter Falk with a mustache. Not far to walk, thank God, Terminal 3 international departures building is just next door, in we go.

Now we're standing in the crowded lobby, I'm still dying, I'm blowing into my hands, I'm stamping my feet, Nuz looks off to our right, shakes his head back and forth like he can't believe what he sees.

"What's the matter?" I ask.

"Jesus H. Christ."

"What?"

"The fucking terminals are connected."

"Connected?!"

"Yes. See there? We didn't have to go outside."

"Nuz, you said you knew exactly where you were going!"

He touches his mustache, smiles, and a diabolical twinkle is in his black Arab eyes. "Yes, well, sometimes I lie."

Nuz and I go back a long way, he's been a cop almost as long as me, and a good cop, a real good one, and sometimes I love him like a brother, but I'm just not in the mood to make a joke out of anything else tonight. Not tonight. Not after what happened. Now would be the ideal time to go into the men's room and change into our *galabiyyas* like Vadney wanted, but I just don't want to do that, orders or no orders. Nuz tries to talk me into it, explains what handsome garments they are and all, and that most of the men on the flight will probably be wearing them, and how comfortable they are for a long flight, but I tell him no, period, end of conversation. And I think he knows where I'm coming from, I think he understands. At least I hope he does and I try not to take it out on him. It's just that this thing in the Customs Hall is really beginning to get to me now. Maybe the walk outside in the cold shocked some common sense back into me, I don't know. For some reason, I feel terribly angry, I feel like yelling at someone, I feel like a fool, I feel like a dumb local-yokel cop who's out of his league. I really do. I mean, the truth is, I don't belong here, I belong home with my family, I'm really and truly too old for this shit. Christ, it's Christmas week, next Wednesday will be Christmas Day, my wife and son are home alone, they'll have to celebrate it alone, there's not a prayer in heaven or hell that I'll make it home in time for Christmas, and here I am, standing here at the airport in London in this ratty old blazer and a shirt I haven't changed in three days, about to board a plane to Cairo. I mean, who the hell am I kidding? If I was twenty-five or thirty years old—hell, even forty—I suppose I'd still find it exciting and glamorous and challenging and all that crap. But I'm past that. I'm serious, I've had all that. It was fun while it lasted, I enjoyed it for the most part, I really did. Now, standing here for just these few minutes, holding my bag and case, feeling cold and dirty and tired and angry, the thought flicks through my mind again, like it did last autumn when I finally sat down and talked it over with my wife, the serious, sobering thought that I've tried not to give in to: It's time. It's been thirty years. Good years, on balance, relatively happy years. Can't believe it's been that long. Can't believe I'm fifty-two. That's still considered young enough to be productive in a lot of rackets. But it's not young for a cop. A cop like me has to do things that would make a fifty-two-year-old corporate executive throw up. That's the plain, simple truth. Maybe it's time to get out. While I can still do it with pride. Whatever happens in this case, I'll stick with it like I always have. Give it my very best shot. But then, that's it. I'll retire. I'm ready for it. I've earned it and deserve it. Maybe it's time.

Nuz has our tickets, we go to the Egypt Air counter and check our two bags, keep our attaché cases, get our boarding passes, walk down the hall and through the security station's metal detector, then through Immigrations, where they check our passports again, and finally we take the long walk to Gate 34. Get there at 10:32 and the lounge is fairly full, most look like businessmen, about half are wearing spotless-white *gala-biyyas,* of which there are three basic styles, as Nuz tells me, the *baladi* (peasant) style, with a low rounded neckline and wide sleeves; the *saudi* style, much more form-fitting, with a high buttoned neck and cuffed sleeves; and the *efrangi* (foreign) style that looks like a regular shirt with collar and cuffs, but reaches down to the floor like the others. Majority here seem to have the *saudi* style and I have to admit they look good—on these particular men, almost all of whom look like Arabs and wear mustaches and/or beards. Me, I still think I'd look like a fool in one of these things.

Flight starts boarding at 10:40, by row number, announcements are in Arabic followed by English. This aircraft's a 747, Nuzhat and me are way back in economy, 43-A/B, smoking section, so we're among the last to board. Despite the crowded lounge, when you get on this thing, it seems about half full, lots of room in back, many empty rows. Before the doors close and the announcements begin, I decide to ask Nuz something that's been worrying me and that I've been trying to push back in my mind.

"What was that you said about translation?" I ask. "About the difficulty in translating the name Shabah al-Mayyit?"

"No, I said the problem of transliteration was difficult. That is, to change words, Arabic words, into the corresponding characters of another alphabet or language, especially English. The frustrating fact is, there's never been a completely satisfactory system for doing this."

"Reason I ask, when this—you speak German?"

"No. No, just enough to get by. My native language is Arabic, and I speak English, French, and Spanish with a reasonable fluency."

"Reason I ask, Nuz, when this guy signed a hotel register down in the Keys, he signed it 'Abbild von Todesfall.' In German, that means, literally, 'Image of Death,' and there's no question about its meaning."

"Yes, Chief Vadney told me about that. Now, John, let me explain something to you."

"Wait'll I finish, just let me finish. Now, under that, he wrote the day and date in German, Wednesday evening, eighteen December. Then he wrote the name of a restaurant, again in German, the Green Turtle. That very night, he killed the girl. At the Green Turtle."

"Laila Mustafa, yes."

"So, what I'm saying, he—in effect, he predicted her death. The exact night, the exact place."

"Yes, I understand what you're saying, John. He wrote today's date on the certificate."

I glance around. "That's right. And the time, between 'light and darkness.' "

"Now, I want you to listen to me, John. Listen to me. I want to explain something. I'll tell you the truth, I don't think he meant it that way. I'll tell you why. And, again, it's a basic problem of transliteration. In Arabic, the word *shabah* has several meanings, all somewhat similar, depending primarily on the way in which it is used. For example, in ordinary vernacular usage, it would mean, 'look for.' Now, follow me, this is important. The Arabic term that is transliterated as *mayyit* means both 'dead' and 'death.' All right, if we assume that this man is fluent in Arabic, which would not surprise me in the least, since he is obviously brilliant, given what we know about him, if we assume he is fluent in Arabic, then he would understand these important differences in meaning. It would depend on the context, the intended context. Therefore, it is quite possible that he meant, literally, 'look for dead' between 'light' and 'darkness.' "

"Okay, two questions. One, how come you read it first as 'image of death'?"

"Simple. Because I already knew about *Abbild von Todesfall,* it has been on my mind ever since Vadney told me. So I reacted automatically."

"Makes sense, okay, question two. If this guy was so determined to get a message through to me, why the hell would he write it in Arabic? Why not in simple English? I mean, for all he knows, I still don't know what the fuck it means, right?"

Nuz frowns, pushes on the nosepiece of his glasses. "Excellent question. The only possible answer, knowing what we know about him, is that he may—and I stress *may*—be attempting to convey several messages. One, that he not only knows your name, but he knows your eventual destination. Two, and this just occurred to me. I don't, I *can't* really believe this, but it just occurred to me. The man may know who *I* am."

"I can't believe that, Nuz."

"I don't *want* to believe it. But, John, listen. Just for the sake of argument. If we admit there is even a remote possibility of that, then we may have an insight, a piece of intelligence, that could be very valuable to us. Because, if the man knows who *I* am, knows me on sight, then he has—accidentally or otherwise—told us something about his identity. He has effectively narrowed the possibilities."

"That's true."

"A case we worked together?"

"Could be, but nothing recent."

"Why do you say that?"

"I'm fairly good on faces, but I just can't seem to place this guy. I think I've seen his face before, but it must be from long back."

We got a six-hour flight ahead of us (Cairo's an hour ahead of London), so as soon as we take off at 11:05 and I get my very dry Beefeater martini on the rocks, I turn on the reading light, get *The Riddle of Cheops* out of my attaché, and pick up where I left off, end of Chapter 5. Tell you what, this is fascinating stuff, this Ismat Farah's got an idea here that really knocks my socks off. Remaining five chapters take me only two and a half hours, can't put the thing down, real page-turner. I mean, if he stuck in just a smidge of sex, violence, and maybe the obligatory chase scene, he might be able to sell this sucker to Hollywood. Substance is there, story is there, but the guy's style is so academic it reads like a speech from Henry Kissinger.

Tell you about it in my own words. First off, some basic information. The Great Pyramid was built by Cheops (also known as Khufu), the second ruler of Dynasty IV, about 2650 B.C. It's the largest of all Egyptian pyramids, measuring 480 feet high, 748 feet square, contains about 2,300,000 blocks of limestone, each weighing about two and a half tons. Ranks among the oldest surviving structures erected by man. *How* was it built? Knew you'd ask. Truth is, nobody knows exactly how it was built. Lots of people have had theories, including Herodotus. Remember him from high school, the Greek historian? Tell you what he said, then we'll drop the subject. Herodotus said it was built during the twenty-two years of Cheops's reign by 100,000 workers and 4,000 stonemasons. I mean, he didn't know for sure, he admitted that, he wasn't even around until 484 B.C., but he made an educated guess. Now, the latest thing, believe this, American engineers just don't buy the logistics of all those workers. They ask questions like, how would you *feed* 100,000 workers in one small area? How would you *house* them? This is no shit, this is straight,

American engineers. Leave it to us Americans to tell the Egyptians and Herodotus and them. Ismat Farah goes into most of the major theories, of course, him being an egghead and all, but he concludes that nobody knows the answer. Cheops knew, of course, he built the thing, he recorded all the details, which were buried with him, along with treasures that would make Tutankhamen look like a ragpicker. Turns out Farah doesn't really give too much of a shit exactly how the thing was built, that's not the riddle he's trying to solve.

Bottom line, it got built, it's standing there, it's now about 4,630 years old, give or take a couple of decades, it was supposed to be the tomb of Cheops, that's the whole reason it was built in the first place—but nobody's ever found Cheops. And his tomb wasn't robbed, like all the others were. Because it was a physical impossibility to get into the tomb itself, located near the center of the pyramid, before it was officially opened by Caliph al-Manum in A.D. 820. This is all historical fact, you can look it up. At this point, you really need a diagram from Farah's book to understand what he's talking about.

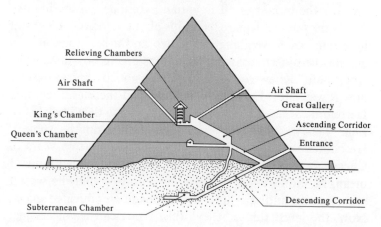

Okay, there are three chambers inside the pyramid, the Subterranean Chamber, the Queen's Chamber, and the King's

Chamber. Now, for openers, we'll concentrate on the King's Chamber. When Caliph al-Manum got to the entrance of that chamber, where Cheops was thought to be entombed, he found that it was plugged from the *inside* by a gigantic slab of granite larger than the entrance itself. Therefore, the granite plug had to be placed there *during* the building of the pyramid. How could grave robbers get in? They couldn't. It was clearly impossible. Caliph al-Manum had to break through the granite plug, a task that took twelve men (working in two-man teams and four-hour shifts around the clock) three days to complete, using relatively primitive pickaxes. What did they find when they finally stepped inside the King's Chamber, sealed until that day for approximately 3,470 years? A sarcophagus of highly polished red Aswan granite. Lidless. Inscriptionless. Empty. Nothing else was in the chamber. Nothing.

The so-called Queen's Chamber was also empty and the entrance wasn't plugged. As a matter of historical accuracy, Farah points out that the Queen's Chamber was actually a misnomer, as there's no evidence that queens were ever buried within the major pyramids during the Old Kingdom period (3000–2270 B.C.); however, there are three small pyramids near the Great Pyramid that probably belonged to Cheops's queens.

Subterranean Chamber was also found to be empty. Herodotus claimed that it was abandoned as the original site of the tomb because it was subject to flooding by the Nile.

Where is Cheops actually buried? Where are his treasures? Why did he leave the chambers empty? Nobody knows. According to Farah, modern archaeological investigation of the interior of the pyramid continues to be hampered by the government's reluctance to permit scientific study that would in any way alter or damage even a minute part of the interior. In addition, there are substantial physical difficulties involved in attempting to work in the extremely hot, unventilated, poorly lighted (no electricity is allowed) atmosphere of the corridors.

Parts of the book are autobiographical and give insights into Farah that might prove valuable to us. Born in Cairo in 1942, the guy was deeply influenced by his father Jamal, a government Egyptologist who was eventually appointed to be a curator at the Egyptian Museum. As a teenager, Ismat Farah became fascinated with all aspects of the Great Pyramid and it became a lifelong obsession. By the time he graduated from Cairo University in 1963, he'd already formulated a theory about the contents of the pyramid, based on an exhaustive study of Dynasty IV, the life of King Cheops, and the known facts about the construction of the pyramid. His theory became the catalyst for graduate study, not in archaeology, but in radiology. The leading institutions in that field were in the United States, and Farah chose Columbia. His master's thesis and doctoral dissertation were in the advanced areas of EMI X-ray scanning and the practical application of lasers.

In 1969, he was one of the American scientists selected by Nobel laureate Dr. William Alvara to assist in setting up and monitoring cosmic-ray detectors around the Great Pyramid in the attempt to discover hidden chambers. That's a weird story in itself, tell you a couple of things about that. Dr. Alvara and his team spent months surrounding the pyramid with this complicated network of cosmic-ray detectors on the proven theory that the rays would pass through empty space faster than through solid stone. Therefore, if there were any hidden chambers, bingo, they'd discover them, right? Hell of an idea, why didn't anybody think of it before? Now they got it all set up, they're watching their fancy computer screens, something very strange starts happening. Readings for the first day are out of whack with readings for the second day. Readings for the third day are out of whack with the first two days. And on and on and on. Completely whacko readings, what's going on around here, the curse of the Pharaohs? All these expensive egghead scientists, they're standing around the pyramid, playing pocket-pool, studying the computer readouts, they don't know to fart or whistle, this computer's spitting out garbage. Totally useless gobbledygook. Take a couple days off, check the computer inside out, it's in absolutely perfect working order. Try it again. Can't get one day's readings to agree with another. Can't do it to save their asses. I'm laughing out loud reading this shit. Finally, the head egghead in charge of the IBM 1130 computer, he gives up, he says it simply defies all known laws of electronics and science. Says it's got to be one of two things, either the geometry of the pyramid is in substantial error (it's not, they double-checked that too) or there's a mystery that's beyond explanation. Says there's some influence at work in the pyramid that's totally unknown to science. He goes home. Everybody on the team goes home to the States. Old Cheops, if he's inside the pyramid, he's got to be laughing his wrappings off. I mean, maybe it's the martinis on this flight, but I can almost hear his ancient voice echoing through the hidden chamber: "Fuckin' American eggheads, hahahahaha!"

Last chapter in the book is the best, in my opinion, because Farah gets down to cases with a theory that's based on three heavily researched assumptions: (1) Cheops never intended to be buried in the King's Chamber; he was a widely recognized genius, far too bright to believe his remains would be safe— from robbers or rulers—in such an obvious location, particularly because, like all Pharaohs, his mummy would be surrounded by all the most priceless possessions of his reign for "the long voyage into darkness, towards eternity"; (2) therefore, the three chambers were all fabulously expensive decoys: Cheops had projected ahead thousands of years to the time when, inevitably, under the authority of a corrupt ruler, his pyramid would be officially opened, the three chambers discovered, and they would be found to be empty, long since robbed, as almost all other Pharaohs' tombs had been throughout the long chain of dynasties; his foresight had been remarkably accurate, because that's precisely what's believed to this day; (3) Cheops designed the subterranean corridors and chamber to give the *illusion* of an intentional decoy, leading potential robbers away from the upper chambers, one corridor leading in a straight line down from the pyramid's entrance to the huge chamber, and, if that failed to deceive, the other corridor was located at the end of the small corridor leading to the so-called Queen's Chamber, a logical connection and an easy journey downward.

Conclusion: Somewhere in one of the long subterranean corridors, both largely ignored by modern archaeologists, was an ingeniously concealed entrance to the real King's Chamber, hidden for five thousand years, the discovery of which would be the greatest archaeological find of all time: King Cheops himself, ruler of the wealthiest dynasty of all, builder of the Great Pyramid, his chamber intact with treasures to blow your mind.

And Ismat Farah knew how to find it.

12

THINK NEW YORK IS BIG? Crowded? Noisy? Dirty?
Cairo's got to be the most sprawling, teeming, roaring, reeling,
reeking, wretching twelve-mile stretch of humanity I've ever
seen in my life. Don't know what I expected, but bouncing in
from the airport in this steamy beat-to-shit taxi, it's a shock
to my senses, it's just positive chaos in the streets here, they
drive like maniacs, they got people hanging out of cars, cabs,
trucks, buses, vans, donkey carts, crazies on motorcycles,
scooters, bicycles weaving in and out, sidewalks are jammed
solid with men, women, children, dogs, cats, yelling, screaming, gesturing, barking, biting, spitting, laundry's strung up in
all the windows, makes Delancy Street seem posh. Horns?
You think they blow horns in New York? I mean, if there's
a single dominant impression here, that's got to be it. *Horns!*
I'm talking serious horns, nonstop horns, a calliope of held-
down horns, absolutely deafening, Nuz and I have to shout at
each other. Official population is ten million now (New York
has seven), but Nuz says there's been a staggering growth over

the past decade—some say it's up to fourteen million—because of the migration from the Suez Canal towns that were
so badly damaged during the wars with Israel. Sum it up, this
is the largest city on the continent of Africa, the biggest and
most important metropolis in the whole Islamic world, and
the horn-honkingest hellhole in the universe. Of course, we
just happened to hit the morning rush-hour traffic. Nuz, he's
laughing all the way, cigar stuck rakishly in his teeth, he loves
this Arab shit. Says it'll get more "tranquil" as the day wears
on. Tranquil?

Still, one thing I'll say for Nuz, he knows how to pick
hotels. I mean, Vadney left it up to him, he's an Arab, he
knows the city, what's the difference, long as we get a minimum-rate room, right? Nuz selects the newest luxury hotel in
town, Ramses Hilton, *the* tallest building in Cairo, thirty-six
stories of conspicuous Egyptian. You wouldn't believe this
place, it's Karnak the Magnificent, 1115 Corniche el-Nil, fashionable east bank of the Nile. Heart of town, walking distance
to all the best restaurants and nightclubs, whole tony shot.
Got to hand it to Nuz. Don't know how much our room costs,
don't want to know. Nuz speaks the language, he's the tour
guide, he'll use his Amex. Me, I left mine home. I tell him that
up front. Sometimes I lie.

Okay, we stroll into this spacious marble lobby, decor by
Cleopatra, we register, bellhop takes us up to our room, 2722.
Walk in here, luxury befitting a Pharaoh. Red-orange color
scheme, original Egyptian paintings and ceramics. Bellhop
shows us our mini-bar, says every room has a mini-bar. Pulls
the graceful curtain, pulls the sliding-glass door to our terrace,
says every room has a terrace. I go out there, I take one look
around, I laugh out loud, I can't help it. We're facing southwest, below me spreads the Nile (looks dirtier than the East
River), the green sporting fields of Gezira, and, beyond the
Bridge of 6 October, the modern Cairo Tower looks something like the Eiffel, but smaller and definitely Egyptianesque.

Now, in the distance to the south—holy shit!—there they are, bigger than I ever imagined, the three pyramids and the Sphinx, yellow-gold in the early morning sun.

Nuz comes out for a look, cigar still in his jaws, points out the fact that the Cheops Pyramid is the largest (thanks, Nuz), next in size is the Pyramid of Chephren, the only one still left with its original polished limestone facing, like a cap at the top, and next is the Pyramid of Mycerinus, which ain't exactly small itself. All rulers of Dynasty IV (2600–2500 B.C.), the most powerful of all. Note how much I know about all this after reading one lousy book? Sphinx is relatively close to Chephren, just east of it. Naturally, I'd seen a lot of pictures of the Sphinx, but now, in person, from this distance, the only word that comes to mind is majestic. Doesn't look so disfigured from here, bathed in sun and shadow, head of a Pharaoh, body of a sitting lion.

Nuz leans on the railing, puffs his cigar, explains somewhat patiently, as to a child, that Chephren was Cheops's son, and that he built the Sphinx. Didn't know that. Seems when the Great Pyramid was almost finished (took more than twenty years), Chephren had a suggestion for his old man. Down in the nearby quarry from which Cheops got many of the limestone blocks for his pyramid, there was this huge outcrop of gray and yellow limestone that was left, not suitable for the pyramid, but still intact as a single mountain of rock. Chephren says, "I want to make a figure out of it, a monument to the sun-god Horus." Dad Cheops smiles and says, "Good thinking, boy, go to it, it'll keep you out of mischief, hahahahaha." Chephren goes to it. By the time old Cheops buys the farm and gets entombed someplace in his Great Pyramid, this figure of Horus hasn't really taken shape yet. Now the old man's gone, Chephren takes over as Pharaoh, this kid's no dummy, he orders the Sphinx's face to be his *own* exact likeness, complete with his royal headdress and sacred cobra on the forehead. While that's being done, he goes ahead and orders his own pyramid to be built next to his dad's, just four feet lower, of course, he doesn't want to seem egotistical. Now, by the time Chephren's ready to voyage into eternity, about 2630 B.C., there's his smiling puss on what he names the Colossus of King Chephren, and, right in back of that, his own Pyramid of Chephren, looking every bit as big as his dad's. Sharper than a serpent's tooth, this kid. When the Greeks took over (332 B.C.–A.D. 395), they named the figure Sphinx, from classical mythology, meaning a lion's body but the breasts and head of a woman who proposed a riddle to travelers, killing them if they answered incorrectly. Leave it to the Greeks to turn Chephren into a transvestite killer, right?

Nuz is telling me all this, he's leaning over the railing, his eyelids are at half-mast, his stogie's about to give him hot lips. Takes it out just in time, says he's going to bed. Me, I could use a little shut-eye too, it's 9:20 A.M. Cairo time, 3:20 A.M. our time. So much for Vadney's schedule. Still, we can grab eight hours, which we really need at this point, since we'll probably be up quite late tonight, wake up at, say, 5:30 this afternoon, have plenty of time to get over to police headquarters, check in with them, pick up a local detective to work with us, if that's required, look around town, get our bearings before we go to the airport tonight.

That's exactly what happens. Nuz, he's up at 5:15, he gets on the phone immediately and orders two pots of *kahwa* (coffee) from room service. Tells me it's like Turkish mocha: "Black as the night, hot as hell, sweet as love." Orders it *masbuth* (medium sweet). We both shower, he shaves, reminds me not to, Vadney's orders. We're all unpacked, of course, he's got our full-length *galabiyyas* hanging up in the closet to get the wrinkles out, now he insists we get dressed, see how they fit. Oh, shit, here I go, jumpsuit in Miami to *galabiyya* in Cairo. Actually, to be honest, these things aren't half bad. He's got the *baladi,* or peasant style, white, with wide sleeves and a low rounded neckline; I would've preferred the *saudi* form-fitting style, but he says we'll buy those if the occasion demands. Guess what we wear underneath? Just our skivvies, T-shirt and shorts, because the December afternoons are ideal here, low seventies. Okay, we get into these things, now he gets out two pairs of ratty old thong sandals, mine are at least a size too big, but he says we'll buy some for me cheap in one of the shoe shops along the Sharias Qasr el Nil. Finally, he gets out a couple of small red caps, each with a tassel, called the *tarboosh,* traditional headgear for men. Straightens the thing on my head, hangs the tassel just so, he's having a conversation with himself in fast Arabic. Now we go over and look at ourselves in the full-length mirror.

Laurel and Hardy in Egypt.

Laugh so hard I damn near piss my drawers.

Room service guy knocks at the door, Nuz goes to open it, I take a long hard look at myself in the mirror, shake my head. Today's Friday, December 20, I can't believe all this happened in just four days: New York–Miami–Washington–London–Cairo. Tonight and this weekend, everybody in New York will be swept up in the most exciting time of the year, doing last-minute Christmas shopping, going to parties, celebrating in a thousand ways, my family and all my friends included. Fifth, Madison, Park, Lexington will be jammed with cabs and cars and bundled-up people with packages and shopping bags and children galore. Bloomies and Saks and Macy's and Lord & Taylor and all the rest will have their fabulous window displays and dazzling lifelike mannequins and the sidewalks will have Santa Clauses ringing bells and Salvation Army bands playing carols off-tune and street vendors cooking chestnuts and pretzels and hot dogs and the cold air will be heavy with those smells. All the theaters on Broadway will be ablaze with lights and limos, restaurants and bars will be overflowing with T.G.I.F. office workers, young and old, and Rockefeller Center will have crowds around the skating rink with another gigantic Christmas tree towering into the skyline. Wednesday will be it, Christmas Day. And here I am in Cairo, of all places, standing in front of a hotel mirror, unshaven, looking like a tired clown in a tasseled *tarboosh,* full-length *galabiyya,* and beat-up oversized sandals. What the hell am I doing here? How dangerous is all this really going to be, trying to anticipate the mind of a paranoid who's obviously toying with me now, baiting me, taunting me? New questions keep coming to mind: Why hasn't he tried to kill me yet? Why hasn't he done anything to discourage me from coming down here?

While we're having coffee (which I have to choke down), Nuz calls police headquarters to set up an appointment. He'd packed the three business letters to Ismat Farah in his suitcase, which was checked on the flight, so now is the first good opportunity I've had to read them. Take them out of the manila folder marked "Cairo," start with the one from GE, a three-page job. Letterhead reads General Electric Credit Corporation, and it's addressed to Farah at his Columbia University office, dated November 21, 1985. After reading the first paragraph, it's clear this is a covering letter that was attached to a standard retail installment contract for the purchase of scientific equipment, to wit: One General Electric 770 Helium-Neon Gas Laser Drill. Letter's written in legalese language, but here are a few highlights. Total cost of this thing is $804,511. Down payment of 20 percent is required, amounting to $160,902.20. Total to be financed over a period of sixty months, including finance charge and insurance, $759,458.38. Equal monthly installments of $12,657.64. Down payment by certified check due on or before December 6, 1985, to ensure air-freight delivery on or before December 17, 1985. Delivery via Egypt Air Freight to: Dr. Ismat Farah, 21972 Shari Gammaiat el-Qahira, Cairo, Egypt. Presumably, he made the down payment by certified check on or before December 6, ten full days before the robbery took place. How? How would an associate professor of radiology at Columbia get his mitts on

a cool $160,902? Better yet, how would he get the credit rating
and equity security that would qualify him to finance $759,458
over five years? Unless he's independently wealthy, which I
somehow doubt, although it's possible, he obviously had to
have a co-maker, a guarantor, an individual or corporation
with the financial resources to underwrite the total commitment, which happens to be $920,360.58. Wonder who that
might be? Keep reading to the end. No mention of an under-
writer in the covering letter, so I can only assume that's long
since handled in previous correspondence. Apparently, the
contract that was attached was signed and fully executed by
all parties concerned, so there's no need to mention the co-
maker here.

Second letter is from the IBM Corporation, Office Products
Division, also addressed to Farah at his Columbia office, dated
November 14, 1985. Another covering letter for an approved
retail installment agreement, this one for the purchase of an
IBM 2260-B EMI X-Ray Scanner and 1130 PC-AT. This package goes for a mere $742,116. Required down payment of 25
percent this time, comes to $185,529. Remainder to be financed
over sixty months, including finance charge and insurance,
just $656,772.66. Easy equal monthly payments of only $10,-
946.21. Down payment by cashier's check due December 2,
1985, to guarantee air-freight delivery (again by Egypt Air) by
December 19 to Farah at the same address. I add up these two
down payments, come up with a figure of $346,431.20. More
quick arithmetic, find out the combined total commitment is
up to $1,762,662.20.

Last letter's from General Motors Acceptance Corporation,
same folks who finance those cars, Farah buys American all
the way. Addressed to him at Columbia, dated November 15,
1985. Covering letter for another fully executed retail installment contract, now he's into heavy equipment, a 1985 GM
Generator Truck with 9120 Induction Motor. Makes sense, a
generator to provide the electrical power necessary to operate

the scanner, computer, and laser. Wonder what color he got, doesn't say, most I've seen are white, TV networks use them for location shoots, football games, like that. Retails for $585,-633. Down payment of 20 percent comes to $117,126.60. Remainder to be financed, including finance charge but *not* insurance (must have to buy his own in Cairo), is $552,837.55. Sixty monthly installments of $9,213.96. This one represents a commitment of $669,964.15. Down payment due November 28 (no mention of a certified check) to ensure delivery to Farah at Cairo International Airport, via Egypt Air Freight, by December 18.

Add up the three down payments, come up with a total cash outlay of $463,557.80 up front. Add up the combined total financial commitment, comes to a nifty $2,432,626.30. Science ain't cheap these days.

When Nuz finishes his phone call, I give him the three letters, we sit out on the terrace in the shade, drink the coffee (gets a little better with the second cup), and he reads each letter carefully. Says he knows the street Farah gave as his Cairo address, Shari Gammaiat el-Qahira, it's a major route, the main drag through Cairo University, southwest across the river, just north of Giza, where the pyramids are. Even points out the university, from this elevation we can see most of the buildings clearly across from the Botanical Gardens and the big green expanse of the Cairo Zoo. Ironic location, cheek-to-jowl with the zoo, must give the eggheads a healthy sense of perspective.

Off we go at 6:10 in our flowing *galabiyyas,* our appointment at police headquarters is set for 6:30. Grab a stinkbag cab from the hotel, head south on Corniche el-Nil, past the Egyptian Museum and the old Nile Hilton, hang a squealing left on Shari el-Tahrir, smack into the center of town, hub of the city, Midan el-Tahrir (Liberation Square), which is actually a gigantic circle where all the city's main traffic arteries meet, bustling bus terminus in the middle, plus now they're building Cairo's first subway system directly below, so this is going to be the central terminal, like Grand Central. Ever been caught in gridlock traffic in Manhattan? Take that scene at its worst, with no traffic lights, add an earsplitting, bowel-freezing caterwaul of horns, jackhammers, pile-drivers, add billowing dust and smoke and exhaust fumes that blur and bend buildings like funhouse mirrors, add the stench of sewers and garbage and donkey droppings so acrid that your eyes sting and your throat gags, now you got Midan el-Tahrir, Cairo's first real plunge into the joys of modern industrialized society. Lovely to be liberated. Times Square, New Year's Eve, is a garden party. Off to the southwest, so Nuz shouts, are the Ministry of Foreign Affairs and the government buildings; police headquarters is located in the Mogamma Government Building. Cabbie defies imminent death by maneuvering within a block of the place, now Nuz haggles with him about the fare in Arabic so fast I can't catch one obscene gesture in three.

Mogamma is a horseshoe-shaped, sand-colored building that houses the public departments of ministries such as Education, Health, Interior, plus the Cairo governate, so the lobby's crawling with police in black uniforms (white in summer), black beret-style caps, wide black belts and holsters with automatics that look like .45s, and black boots worn inside the trousers. Most of these guys seem very young to me and almost all have mustaches. As Nuz tells it, the police, or *askari,* are part of Egypt's 250,000-man (no women) Central Security Force created by former president Anwar Sadat and maintained, sometimes precariously, by President Hosni Mubarak since Sadat's assassination in 1981. Nuz says "precariously" because the huge majority of these young cops are conscripts. That's right, they're drafted. Three-year tours of duty, very low pay, and they actually live in barracks, just like the regular army here. Thing is, these kids don't like the conscription duty, they can't even begin to live on their pay, so they have a nasty little habit of periodic rioting. Yeah, they riot in the streets every so often to protest the draft, the pay, the living conditions, you name it, including frequent rumors that their conscription might be extended to four years. When they riot, they're immediately joined by mobs of civilian kids, looters, leftist students, and Muslim fundamentalists. I mean, we think civilian demonstrators are bad, these kids get pumped up by something, they run through the streets screaming, they break windows, they rob stores, they burn cars, they mug tourists, everybody goes and hides from them until the regular army itself steps in with tanks in the streets, the whole bit. Then, according to Nuz, these mobs of kids will sometimes decide to take on the *army*. Yeah! Open gun battles, rock throwing, hand-to-hand combat, police against the army. Sometimes lasts days. Sometimes a city-wide curfew has to be imposed, everybody off the streets by dark. Think the ten to fourteen million residents are intimidated by all this? Naw. Every time it happens, it's always the superior firepower of the army, supplied with armored personnel carriers, helicopters, and U.S.-made M-6o tanks that ensures the ultimate victory. Police kids are thrown in jail once again. Everybody goes back to horn honking as usual. Must give civilians and tourists a feeling of great domestic security.

Police headquarters is on the ground floor, impressive entrance. Inside, there's a long counter manned by three young cops. Nuz explains that we have an appointment with Chief Osama el-Kez. Mustachioed kid cop with jet-black eyes looks it up in his book, picks up a phone, speaks a few words, then escorts us personally to Chief Kez's office. Follow him back to the right down a long dark-gray marble corridor, his polished boots clicking smartly, our sandals slapping sloppily, hats in hands, I feel like a weird vagrant in a nightgown. All offices in this area have doors of elaborate black wrought-iron

grillwork, interiors lighted by lamps, quietly elegant, Doris
Banks would love this shit.

Chief Kez's mustachioed kid cop secretary with jet-black
eyes greets us quietly: *"Mesakum bil-kher."*

"Allah yimesikum bil-kher," Nuzhat says.

Kid walks around his desk, opens Chief Kez's grillwork
door, motions for us to enter. We nod, slap in softly.

Chief Osama el-Kez rises from his long mahogany desk in
soft yellow lamplight, distinguished-looking man, mid-fifties,
lean in a spotless-white form-fitting *saudi-*style *galabiyya,*
high-buttoned neck, cuffed sleeves. Smiles as we come closer,
bald pate, oval face, sparkling eyes with crow's-feet, trim gray
mustache, and the smile is tight-lipped but genuinely warm.
Ed Koch with a mustache.

"Es-salamu 'alekum!" he says.

"We-'alekum," Nuz says, *"es-salam warahmet allah
wabarakatuh!"*

"Idrissi, Rawlings," he says, "let us speak conversation
English. I am under your protection, save me. Recline, I am
welcome. My house is your house."

Nuz and I exchange a glance as we sit.

"May you desire a coffee cup?"

Decline, politely, do we.

"Valtadney explains your serious condition by telephone."

"Valtadney?" I ask.

He nods, smiles. "May you enjoy it."

"Waltvadney?" Nuz asks.

"Ah, yes, Valtadney. May God preserve you in safety."

"Walt Vadney," Nuz says slowly.

"Valtvadney," Kez says smiling. "Welcome. May your day
be a happy and blessed one."

Goes like so. Just as I begin to think we're up to our hips
in sand, Nuz makes a transition, slowly, carefully, respect-
fully, a word here, a sentence there, back to Arabic, and before

long they're into fast and serious conversation. As we suspected, under the law, we'll have to be accompanied by an armed undercover detective from the Central Security Force during all surveillance and other official police duties. When Nuz explains that our primary locations will probably be in and around Cairo University and the general vicinity of the pyramids, Kez selects an outstanding young officer from the Tourist Police, a special branch, all of them speak at least two foreign languages. Kid by the name of Abu Ben-Adam, a 1982 graduate of the university who's fluent in English and is presently assigned to the Pyramids Station in Giza. Kez phones that station house, speaks to the officer in charge, arranges for Abu Ben-Adam to meet us there at 7:15 tonight.

It's about 6:45 and dark when we grab another cab at the edge of terrible Midan el-Tahrir. We have to cross the Nile and then head south to Giza, but instead of fighting our way around the circle to go back the way we came, Nuz tells the driver to take Shari el-Qasr el-Aini south; it's a major artery that joins Corniche el-Nil down near the Giza Bridge. We cross the bridge heading west, then continue straight on Shari el-Roda into the Giza area, packed with taxis, headlights, horns honking, all headed for the pyramids to see the nightly *Son et Lumière* (Sound and Light) show that starts at 7:30.

Turns out the Pyramids Station is just off Shari el-Akhram, overlooking the pyramids, a simple one-story gray stone structure with a sign over the front door: "Tourist Police, *Askari.*" Three or four young cops are outside, talking with tourists. They wear the same black uniform as all the other cops around town, except for a small blue cloth stripe on their left chest and a green armband with white lettering that identifies them as tourist police in English and Arabic. According to Nuz, their principal job, outside of giving directions and information in a wide range of languages, is to keep tourists from being ripped off, particularly by the thousands upon thousands of merchants, "guides," and cabbies who hang around tourist haunts in hordes. Also, I assume, to protect tourists from rioting policemen, when the occasion demands.

No meters on any of these hacks, so Nuz haggles with the cab driver again, and they both seem to delight in the experience. We have enough Egyptian pounds for the time being because each of us was required to exchange a minimum of $150 at the airport. There's a special exchange rate for tourists, £E1 = US$1.43, so we each started out with £E105. Me, I still have it all, I haven't spent one thin *piastre* so far. I mean, I'm a common tourist, what do I know, I don't know what anything's worth, right? Nuz, he's the guy, he knows everything, so I let him pay for everything, put it on his expense report. Of course, he'll have to explain it all to Vadney, every freakin' penny, so I hope he's keeping careful records.

We climb out, go inside, flip-flop up to the desk, I decide to test the English fluency of the kid cop up there. Get my gold shield and ID from the deep pocket of my *galabiyya* (yeah, they have pockets), show them as I speak.

"Good evening, Officer. We have an appointment to see Officer Abu Ben-Adam."

Black-eyed kid smiles. "You guys the detectives from New York?"

"That's right."

Couple of young cops sitting nearby get up and stroll over now, take a good look at us, try to be casual about it.

"We've been expecting you," desk cop says. "Chief Kez called our station commander. Most of us have never met New York detectives before." Glances at Nuz, then back at me. "You must be Detective Rawlings and he's Detective Idrissi?"

"That's right."

He comes around the desk, shakes hands with us. "I'm Officer Haleb. Pleasure to meet you. Welcome to the Pyramids Station."

"You speak perfect English," Nuz says.

"Thank you very much. We get a lot of tourists from New

York, y'know, we try to keep current on the vernacular. Abu's in back, I'll go tell him you're here."

Word must've spread fast, several other young cops come in now, take a silent gander at us, try to be nonchalant. Me, I yank off my *tarboosh,* try to be nonchalant. My guess, these kids have probably seen a shitload of movies and TV shows about tough-guy New York cops, probably even studied the dialogue, probably expect me to talk like that. Hate to disappoint them, but I just don't fit that stereotype. All these tough-guy New York movie-star cops, you take away their shootouts, you take away their fistfights, you take away their high-speed car chases, you take away their four-letter words, what've you got? Quiet, smooth-talking little guys like me. All right, okay, with steel-blue killer eyes, I'll give you that, but I can't help that, I was born with them. I mean, I don't *flaunt* shit like that, know what I mean?

Officer Haleb comes back with Abu Ben-Adam, who's wearing a peasant-style *galabiyya* like ours and sandals; he was probably off-duty when he got the assignment. Sharp-looking kid, mid-twenties, about five-eleven and 160, thick but well-trimmed black hair, dark eyes with life in them and humor, aquiline nose, no mustache. Smiles when he sees us, walks over confidently, shakes our hands.

"I'm Officer Ben-Adam. Nice to meet you."

"John Rawlings."

"Nuzhat Idrissi, it's a pleasure."

"I'm at your disposal, my car's just outside."

Can't help noticing, all these young cops standing around, they're staring at this guy, their eyes say it all, like he just won the national lottery or something. Makes me wonder exactly how much they know about this case. We thank Officer Haleb, follow Abu out to his car in the lot just behind the building.

It's quite dark now, just past 7:30, and the *Son et Lumière* show is beginning down at the pyramids, no more than two hundred yards beyond the parking lot. All the tourists (I'd guess several hundred) are sitting on a terrace close to the Sphinx, facing the Pyramid of Chephren. An overture is playing softly, amplified by an excellent sound system, and all three pyramids are outlined in deep blue lights from below. We got all the time in the world, so I ask Abu and Nuz to wait just a minute, I want to see the start of this thing. We walk to the far end of the lot, lean on the railing and watch. Abu says I'm in luck, happens to be the English-language program tonight; other nights the show's given in French, German, and Arabic.

Overture softens now and a narrator's voice is heard, deep and resonant: "You have come tonight to the most fabulous and celebrated place in the world. Here, on the plateau of Giza, stands forever the mightiest of human achievements. No traveler—emperor, merchant or poet—has trodden on these sands and not gasped in awe. The curtain of night is about to rise and disclose the stage on which the drama of a civilization took place. Those involved have been present since the dawn of history, pitched stubbornly against sand and wind. And the voice of the desert has crossed the centuries."

Suddenly, the face of the Sphinx appears, huge and bright gold in the night, as if colored by the light of dawn.

And the voice of the Sphinx is heard: "With each new dawn I see the sun-god rise on the far bank of the Nile. His first ray is for my face, which is turned towards him. And for five thousand years I have seen all the suns men can remember come up in the sky. I saw the history of Egypt in its first glow, as tomorrow I shall see the East burning with a new flame. I am the faithful warden at the foot of his Lord—so faithful, so vigilant, so near him that he gave me his face for my own. I am a Pharaoh's companion, and I am he, the Pharaoh. Through the ages I received many names from the people who came to me in adoration. . . . But the name which has re-

mained with me is that given to me by a Greek traveler: the
Father of History, Herodotus. He called me Sphinx, as if I
were from his land. And that name is now mine."

Continues on like that, we watch a while longer. To be
honest, I don't exactly "gasp in awe" at this spectacle, although I'm sure some people do, but I can't help but be deeply
impressed by it, almost hypnotized by the sheer scale of it. I
mean, these pyramids are just positively gigantic, you'd have
to see them to believe them. Give you an idea what I mean.
When the narrator (sounds a little like Richard Burton to me)
starts talking about the Great Pyramid, and it suddenly ex-
plodes in brilliant gold light against the dark sky, he says the
area it covers—get this!—the area it covers is vast enough to
hold St. Peter's Cathedral in Rome. That's a fact, that's what
the man says. So, what I'm trying to bring out, I'm standing
here, I'm looking at these mountains of stone, I'm listening,
and the combination of voices, music, sound effects, colors, all
against a backdrop of the desert night, it just sends an ice-cold
shiver from my neck clear down to my asshole. That's the
truth, that's how it affects me, I don't know about anybody
else. And hearing the Sphinx talk about all this stuff, five
thousand years of history, it makes you feel like Snoopy racing
at Aqueduct. Sphinx says stuff like he bears witness to the will
of Cheops, his father, to defy time forever. Says he saw Anthony and Cleopatra bow before him. Says Alexander, Caesar,
and Napoleon took one look at him and felt like Rodney
Dangerfield. Words to that effect. Says he chose as his motto
an old Arab saying: "The world fears time, but time fears the
pyramids." I mean, stuff like that can spook the crap out of
you. Gives you a perspective on civilization as we know it.
Reminds me of that famous shot of Ed Koch riding a camel
past the Sphinx some years back. All these New York tourists
wave at him, photographers crowd around, he rides past the
Sphinx, he shouts, "How'm I doin'?" Remember that? What
I'm saying, legendary people like Anthony, Cleopatra, Alex-

ander, Caesar, Napoleon, they all gasp in awe before the majesty of the Sphinx here, right? Ed Koch, he rides past this colossus, he yells, "How'm I doin'?" Don't get me wrong, I'm not taking anything away from Koch, happens to be my favorite mayor, best mayor New York's ever had, at least in my lifetime, but I can't help thinking of what he said here. *How'm I doin'?* Come on, Ed. Sometimes you got to show some respect for your elders. Least you could've said was, "How're *you* doin'?"

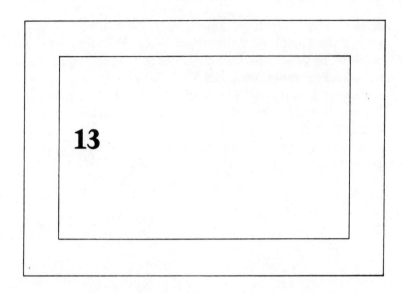

13

AM I GOING CRAZY? That's what I start asking myself
when we get talking to Abu in the car. We're headed north
to Ismat Farah's address at Cairo University, we want to
check that out before going to the airport, and Abu asks us
a basic question. Asks us for Farah's description. Nuzhat's in
front, he turns, glances at me, clears his throat. Farah's description, Farah's description. That's all the kid wants, simple
enough question, since we'll be waiting for the man outside
Customs at the airport in about three hours. Can't start surveillance on a subject till you know his basic description,
right? So, go ahead, John, give the kid a rundown. Oh, boy.
Ohboyohboyohboy. We don't have Farah's description. All
we have is the information we got from Morningside Motors
on his lease of the 1985 Chevy van: Age, forty-three; height,
five-eleven; weight, 154. That's it. Never saw the man, never
saw a photograph of him. Probably looks like an Arab, which
is a big help when you're in Cairo. Don't know what's wrong
with me. Honestly don't. Allowed myself to get sucked in and

carried along in this whole raging river of uncertainties that's been gaining momentum over the past four days, not having enough time to check out even the essentials, playing almost everything by ear. Flat-out unprofessional behavior. Worse than that, if I'm honest about it. Sloppy, lazy, potentially dangerous. No excuse for it. I could blame Vadney for not digging, not doing even the minimum research on this guy, but I won't. Vadney's too easy a target. He's not a cop anymore, he's a politician, a publicity junkie. I blame myself. Not too long ago, before this case, I still went by the book, as I'd done throughout my career, I was still disciplined enough to conduct myself as a trained professional. What happened to me?

"John?" Nuz says.

"Yeah?"

"Are you falling asleep?"

"No, I heard the question. Good, sensible question, Abu. Unfortunately, the description we have is almost totally useless. Ismat Farah is forty-three years old, five-foot-eleven, and weighs one-fifty-four. From a physical standpoint, I'm afraid that's all we have."

Nuz turns around again, clears his throat, and reflections from headlights move across his glasses. "Somehow I thought —excuse me, John, but somehow I assumed that you had a full, detailed description."

"Nope."

"We cannot go to the airport with this description."

"Obviously."

"Well, at least we know where he's staying," Abu says.

"It's enough for the time being," I tell them. "In fact, it's probably better than trying to pick him out at the airport."

Nuz nods, shrugs. "It would have been very difficult even with a complete description."

We drive along in silence for a while, Abu's car is an old VW Bug, but comfortable enough, clean, and the engine sounds good. I start thinking about the description taken from the lease of the van. Thing that bothers me, it's not based on anything solid, like a driver's license, as far as I know. When I call Vadney tomorrow, I'll ask him to check DMV, Columbia University, Social Security, the whole shot, see if we can nail down some dependable intelligence about this guy. Personnel Department at Columbia must have a fat file on him, including duplicate ID photos, Vadney could give me a detailed description over the phone, everything we'd need.

As we approach the vicinity of Cairo University about 7:55, traffic becomes very congested, although the horns aren't nearly as bad as around Midan el-Tahrir, and bicycles outnumber cars by at least five to one. As a 1982 graduate, Abu tells us some basics about the place, most of which I knew through Doris Banks's research. It's a fact that this is generally considered to be one of the great research centers in the world, eleven faculties, more than 3,300 teachers, over 62,000 students. Farah's address, 21972 Shari Gammaiat el-Qahira, is right on the main drag and Abu seems to remember that the building itself is actually a graduate-student dormitory, although he'll check it out to be sure.

It's a long, fourteen-story structure fronting right on the cobblestone street with just a narrow sidewalk and many of the windows are lighted. Entrance is off to the right through a stone archway leading to a courtyard. Question hits me immediately: How could Farah have all that heavy equipment delivered to him at a dorm? Abu double-parks directly across the street, sticks a "Tourist Police" sign on his dashboard, and we wait in the car as he goes into the building. Horns begin honking behind us, but cars are double-parked on both sides and there's enough room to pass in either direction. Hundreds of students flow past us on bikes and on foot, almost all male, majority wearing jeans and shirts, jackets, sweaters, sneakers galore, and there's a continual din of fast Arabic music from portable radios, same general beat as rock. One thing Nuz didn't remember from his last visit, this desert air gets chilly at night. Our *galabiyyas* aren't really thin, but all we got under are skivvies. Me, I could do with a sweater. Not Nuz. Nuz, he's got insulating layers of fat, he looks happy as an Arab in heat, puffing on a cigar now, checking out the students, enjoying the academic ambience. At exactly eight o'clock, we hear this loud, lovely melody of chimes sounding the hour; Nuz says they're from the old clock in the central quadrangle, one of the most familiar sounds throughout Egypt because they're tape recorded now and heard on Egyptian radio every hour.

Several minutes later, Abu crosses the street, weaving his way through the crowds of bikes and cars and pedestrians. Looks so young he melts right in, he could easily pass for an undergraduate. Hops in, slams the door.

"Ismat Farah will be in Room Ten-thirty-eight," he tells us. "He's expected around midnight."

"How'd you get the information?" I ask.

"Simple. I told the clerk I'm one of his research assistants."

Good sharp kid, Abu, have a feeling he'll work out fine. Nuz and I breathe a sigh of relief, we feel much better about the whole situation. It's just past eight now, we have about two hours to kill, we're all hungry, so Abu suggests we have dinner at his favorite restaurant (when he can afford it), which also happens to feature belly dancers. Place is called the Bateau Omar Khayyam, a large old vessel moored by the Sporting Club at Gezira, perfect spot for dining quietly on the Nile, and just a short drive northeast of the university. Off we go in the VW Bug for my very first taste of authentic Egyptian cuisine and dangerously undulating hips. Wouldn't mind a genuine Egyptian martini to warm the old loins, or a reasonable facsimile thereof, just to get in the mood.

Mood? Tell me about it. Soon as I take one fast gander at this softly lighted old *dahabeah,* as Abu and Nuz call it, which is like a large houseboat, and listen to the sensuous violins wafting across the sparkling Nile, I feel strangely rejuvenated, transformed, as it were, from a disheveled middle-aged clown in a nightgown to an impulsive, almost shockingly virile cross between Omar Sharif and Bill Cosby. We board via the gangplank, Abu knows the maître d', of course, no reservations needed, even on a Friday night, Tourist Police have their perks. We're shown to a candlelit table next to the railing, fine view of the dance floor as well as the Nile. First things first, I order a Beefeater martini on the rocks with a twist (in English), glance at the waiter, fully expecting a puzzled frown ("Twist beef in martini?!"), forgetting I'm in a chichi international joint here. Know what he does? Eyelids go half-mast in disdain, lips curl in a condescending smirk, he jots it down without a word. Nuz orders vodka, rocks, Abu orders white wine, Cru des Ptolémées, says it's his usual. My guess, his "usual" is a beer, but he figures, screw it, we're on full expenses, we'll pick up the tab. Which we will. Nuz will. Me, I left home without it.

Drinks are served, hold on, wait a minute, we have to go through a ritual here, polite Arabic toasts. Abu takes the first sip, nods at us, I watch Nuz, copy from him, we touch our forehead with the right hand, we say, *"Hani'an ya sidi!"* Means, "Enjoy your drink, sir!" Now Abu says, *"Allah yehannik!"* Means, "May God grant it pleases you!" I mean, I don't know how they get that much out of two words, but I go along with the gag. Finally, we get to drink. Ahhhhh. First swallow burns nicely, it's the genuine stuff. Praise be to Beefeater, it pleases the crap out of me, sir.

Okay, we're sitting there, agreeable atmosphere, violins squeaking softly, no belly dancers as yet, Abu and Nuz study the menu, now they give me a fast crash course on Egyptian cuisine. Turns out there's no characteristic Egyptian cuisine, it's almost identical to the food in other Arab countries. Most dishes are fatty and usually too highly seasoned for Western tastes. Staples? Ready for this? Mutton, poultry, beef (pork is forbidden), normally grilled, sometimes stewed in an herb stock, served with rice, black beans, brown bread, choice of various salads, vegetables, sauces, always grossly seasoned with spices and herbs. They warn me about dessert. Seems all sweets and pastries are loaded with sugar, syrup or honey, oil, all kinds of nuts. I pass before the fact, don't happen to have any Rolaids with me.

Another round of drinks, we give Abu a brief chronological rundown on the case to date. He's fascinated, he's a good listener, and he asks damn good questions, some we hadn't even considered. Time to order, I play it safe and have the same as Nuz and Abu, entrée called *fata* (appropriately), consisting of boiled mutton and rice mixed with breadcrumbs, rissoles of minced meat, and broad beans. While we're waiting, I give both of them a synopsis of Farah's book, *The Riddle of Cheops*. Must say, the combination of martinis, music, candlelight, and exotic atmosphere really pumps me up here, I'm telling this story like Rod Serling used to narrate the adventures of Jacques Cousteau, these guys are hanging on my every word, visualizing the whole incredible canvas I'm painting. Dinner is served, I get so involved in my eloquent martini rhetoric, explaining Farah's theories, I hardly notice how dreadful the mutton dish is, just shovel it in and keep talking. Lastly, Nuz and I explain the business letters from GE, IBM, and GM, plus the expected dates of arrival of the equipment, December 17, 19, 18, respectively.

"That's very heavy equipment," I tell Abu. "Obviously, they wouldn't deliver it to him at a dormitory complex."

"Of course not," he says. "Undoubtedly, it's all in the Egypt Air Freight hangar with instructions to hold it for his arrival."

"Know anybody at Egypt Air Freight?" I ask.

"No, but it's no problem, they'll cooperate with us."

"Would the hangar be open now?" Nuz asks.

He thinks about it. "I'd have to call and check. As I under-stand it, most regular air freight flights are scheduled for lowest-peak periods, late night, to reduce air traffic congestion with passenger flights. So, yes, I'd think the freight terminals and hangars are open right now, probably all night."

"Would you call and check after dinner?" I ask. "If they're open, I'd like to get out there and take a look tonight."

Abu makes the call right after dinner, confirms the fact that Egypt Air Freight's terminal and hangar are open. Nuz asks the waiter when the belly dancing starts. Eleven o'clock nightly. It's now 9:25. So much for undulating hips, have to catch them another night.

Off we putter in the Bug, across brightly lighted 6 October Bridge, then head northeast on Shari Ramses, a wide, modern four-lane highway, all the way to Cairo International Airport. Egypt Air Freight is located in Hangar 23, about a mile north-west of the main passenger terminal. Arrive about 9:50. Enor-mous white floodlighted building with the Egypt Air logo up on the left corner in red-orange letters, Arabic on top, English under. Park in the big lot, go in the office, up to the long counter, Abu shows his ID, asks to see the night manager. Muscular clerk picks up a microphone, pages a guy by the name of Kareem Hassia, we can hear the voice echoing back through the hangar.

Couple of minutes later, Hassia comes out through the swinging doors, short, chunky, middle-aged man in a dirty white jumpsuit, full head of graying hair, gold-frammed glasses, gray mustache, neck so thick it's like part of his shoul-ders. Fireplug type guy. Holds a white hardhat under his left armpit, wipes his mitts on a rag as he approaches the counter, dark eyes dart to each of us. Abu goes through the ID routine again, tells him who we are, fast Arabic, asks about the three international shipments to Ismat Farah. Hassia walks down the counter to a computer terminal, punches up the name and address. Face flickers blue-green as he watches the screen flash up data. Carries on a conversation with Abu, then punches up details on each shipment; Abu takes notes, air waybill numbers, equipment serial numbers, description of equipment, platform storage numbers in the hangar. Translation: Shipments from GE and IBM arrived on the same EAF Flight 398, December 18, F.O.B. New York; third shipment, 1985 GM Generator Truck, arrived yesterday morning, December 19, EAF Flight 473, F.O.B. Detroit. Waybill instructions on all three: Hold at hangar until claimed by Dr. Farah on or about December 21. Hassia also tells Abu that import duties must be paid on the shipments before they can be released. So far, so good. Now Abu requests that we be allowed to view these shipments in the hangar. No problem, no questions, Fireplug is all cooperation, long as you don't piss on him.

Buzzes us through the little gate in the counter, we follow him back through the swinging doors, he hands us each a steel hard hat (insurance regulations), plus plastic visitors' badges that we pin to our *galabiyyas*. Hangar is gigantic, noisy, wide cement aisles are like streets between canyons of storage bins, steady stream of fork-lift trucks haul pallets of cargo large and small to and from the far end, where open-nosed 747 freighters wait. Hassia loads us aboard a four-seater electric cart, nice red job with a roof of steel bars, drives us along a main drag for maybe seventy-five yards, honks greetings to passing fork-lifts, they honk back (yeah, even in here), hangs a left, now we're headed toward Platform 29, storage area for heavy industrial equipment. I spot the generator truck easily, big white van-type vehicle, looks exactly like the TV trucks I'd seen outside ballparks.

We stop, slide out, stroll over for a look. Abu checks the truck's serial number just inside the windshield, driver's side. Hassia points out the other two shipments alongside, both crated in heavy pine, bonded with steel tape, lots of neatly stenciled ID, large waybill packet on each. Truck's locked, of course, but the side and rear doors are double, plenty wide enough to accommodate the two crates. No license plates, but I assume Farah must have temporaries. All he'll have to do is pay the import duties, get the crates loaded aboard via fork-lift, gas this beauty up, and move her out. To his address at the university?

No way.

No way.

Have to smile when that dawns on me. Not that I anticipated that move, far from it, I'm not anywhere near as sharp as these eggheads, all I'm doing now is learning not to underestimate them. Didn't know the address was a dorm, had no way of knowing, never even entered my skull. But now I know, now I'm standing here looking at the truck and crates, something happens to me, radar begins picking up blips again, feels good, feels refreshing. Maybe, just maybe, I'm not as stale, old-fashioned, and inhibited as I thought. Okay, I stumbled into it, I admit it, sure, but a broken-bat Texas League dying quail looks as big in the box score as a line drive banging off the center-field wall. Pete Rose will tell you that. You take 'em any way you can get 'em. Now, next question: If Farah has no intention of driving this mother to his dorm (where we would've been waiting, without a description, till the Sphinx spit Red Man tobacco juice), then what's his real destination? And when?

Anticipate this guy. Just like you should've done all along with Todesfall/Mayyit. What would you do in Farah's place? If he's on that British Airways flight tonight, and I'm not at all sure he will be, what's the most unconventional, unexpected, totally off-the-wall move he'd make? Me in his place, here we go, pull on the skullcap of a real egghead. Me, I'd take a sleeping pill on that flight from London, even if I got a good night's sleep last night, I'd sleep all the way, before I ate or

drank anything, I'd ask to be awakened an hour before landing, say nine, then I'd have plenty of strong coffee, something
light to eat, and I'd be pumped up like crazy when the plane
touched down, energy to burn. Sail bright-eyed through Immigrations and Customs, pick up my luggage, grab a cab from
the international arrivals terminal to Egypt Air Freight, Hangar 23. Greet that clerk with all the ID he'd ever want to see,
pay the import duties in cold-cash Egyptian currency, sign the
necessary documents, produce my temporary license plates,
slip the clerk enough cash to go around, to ensure that the two
crates would be loaded aboard the truck safely, the gas tank
filled, the oil and water checked, the windshield wiped, the
engine revved and purring, then a little something extra for all
hands concerned, before I took off into the night.

Where to?

Outlandish as it seems, me, I wouldn't waste any time now,
my master plan wouldn't allow a pause in the momentum, I'd
go straight to work. Because the time would be perfect. When
I drove out of the hangar, it'd be well after midnight, probably
close to one o'clock or later, so I'd drive straight to Giza, to
the pyramids, where the whole area would be dark and de-
serted for the night. Except—and this is an educated guess—
except for the guards, token guards, undoubtedly from the
Central Security Force, as the pyramids and Sphinx are national treasures and there are no fences of any kind around
them or around the area. Now, question: Which individual
cops from the CSF would pull the all-night shift guarding
these treasures, that obviously can't be stolen anyway, but
might possibly be the targets of terrorist bombing? My guess,
Chief Kez and his brass would select a bunch of cops with the
lowest seniority, the youngest conscripts, and/or "problem"
cops who participate in the periodic riots, cops who protest the
draft and low pay and living conditions, cops who've been
jailed for demonstrations, cops who need discipline. To wit,
precisely the kind of cops who could be bought. Not that it's

phrased that way, of course. According to Nuz, one of the most important words in the Arabic language to the average Egyptian today is *bakshish,* meaning "tip" or "gift" or "gratuity" for an almost infinite variety of services rendered, because the average income here is so low. In fact, the rank and file of Egyptian workers in "service" industries today depend on *bakshish* just to make ends meet. And my radar blips strong and constant on this word, on this point, because I'm sure it's a critical factor to the success of the master plan. In more ways than one.

Because, of course, I'm not only talking about *bakshish* to young conscript cops here, that's just the tip of the iceberg as far as money's concerned. No, to pull a caper of this magnitude, to even contemplate something this Machiavellian, involving national treasures that are, in fact, literally priceless, let's face it, you've got to be talking major money. To major government officials. Up front. Cash. You've got to understand and accept the political and economic reality that the so-called untouchable hands will turn palms up. To be touched. But not seen. With how much? My judgment, millions. Dawns on me gradually, as usual, but at least it dawns: That's the major business expense in this whole operation. Not the Bancaro International money laundering commission of $2.4 million, but the total committed *bakshish,* probably approximating a cool £E3.5 million cash, which, considering the current exchange rate, adds up to virtually all they had left of the $8 million after conversion, not counting peanuts for the conscripts. Okay, maybe I'm cutting it too fine, maybe the major-money *bakshish* isn't that much, maybe I'm manipulating the figures to make them add up, but I have a strong gut feeling I'm on track now. For the first time since this case began, I'm beginning to think I can actually see some light at the end of the tunnel. Hope it's not the headlight of a subway train speeding straight at me.

But if I'm right, and if Farah's on that ten o'clock flight from London, and if he comes to Hangar 23 to pick up his equipment, things are going to happen fast. We've got to anticipate that possibility, we've got to be ready for it well in advance, which means we'll have to arrange convincing cover through Hassia to start surveillance in the hangar before 10:30, depending on whether or not Farah's flight is on time.

Now I call a quick confab with Nuz and Abu, explain what I want to do and why. Abu sees no problem with it, he takes Hassia aside, explains carefully what we need. Fireplug squints, nods, shrugs, motions for us to climb back in the electric cart, drives us to the employees' locker room near the office.

Tell you what, when we come out of that locker room at 10:02, I feel like a new man. Fireplug's raided the storeroom and outfitted us in white EAF jumpsuits that actually fit pretty good, battle-scarred white hard hats with the EAF logo, and old, high-topped, steel-toed safety shoes that are relatively close to our sizes and, with heavy wool socks, even afford a tad of comfort. Only problem, the jumpsuits are freshly washed and look too clean; easy to remedy that. Next thing, we've got to have jobs, right? First, Fireplug says we should be "sweepers," he gets out three long-handled pushbrooms; Abu says no, we've got to be in the same area, it's too obvious to have three sweepers in the same area. Fireplug sees the logic to this, he's not too good a detective yet, but he's trying. Now he commandeers three fork-lift trucks, gives us formal instructions on how to operate them, how to lift and release various pallets of cargo safely, to look like we know what we're doing, and finally he assigns each of us a "job" over in the general vicinity of Platform 29, where Farah's truck and equipment sit. What kind of jobs? Okay, this is the storage area for heavy industrial equipment, so my job, for example, will be to pick up two giant Goodyear farm tractor tires, bonded with steel tape, drive them down a numbered aisle, maneuver them into a numbered steel bin, release them, shut off the engine, get off the truck, check the waybill, check the condition of the tires, get back on the truck, start the engine, pick up the pallet, drive it back to its original position, release it, then take a coffee break. I figure, hell, these Arabs are obviously bona fide members of the Teamsters, makes me feel homesick. Nuz and Abu have similar responsible jobs.

Moment of truth comes at 10:09, when Abu, who's been calling British Airways from the front counter every thirty seconds, finally gets the confirmation that Flight 155 from London just landed. As usual, following international regulations, British Airways could not reveal the names of any passengers aboard until the flight landed safely (not even to a cop, without the official station call-back number), but now they cheerfully confirm that Dr. Ismat Farah is definitely aboard.

Bingo! Hate to admit it, but we all start to get excited now, Nuz and Abu take their cue from me, I'm so happy I give 'em both high-fives; if I had a football, I'd spike the sucker. Fireplug, he's been standing around all serious, observing us super-cool detectives with dark envious eyes, now he can't believe what he's seeing, we're acting like kids, Nuzhat's even shouting salutations: *"Kattar allah kherak!"* Over and over. I ask what it means, he says, "May God increase your good deeds!" Religious people, these Arabs, got to give them credit.

Okay, down to business. When Nuz and I landed this morning, it took us about forty-five minutes to clear Immigrations (we had to get our visas) and Customs, so we figure Farah to take a minimum of thirty, maximum of forty-five; he probably has a visa, but he's a naturalized American citizen, so he'll have to go through most of the red tape that we did. That would mean he'd be able to grab a cab no earlier than 10:40 and, if he's coming to Hangar 23, a one-mile drive, he'd arrive here well before eleven. Abu takes Fireplug aside again, explains the situation, asks him to man the front counter together with his regular clerk now, to remain perfectly calm, because there's absolutely no danger involved, and to assist Dr. Farah in any way possible. Fireplug wants to know if he should give us a signal when the man arrives. We tell him no. Nice thought, but no. No signal of any kind. We'll be wheeling our fork-lifts around back in the vicinity of Platform 29, there's no possibility we could miss him. If he comes.

He comes.

Ismat Farah comes.

Later than we anticipated, 11:12, but he had a lot of paperwork at the front counter, and it's all completed now, the documents signed, the import duties paid, and he's ready to take possession of his equipment now, all perfectly legal. I'm sitting in my fork-lift truck, parked in an aisle facing the main-drag aisle from the office. And I see Hassia's red electric cart flash past in the distance. I start my engine and drive in the same direction, parallel to that main-drag aisle, seeing that cart flash past between the tall canyons of bins. He comes. Silently, amid all the noise and movement of that hangar, I see Hassia gliding along in the little red electric cart, pulsating into view rhythmically between the tall storage bins, disappearing behind them, appearing again, heading for Platform 29. And I catch glimpses of the man sitting next to him, I see the man with the hard hat and big plastic visitor's badge, towering over him, face rawboned, weatherbeaten, deeply wrinkled, lean, tanned, tired maybe, that was it, tired, exhausted even, the face of a man in his mid-fifties who was working himself sick, the face of a heavy drinker who, if he didn't have that deep bronze color that made you look like a million bucks, might have the telltale red and purple blotches at the end of the nose and across the cheeks, and hangdog circles under eyes that were beaten and admitted it. My mind gropes for just a moment, names and places and years spinning, and I experience the same sick feeling in my stomach and visualize the same strange image that the face triggered before:

Farah, Farah, Farah. Slender figure of a Brazilian street cleaner pushing trash with a long-handled brush, Where do I come from? *all dimly seen in the orange-yellow glow of a streetlight.* Nobody knows. *Man appears to wear light-blue work clothes, maybe denim, and heavy boots or shoes.* Where am I going? *Curb of the narrow sidewalk is high red brick.* Everybody goes. *House behind him has a low, narrow doorway and a narrow blue-green window. Almost invisible, the outline of a person standing in the doorway; I think it's a woman, but I'm not at all sure. In the dark-brown shadows to the left* The wind blows *is the man's old wooden-wheeled trash wagon and, beyond that, the bare branches and trunk of a small tree.* The sea flows. *It's possible the street cleaner might be wearing a skullcap of some kind, it's hard to tell,* Nobody knows *but one thing is for certain: The man has no face. His head appears to be wrapped tightly in slender rolls of brown cloth painted in intricate detail.*

Electric cart stops at Platform 29, the man gets off, goes directly to the generator truck, unlocks the front, side, and rear doors. I stop now, partly concealed by a bin, I'm about thirty-five yards away, but I can see him clearly. It's him all right, the man I've been calling Todesfall and Mayyit, but is he actually Ismat Farah after all? Is that possible? Is it logical? Could it have been one man all along? Would all the dates and times and places fall in line without reasonable doubt? One critical date, time, and place comes to mind instantly, the first time I saw him from the elevator at the Fontainebleau. Date? Tuesday, December 17. Time? About 5:30 in the afternoon, I'm sure of that, because we were on our way to a 5:30 appointment to interview R.T. Mustafa. Okay, the robbery itself took place Sunday night, December 15, between 11:15 and midnight, but wasn't reported until 2:32 A.M. Now, if this guy left New

York immediately after the robbery and drove the Chevy van virtually nonstop to Miami, how many hours would it take? Distance is roughly 1,100 miles, as the crow flies, let's call it 1,200 miles. If he stayed under the speed limits all the way and averaged, say, fifty miles an hour, only stopping for gas, food, and a leak now and then, he could make it in twenty-four hours, let's say just after midnight, Tuesday, December 17. So, yeah, he could've done that. He could've participated in the robbery himself, along with the single accomplice, probably Laila Mustafa, then driven his own leased van to Miami with the fifteen to seventeen moneybags, and still have more than seventeen hours to spare before I saw him in the lobby at 5:30. That checks out. And if that checks, most of the other dates, times, and places fall in line too because of the frustrating fact that we've never actually seen the Ismat Farah who's listed on the Morningside Motors lease as forty-three, five-foot-eleven, and 154. The man who's now opening the engine hood on the generator truck is easily fifty-five, six-foot-three, maybe 175–180. Hair showing under the hard hat is gray-white, worn short, and his features are anything but Arabic, although he's wearing a classy white *saudi-*style *galabiyya.*

But there's one major date-time-place that definitely doesn't check out, if our intelligence is accurate. That's Thursday, December 19, 8:10 A.M., Nassau. Ismat Farah was confirmed by Mort Cooper to be on British Airways' Flight 262, Nassau-London, seat number 5-J, nobody in the seat next to him. The flight took off at 8:10 with his ass in that seat. So the same ass couldn't have been in seat 1-A on Concorde in Miami at eleven o'clock the same morning. Of course, I shouldn't be so glib about it, because there's an unknown factor here that could screw up the whole equation. When Mort called British Airways at the airport that morning, identified himself, requested the manager on duty, told him we had some confidential questions, asked him to go through the call-back routine, then had him check the PNL computer to see if Ismat Farah was on Flight 262, Nassau-London, the guy told him yes, Farah was aboard the flight, seat 5-J. Unknown factor? Airline computer listings are not proof positive that any given individual is physically aboard any given flight. In theory, it's supposed to be proof, and I've been assured by airline authorities that it's accurate 99.9 percent of the time. But I've worked cases in the past when it wasn't. Trick is, you get your seat assignment, as usual, computerized right on your boarding pass, you wait until the flight's actually boarding, hand it to the gate attendant just before you board, have the stub torn off for you, standard stuff, get aboard, show the flight attendant your stub, get directions, go to your seat, put down your coat and bag, whatever, then—oh!—you forgot something, left it in the lounge, have to go back for it. Works best on jammed jumbo jets. Especially if you look like a nice elderly gentleman.

Would this guy do that?

This guy would do that.

Would he have a forged passport in Ismat Farah's name, a forged driver's license, a variety of totally convincing backup ID, all masterpieces of craftsmanship, state-of-the-art high-tech Silicon Valley microchip wizardry?

Would this guy have that?

This guy would have that.

Which leads to the inevitable question: What happened to the real Ismat Farah? Call the Department of Radiology at Columbia, speak to the head honcho, he'll tell you Farah's on a term-long sabbatical, effective December 13, to research a new book at Cairo University, be back for the fall term. Stop in the graduate-student dorm at Cairo University, speak to the desk clerk, he'll tell you Farah's registered in Room 1038, expected around midnight tonight. Ismat Farah? No. Seeing this guy tonight, knowing that he had to show heavy ID to Hassia for the equipment, I'm finally convinced that Farah's dead. Where or when, I don't know, but I'd guess this guy took him out back in New York, sometime around December 13. Like Laila Mustafa, he was a potential canary. This guy blew his egghead all over the birdcage.

Would this guy do that to us?

This guy would do that to us.

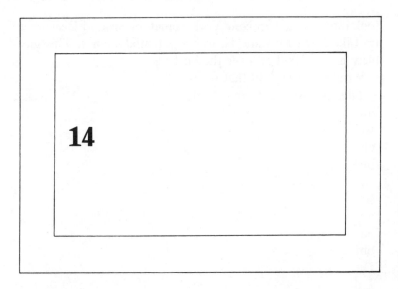

14

SPEED INTO TOWN on the Shari Ramses now, wide and straight and jammed with traffic even at 12:25 A.M., horns blasting as the maniacs snake in and out, suicide style, we follow the big white generator truck, temporary license stuck in the rear window, and Abu stays four to five cars back because this guy's got giant side-view mirrors like you see on the cabs of eighteen-wheeler rigs, we actually catch fast glimpses of his rawboned face in the one on the driver's side. Reason it took him so long in the hangar, he pays two cargo jockies to pry open the pine crates so he can open the boxes and check out the scanner, computer, and laser before they're loaded aboard. Then it takes over half an hour to get the truck going, it's got all kinds of problems that should've been caught at the factory, so he passes out the *bakshish* with such abandon that, in the end, he's got seven gorillas in hard hats climbing all over this ice-cream wagon, fighting to fix something, anything, even if it ain't broke, while he plays with his new toys inside. Now he stays in the fast lane on Shari Ramses southwest into town, hangs a right near the Egyptian Museum to avoid the chaos at Midan el-Tahrir, crosses the 6 October Bridge west into Gezeria, Cairo Tower ablaze to our right, crosses the bridge to the west bank, hangs a left, follows Shari el-Nil south along the river, which means he's not going to the university, hangs a right into Shari el-Akhram, follows it southwest, now we're in Giza, so maybe I guessed right for a change, maybe this guy's actually planning to start work tonight.

Can't keep calling him "this guy," we're stuck for a name, so Nuz thinks on it, puffs on a new cigar in the front seat, finally comes up with a temporary moniker he likes, a code name, says it fits, says we should call this psycho what he obviously thinks he represents, in his sick brain, the Image of Death, or just plain Death, period, and be done with it. Me, I don't happen to like that code name for this particular whacko, I have my reasons, tell you later, but I go along with it for now.

It's around 12:45, traffic's much lighter along Shari el-Akhram, so we play it cautious, we hang way back, all we can see are the truck's distinctive tail lights, pinpoints in the distance. Abu knows every inch of this area, his station's just up the road, he says we're entering the village of Nazlat el-Samman, dominated by the pyramids, we can see them up ahead, unbelievably huge and dark against the sky. Says the lights in the distance way up to the right are from the Mena House Oberio, closest hotel to the pyramids and one of the oldest; across the road to the left are the Post Office and Tourist Information Office, closed and dark, of course, and his Tourist Police station, which never closes.

Next thirty seconds are critical because there are only two alternatives for the truck: Pull into the driveway of the Mena House or continue just past it, where the road curves sharply left, mounts a slope, and finishes at the north end of the plateau, directly opposite the entrance to the Great Pyramid.

At this point, there's only one car between us and the truck, we've slowed to a crawl, because if the truck turns right, into the hotel, Abu's got it timed so he can then turn left, almost immediately, into his station.

Truck continues past the driveway, starts the sharp left curve up the slope, and the car behind it turns into Mena House. We decide to pull into the hotel too, because Abu says there are wings where we can get an unobstructed view of the pyramid from the roof. We park in the lot behind the hotel. We're still wearing our EAF jumpsuits and safety shoes, didn't have time to change, but Nuz grabbed our Arab gear from the locker room just before we left, so we can change later.

Walking around to the front entrance, Abu gives us a quick rundown on this historic old place. Originally, it was a hunting lodge for the Turkish viceroys, converted to a hotel in 1869, and it's where Roosevelt and Churchill created the D-Day plan. Mena House and the famous old Shepheard's were once the great hotels of Cairo and the original section of this one is still considered by eggheads and them to be *the* place to stay because of its unequaled views of the pyramids. New section was added in 1976, called Mena Gardens, but it's not in the old Arab style and the views aren't as spectacular. Still, Abu says it's a five-star hotel, tops, it's got all the luxury stuff, golf course, swimming pool, even riding stables. Each section is only three stories high because they didn't want to interfere with views from behind to the north. Interfere? Great Pyramid looks so huge from here, it makes the hotel seem like a dollhouse.

Only a few people in the lobby this time of night, our outfits get curious glances as we walk to the desk. Abu knows the young room clerk, doesn't have to show ID, explains that we need access to the roof for surveillance. Kid says he can have a room if he wants, two top-floor suites are vacant, very slow weekend for tourists because of the Christmas season. Gives

Abu the key to Suite 300, says we can use it all night if we like. We thank him kindly. Seems like the Tourist Police get full cooperation from everybody in town, nice to know.

Take the elevator to the third floor, walk to the end of the hall, I tell Abu not to turn on the lights when we go in. He leaves the door open so I can see my way to the windows. When I open the curtains—wham!—Great Pyramid is directly ahead, looks like a gigantic mountain against the stars.

Now I look down, blink, squint, wait for my eyes to adjust, I can see the dim outline of the white generator truck. He's pulled it off the road and backed it up to the entrance of the pyramid. Truck looks tiny, looks like a toy down there, if it was a dark color I wouldn't be able to see it. Nuz and Abu come over now, take a look. We can't see any guards around, but their uniforms are black, so spotting them from this distance would be almost impossible anyway.

"Son of a bitch," Nuz says. "The man has actually started."

I glance at my watch. "Abu, what time does the pyramid open for tourists in the morning?"

"Eight-thirty. Eight-thirty to four-thirty daily."

"And what time is sunrise?"

"This time of year, about seven."

"It's almost one o'clock now," I tell them. "That gives him about six hours tonight. What time's sunset?"

"In December, very early," Abu says. "About five-fifteen. And it's a short twilight, barely half an hour. Same in the morning, less than half an hour of predawn light."

Glance at my watch again. "That means if he started at, say, six every evening, he'd have thirteen hours of darkness each night. Thirteen hours to work."

"How long will it take him?" Nuz asks.

I shrug, look down at the truck again. "In the book, Farah didn't go into the possible time required. In the beginning, it'll be strictly trial and error. He'll be working two long subterranean corridors with the X-ray scanner and computer. One corridor leads straight down from the entrance, then levels out just before it reaches the big decoy chamber. That's the longest, but the easier of the two, so that's the one he's probably starting on now. The other one starts way up near the real corridor leading to the so-called Queen's Chamber and leads downward at a slight angle all the way till it joins the first corridor just as it levels off near the decoy chamber. My guess, from reading the book, and it's just a guess, it'll take at least a couple of nights just to find the hidden chamber, Cheops's real chamber—if it's there. Then at least one full night working with the laser drill to cut through the limestone blocks outside the chamber. Finally, if the chamber's plugged from the inside with a granite block, that'll take even longer to cut through, maybe a couple of full nights, I don't know. Keep in mind, I'm guessing about all this."

Nuz looks at me in the dim light from the window. "Now, John, listen to me. This is important. To me, that seems like a very long time. Now, I realize he's paid everyone off, he has no problem going back every night, he's paid millions. But listen. Do you think it may be possible that he already knows where the hidden chamber is?"

"No way, Nuz. Look at it logically. If he knew where it is, why would he go to all the trouble and expense to buy the X-ray scanner and computer? I mean, all he'd need is the laser drill."

Nuz nods solemnly. "That's true."

"May I offer an idea?" Abu asks.

"Absolutely," I tell him.

His eyes sparkle in the half-light. "I think it's a mistake to assume that he has absolutely no knowledge about where the chamber is—except that it's in one of the subterranean corridors. I don't think we should necessarily assume that, because we could be underestimating his knowledge."

When I hear the word "underestimating," I'm suddenly all

ears. "Go ahead," I tell him. "Keep talking, I want to hear this."

"Well, it's possible he may already know the general *area* where the chamber is hidden, but not the precise location. If that's true, he'd only need the scanner and computer for—let's say a relatively small part of just one corridor. Which could cut his total working time from—your guess was four or five nights. From four or five nights to, I don't know, maybe half that time."

"Or less," I say. "Keep talking."

He shrugs. "That's all. That's all I'm suggesting. That we might be wise to assume this man has far more knowledge than he actually has, and therefore could complete the robbery in far less time than we believe he could."

"Excellent suggestion," I tell him. "Abu, keep doing that, keep thinking that way, keep second-guessing us on all this. We need your input. No matter how trivial you think it might be, speak up."

"Yes, sir. I'm afraid I don't have much experience."

"Abu, listen to me," Nuz says. "We are all guessing here, so it's not a question of experience, it's a question of insight. Do not be intimidated by our ages, by our experience. Do you understand?"

"Yes, sir."

We close the curtains now, turn on some lamps, walk around the suite, see what we've got here. Corner suite, two fairly big rooms with high-beamed ceilings, living room with a large stone fireplace that's obviously seen a lot of use, bedroom with a smaller fireplace and twin beds. Old Arab decor throughout, Persian carpets covered here and there with sheepskin rugs, antique-looking sofas and chairs, ornamental camel saddles for footstools, oil paintings of various Egyptian landscapes and hunting scenes. Color television is out of sight in an ornate mahogany cabinet with doors, tasteful touch.

Hello, here's something that could be quite useful, small balcony off the living room enclosed by a low black wrought-iron railing. I open the windowed wooden door, step out carefully in the dark. Gives a slightly different angle on the Great Pyramid, faces more to the south, I can see the dark silhouettes of the other two pyramids now, off to the right. Much clearer view of the generator truck than from the windows. Two wrought-iron chairs with cushions out here, glass-topped table with a fancy cut-glass ashtray, nice tiled floor. Man could sit out here at night with binoculars, sip a martini, smoke a cigar, pull his surveillance shift in comfortable, fine Arab style. Praise be to Mena House, it pleases the crap out of me, sir.

Obviously, this is the spot for us, however long all this takes, we all agree, so Nuz and I will have to check out of the Ramses Hilton whenever we get a chance, check in here immediately, and start the surveillance routine. Abu thinks he can get us a good discount, owing to the vacancy over the weekend, he'll speak to the room clerk on his way to the station to pick up some binoculars. When I ask him if the station might possibly have an infrared night scope, he pauses at the door, turns, gives me this look straight out of one of the American cop movies he's seen, and says, *"Naharak sa'id we-mubarak!"* When he's gone, Nuz says it's a popular expression among the *askari:* "May your day be as white as milk, you rat motherfuck!" Kid's a pisser, like his style.

It's 1:05, we're six hours ahead of New York, it's only 7:05 Friday evening there, so I decide now's a good time to call Vadney at home, give him our first daily progress report from here like he wanted, because we're finally making some headway. Nuz goes out on the balcony for the first surveillance shift while I make the call. Dial the hotel operator, who speaks English almost perfectly, tell him my name and suite number, explain that we just checked in, ask him to put the call on our bill, tell him the area code and Vadney's home number in

Manhattan. No problem getting through this time of night, but there's lots of static, we can't hear each other real clear. After the first few words, we have to practically shout.

"Rawlings! You in Cairo?"

"No, we're in Giza."

"Giza? Giza, *Italy?* What the hell you—?"

"No, no, that's *Pisa,* Chief. Y'know, the Leaning Tower?"

"Rawlings, *speak up!* You're at the Leaning Tower?"

"No! We're in *Giza!* Giza, *Egypt!"*

"You guys are supposed to be in *Cairo!"*

"We *are,* Chief! It's like—like a *suburb* of Cairo!"

"Well, what's happening?"

"We located our suspect, we're doing surveillance on him."

"Good man, Little John! Congratulations! What's he up to?"

"Right this minute, he's in the process of a robbery."

"A robbery? Did you say *robbery?"*

"Yeah, robbery. He's attempting to rob a pyramid."

Pause. "Don't think I heard you right. Say again."

"He's trying to rob a *pyramid!"*

"Rawlings, are you—are you *drunk?"*

"No! I'm telling you, that's what he's—"

"How the fuck's he gonna steal a *pyramid?"*

"Not the pyramid, Chief! What's *inside!"*

"What the hell's inside?"

"Priceless national treasures."

"Like what?"

"Like—there's a mummy in there."

"Money? How much?"

"Mummy!"

"Yeah, I hear ya, but how *much?"*

"A *dead* guy! Y'know, all wrapped up?"

"He's stealin' a *dead* guy?"

"Right. Been dead for five thousand years, y'know?"

"Holy shit. And he's trying to *steal* him?"

"Right."

"What the fuck's he *want* with him?"

"He was a king, Chief, a Pharaoh."

"Farah? Farah was a king?"

"No, the *dead* guy!"

"Come again? Farah's *dead?*"

"Well—yeah. Yeah, I think so, but that's another—"

"If Farah's dead, then who's your suspect, who's the robber?"

"We don't know his name, Chief, but I want you to listen to me for a minute, this is important. I'll talk slowly and repeat words if necessary, because you've got to understand this. Our suspect is the same man who killed Laila Mustafa in Florida. That's a positive ID. We also have reason to believe he killed Ismat Farah, probably in New York. In my judgment, this man is the mastermind behind our eight-million-dollar robbery. Can you hear me clearly, can you understand me?"

"Positive. Now you're making sense, Little John. Good work, buddy-boy. Now, just keep talking slowly and distinctly. I'm taking notes now. Go ahead."

"At the present time, we have this man under twenty-four-hour surveillance. He is working in the interior of a pyramid called—copy this—called the Great Pyramid. It is located in Giza—copy this—G for George, I for Irving, Z for Zack, A for Alice. Giza, Egypt, an area just southwest of Cairo. The suspect is attempting to discover and steal various national treasures of Egypt, believed by him to be hidden in a chamber inside the Great Pyramid. He is believed to be a skilled technician and is known to be using highly sophisticated technological equipment. He is believed to be armed and should be considered extremely dangerous. Description: White, male, Caucasian, fifty-five to sixty, six-foot-three, one hundred seventy-five pounds, short gray-white hair, color of eyes unknown, rawboned features, swarthy complexion. Fluent in English, German, Arabic, possibly others. Known to be a specialist in the use of makeup and disguise. Suspect uses a variety of bogus passports, driver's licenses, and backup identification. Detective Idrissi and I have the official cooperation of the police authorities here, namely Chief Kez—copy this— K for Ken, E for Ed, Z for Zack, of the Central Security Force. We are working in concert with an armed detective of the Tourist Police branch of Central Security. Our present address is Mena House Hotel—copy this—M for Mike, E for Ed, N for Nick, A for Alice. Mena House Hotel, Giza, Suite Three-zero-zero." I glance at the phone. "Telephone number, eight-five-three-seven-eight-nine. Can you still hear me clearly?"

"That's a positive, Little John, excellent work. Now, listen up, I got important questions here. I'll ask the questions slowly and distinctly. Can you hear me all right?"

"Positive."

"Can the Egyptian authorities arrest this guy right now?"

I hesitate. "Negative."

"Why not?"

"First, he hasn't committed a crime here yet, to our knowledge, he hasn't stolen anything yet. And the attempted robbery will probably require at least several days, maybe more. Second, knowing this guy, I'm sure he's obtained all the government permits and permissions necessary to conduct radiological research inside the pyramid."

"How would a guy like this get permission?"

"My opinion, Dr. Ismat Farah did all the paperwork. This guy is now impersonating Farah and has convincing identification. Also, he's obviously got everybody in his pocket."

"Come again?"

"Bribes. Cash gifts to police and government officials. My guess, for something this big, millions of Egyptian pounds. Millions."

"Holy shit."

"He's planned this for years, Chief."

"You got a fugitive warrant, right?"

"Fugitive warrant? Negative."

"Idrissi have one?"

"He hasn't mentioned it, Chief. Frankly, I doubt it. I mean, whose name would be on the warrant?"

Pause. "Ismat Farah?"

"Chief, the real Ismat Farah didn't commit a crime in this case, at least nothing we could prove. Under the law, we didn't even have prima facie evidence of any wrongdoing on his part. No judge in his right mind would sign a fugitive warrant for Ismat Farah."

"Point well taken, Little John. If we'd been thinking ahead, if things hadn't happened so fast, we would've given Idrissi a 'John Doe' warrant. Wait a minute. Wait a minute, did you say the robbery attempt would probably take at least a couple of days?"

"That's right. Maybe more."

"Hell, then I'll get a 'John Doe' fugitive warrant issued immediately. Immediately, with the detailed description, facts, figures, all the shit you just gave me. Christ, this guy's wanted for *murder,* I can get a warrant on him in no time flat."

"We sure could use it, Chief."

"All right, listen up, buddy-boy, you're gonna get it. You're gonna get all the help we can muscle out of the tight-ass criminal-justice system in this city. Here's what's gonna happen here. It's now—let's see—it's now seven-oh-eight P.M., New York time. I'm gonna get on this right now, I'm gonna call Judge Roffman at home. Old buddy of mine, known him for years, lives down on East Thirty-eighth. Now, hold on a second. *Samantha!* Sam, honey, will ya get me the *OAG* out of the desk in there? The *OAG!* Right. Naw, honey, that's *Oui,* that's a skin mag, I want *OAG, Official Airline Guide.* Right. Hold on a minute, Rawlings."

"You coming to Cairo yourself?"

"Fuckin'-A well right I am, buddy-boy! Wrap the biggest cash robbery in history? You kiddin'? Mastermind caught with his pants down in a fuckin' pyramid? This is world-class news we're talkin' here, buddy, wouldn't miss this collar for all the crabs in Casandra's crotch! Hey, thanks a load, Sam, appreciate it, doll. Okay, now, Little John, get a pencil out, let's see what we got here. New York–Cairo, New York–Cairo. Here we go. Nonstops, nonstops. Shit, I can't believe this. No nonstops to Cairo from here. Guess they have to refuel. Wait a minute, here's a direct flight, Egypt Air, one stop in Paris. Okay, Friday, Friday, let's see here. Flight MS-nine-eighty-six, departs JFK exactly ten P.M. tonight, nonstop to Paris, arrives exactly eleven A.M., Paris time, continues nonstop to Cairo, arrives four-thirty P.M., Cairo time. Wait a minute, what day is that?"

"Saturday. It's already Saturday morning here, Chief, December twenty-one. You arrive at four-thirty this afternoon."

"Yeah, that's right, that's tomorrow afternoon, Saturday. Well, okay, that's the fastest way I can get there, that's the sucker I'm grabbing, Little John. Copy that, get somebody to meet me, Egypt Air Flight MS-nine-eighty-six, arrives Cairo four-thirty Saturday. Holy shit, I gotta get goin', no time to pack, I gotta call Dor—I gotta call Judge Roffman right now, gotta get down to his place, gotta grab a cab from there to Kennedy, get out there by nine. Gotta get my passport! *Sam?* Sam, where's my—" *Click.*

Hangs up. Have a nice flight, Chief. Intriguing little slip, "I gotta call Dor—"; probably do it from Judge Roffman's place. Long flight, New York–Paris–Cairo. Lonely, too. If you're all alone. Wonder if—? Naw. Naw, it's just too preposterous to presume that Doris could be persuaded to grab her passport on such short notice and jet off into the starry night. Of course, it's an emergency of the first order and she is, after all, his key assistant, his strong right arm. And, naturally, they'd have to fly first class on a trip that long, oh. Imagine being jammed in with all those crowds of common, scraggy street Arabs in back? And, of course, she'd have to buy a whole new wardrobe in Cairo; inconvenient as hell, but I noticed a few chic shops in the Ramses Hilton that might do in a pinch. Can't help wondering how her husband, J.W. "Will" Banks, would react to such a sudden (dare I say it?) nocturnal rendezvous, emergency or no, smack in the middle of the Christmas festivities. Could be he had plans. Could be he had reservations at posh restaurants and tickets to hit shows. Could be he'd be annoyed. Self-made multimillionaires are seldom pussycats. Hot damn. I mean, somebody could get hurt here. Somebody could get his head pinched off like a bug.

When Abu comes back from the station at 1:15, he brings one pair of high-powered binoculars, three walkie-talkies, a large thermos of hot black *kahwa* with three plastic cups, yesterday's English-language newspaper, the *Egyptian Gazette,* plus our *galabiyyas* and sandals from the car. For the next hour or so, all three of us sit out on the dark balcony, Abu on a camel saddle, sip the *kahwa,* talk quietly, and take turns with the binoculars. Stars seem very bright and close this time of night, few clouds, and there's a half-moon, so we can observe the truck with at least some degree of clarity. Less than five minutes after Nuz starts using the binoculars, he spots two black-uniformed kid cops sitting on a limestone block near the base of the pyramid, north side, not far from the entrance, to the right of the truck. Reason he spots them, he sees the red tip of a cigarette. I take the binoculars now, focus on them, they're talking, once in a while they pass a bottle back and forth and it catches the moonlight. Can't see any light at all from the entrance itself. My guess, entranceway is kept dark purposely, no need for light there, he's got a cable or a series of cables extended from the truck into one of the subterranean corridors. I judge the truck to be about 300 yards away, length of three football fields, so we can't hear the sound of the generator. As I move the binoculars around the pyramid, one thing surprises me a little. This monstrous thing is jagged as hell. I didn't expect it to be smooth, I knew the original polished limestone casing was removed centuries ago, but in silhouette from this distance the edges are so ragged that almost anybody could climb all the way to the top. Abu laughs softly when I mention that. Says tourists climb to the top every day, but it's very strenuous and there's a rule now that you have to hire a "guide" to accompany you. Says years ago tourists were allowed to climb it alone. Says he knows gory stories about people tumbling all the way down, leaving their splattered brains as graffiti. Says he won't tell us details in the dead of night because it'd scare the piss out of New York cops. Thoughtful kid.

We each work one-hour surveillance shifts, try to grab as much sleep as we can, because we've got to be ready to roll before sunrise when the truck leaves. Abu was right about the short predawn light, starts around 6:30, so he wakes Nuz and me at 6:15. We hop into our *galabiyyas* and sandals, Abu takes his walkie-talkie down to the car, drives it out of the back lot, waits near the front entrance. Nuz uses the binoculars from the window now, I test my walkie-talkie with Abu, make sure we're loud and clear on the same frequency.

I've got the binoculars at 6:50 when our man appears from behind the truck, wearing a blue T-shirt, jeans, and sneakers. Walks over to the two kid cops nearby, starts to give them *bakshish.* Nuz alerts Abu on the walkie-talkie, I keep the binoculars as we rush out the door, run down the long hall, press the elevator button. There's only one elevator and the lighted indicator above the door reads "1." Doesn't change for about five seconds. Nuz hits the button half a dozen times, starts cursing in Arabic. Indicator stays at "1." We look around for the fire stairs, see the lighted "Exit" sign halfway down the hall, run like crazy, fling the door open, flip-flop down the cement stairs, I'm tripping over my thongs, reach the ground floor, sprint through the lobby, race past the doorman into the driveway.

Abu's car is gone.

No cabs around this time of morning, of course, nothing. Nuz starts cursing in English now, he's desperate for words. My heart's pounding, I'm out of breath, I'm even sweating now, but I'm not really worried. This kid knows what he's doing, I have complete confidence in his judgment. He did exactly what he should've done, what we would've done under the circumstances. We look at each other sheepishly, realize we both left our walkie-talkies in the room, didn't think we'd need them in the car. Abu undoubtedly called us, said the truck just went past the driveway, that he had to take off. Kid kept his head. I'm proud of him. Glance at my watch: 6:54. Took us four full minutes to get from the third floor to the driveway. Running all the way.

Only sensible thing to do, go back to the room and wait for Abu to call, either by walkie-talkie or telephone. Don't think these walkie-talkies have much range, I'm betting he'll use the telephone, first chance he gets. We go back in the lobby, Nuz uses the housephone to order room-service breakfast for us, light repast, just asks for three *bade masluk* (boiled eggs) each, five *ataif* (pancakes in syrup) each, two pots of *kahwa,* and something called *baklawa,* which has no real English counterpart, he says it's more or less cakes and pastry flavored with nuts, almonds, ginger, icing, and particularly honey. Translates all this shit after he hangs up, says I'll love it, says I need to educate my palate. Me, I'd rather have a dumb palate.

Get up to the room, telephone rings at 7:16, I answer, happy to hear Abu's voice, he's at Cairo University. Yeah. Seems our man drove straight to the campus, parked the generator truck in a lot behind the graduate-student dorm on Shari Gammaiat el-Qahira, carried in two suitcases, registered at the desk, now he's up in Room 1038. Probably plans to sleep all day, he had a busy night. I breathe a sigh of relief.

"Want me to stick with him?" he asks.

"Yeah, I do, Abu. Hate to use your time like this, but we just can't take anything for granted with this guy."

"I understand."

"They got a lobby there?"

"Yes, that's where I am. There are two elevators, right next to each other, serving the whole dorm. I've got an eye on them right now."

"You didn't get much sleep last night, you feel alert enough?"

"Oh, sure. I'll just sit in the lobby, have some coffee, keep my eyes open. The fire stairs are near the elevators, so that's no problem."

"Okay, here's what I want you to do. Call your station about nine, give your commanding officer an update on what you've been doing, tell him I requested surveillance relief for you at ten. Reason I want that, Chief Vadney's arriving at four-thirty, as you know, and I want you with us all the way. You feel all right now, but you'll start to fade before long. I want you to go home as soon as your relief man takes over, get as much sleep as you can, then pick us up at the hotel at three. On the way to the airport, we'll stop at the Ramses Hilton, get our luggage, pay the bill, and check out."

"Sounds good to me, John. You shouldn't have any problem getting Chief Vadney a room at Mena House. This particular weekend is very slow."

"Good. I'll call the desk."

"May I make a suggestion?"

"Sure."

"I realize you and Nuzhat need sleep too, but sometime before I pick you up this afternoon, you should go over to the Great Pyramid and familiarize yourselves with the interior. It opens to the public at eight-thirty. Just buy tickets, hire a guide, go inside, get to know the corridors and chambers. Normally, tourists aren't allowed in the subterranean corridors, but if you slip your guide enough *bakshish* I'm sure he'll arrange it. Maybe you can see what our man was up to last night. Might be worthwhile."

"Good suggestion. We'll do it."

I call the desk, make a reservation for Vadney. We're in luck, Suite 315 is vacant, just down the hall, with a balcony and a gee-whiz view. Ordinarily, he'd insist on the cheapest room in the joint (looks good on the expense report, sets a good example), but there are none available. Also, if Doris just happens to be with him, there's no way she'll chirp in a cage without a view. I can just hear her now: "Walt, what a *dump,* you cheap *wimp!*" Good old Doris, love her style, class act all the way, she don't take no shit from nobody. What we'll do, if she's really with him, we'll tell 'em the hotel's booked solid, no other rooms, they'll just have to share the suite. Make 'em feel good, make 'em feel like innocent bystanders in the whole deal, know what I mean? Jeez, I'm sorry, Doris, place is booked, Chief'll just have to sleep in the living room. Right? I mean, what can a mother do? Caught in the jaws of chance. Chance to dance. Hope his skivvies are clean.

Life of a cop's not all work, of course, Nuz and I sit down to a leisurely breakfast on the balcony about 7:25. I'm no artist, but see if you can picture this exotic-type panorama: Big red-orange sun's still rising behind the massive pyramids, casting long shadows across an endless white sea of desert mist. Mist starts rising now, swirling like foam in slow motion, dreamlike, gradually revealing all these tiny pyramids near the three big ones, where, Nuz says, the many wives of those Pharoahs are buried. Plus there's this huge graveyard to the right of the Great Pyramid, couldn't see it last night, rows and rows of little stone houses (mastabas, Nuz says), where all the great nobles and princes of the blood are buried. In the shadow of Cheops, as it were. So many stone houses, place looks like a miniature city. Nuz says it *is* a city. Says, "John, listen to me, the whole pyramids area is a city." Says, "The ancient Egyptians named it the City of the Dead." Says it low and eerie. Says, "What better place for Death to be, wandering the corridors of the Great Pyramid, searching for Cheops himself, under the cold mantle of darkness?" Now he gives with this Boris Karloff laugh, stuffing his puss with pancakes. Weird Arab. Puts me off my breakfast. Good excuse. But what I'm trying to get across, this whole sunrise at the pyramids deal here is positively breathtaking. No other word for it. Me, I'm feeling happy, I light up a cigar, sit back, let it all wash over me. Not bad for a kid from the Lower East Side, right? Thought occurs to me, maybe I'm not too old for his job after all, know what I mean?

After breakfast, Nuz and I each take a much-needed shower, but don't shave, of course, we want to impress Vadney with as much scrag as possible. Glance at myself in the bathroom mirror, two days' stubble, I'm getting there, I'm starting to look like a Bowery bum, but at least I smell good. Hard to believe, just last Wednesday I looked like Liz Taylor, time sure flies when you're having fun. Haven't worn my *tarboosh* in a while, I try it on now, can't help smiling. Look like a down-and-out past president of the Elks.

Walk over to the Great Pyramid about 8:30, it's just opened to the public, but this is a total madhouse scene here. No tourists in sight, but here's this mob of Arab hawkers coming at us, walking at first, then running when they get a load of me and realize I'm an ugly American in sheik's clothing. I'm telling you, we're overwhelmed by these hustlers, they surround us, they all speak English, they're yelling, they're trying to get us to ride camels, donkeys, horses, they all want to be our guide, our guard, our watchman, they're five deep around us, they're screaming now, they're pushing, they're pulling us toward these ruined little temples along the roadside, they're promising everything from undiscovered mummies to gross Pharaonic porn. Nuz, he's in his element here, he's cussing 'em out in Arabic, he tells me to keep walking toward the ticket kiosk and keep my hands in my pockets firmly gripping my wallet and shield. Buys two tickets fast, shoulders his way toward the entrance, army of conmen still hanging tough, finally he turns and shouts, *"Askari! Askari!"* Magic words, mob starts to split. Last minute before we go in, Nuz motions to this ancient white-haired man who's standing by the entrance with a long aluminum flashlight. Old guy comes over, very dark skin, white mustache, clean white towel around his neck. Nuz says only one word, softly, politely: *"Turguman."* Means guide. Man nods with great dignity, ushers us inside.

Soon as we step through the stone archway and give the lone kid there our tickets, it seems suddenly very quiet. Dark and quiet. Takes a while for my eyes to adjust.

"Welcome, gentlemen," guide says. "Have you been here before?"

"I have," Nuz tells him. "But we need your wisdom."

"I understand." Guide looks at me. "There is nothing to fear, sir. Have you ever suffered from claustrophobia?"

"No, sir."

"That is good," he says. "Some of the corridors are low and narrow. You may experience some difficulty in breathing due to inadequate oxygen. We will therefore proceed slowly. We will use our energy wisely by climbing directly to the King's Chamber first. That is the steepest and most difficult." He turns on his big flashlight, plays the beam on the stone floor. "If you will be so kind, gentlemen, follow me closely."

We do just that, me right behind him, Nuz bringing up the rear. Low, narrow corridor from the entrance heads downward first, guide says it's approximately 110 feet in length. First thing I notice, there are some widely spaced horizontal fixtures with fluorescent lights along the walls, every twenty feet or so, relatively dim but helpful. In his book, Farah mentioned that electricity wasn't allowed in the areas he wanted to explore, the subterranean corridors, and I see what he meant when we reach the "end" of this first corridor, which is descending. What happens, we come to a connecting tunnel called the Ascending Corridor, reached by a staircase, but the Descending Corridor continues, unlighted, and off limits to tourists.

Climb the staircase into the Ascending Corridor, this thing's really claustrophobic, guide says it's five feet high, three feet wide, so we're crouched now, it's quite steep, we're grunting, it continues for 125 feet. Fluorescent lights aren't much good in here and the air is musty. Nobody ahead of us, guide says we're the first visitors of the day. Nice to know. Hate to have some tourist go bananas in a tunnel like this and try to get out in a hurry.

End of this thing, we come to the start of three other corridors: (1) extremely narrow shaft leading downward at a sharp angle, the second of the two subterranean corridors that interested Farah, this one joins the first deep underground just before it reaches the decoy chamber; (2) narrow horizontal corridor that leads to the so-called Queen's Chamber; (3) surprisingly high and wide ascending corridor called the Great Gallery, guide says it's twenty-eight feet high, seven feet wide, 154 feet long.

We enter this one and it's a relief to straighten up for a change. Great Gallery is lighted well enough so you can see the limestone blocks clearly. Guide pauses, plays his flashlight beam on the walls and ceiling. "Gentlemen," he says, "if you will be so kind to take notice, this is indeed a marvel of precision. It has been said of old, and I believe it to be true, that not a needle nor a hair can be inserted between the joints of these stones." Nice pitch, says it with just the trace of a British accent; like the old guy's routine. Okay, we climb up this Great Gallery, make use of the steel handrails along the sides. Now he points out an air shaft, one of only two in the

entire pyramid (the other's in the King's Chamber), located
in the ceiling up toward the end. Says it extends up at a steep
angle all the way out to the upper west side of the pyramid.
Opening at this end looks almost wide enough for a real skinny
guy to crawl through, but I can't see any daylight through it.
Finally we're at the top of the Great Gallery, we walk along
the twenty-five-foot horizontal passage that leads directly to
the King's Chamber.

This is it, we step inside, big room, everything has a pale red
glow, and there's a peculiar odor in here, reminds me of
rotting leaves. Guide plays his flashlight on the precision masonry, says the tomb is thirty-four feet long, seventeen feet
wide, nineteen feet high. Constructed entirely of pink Aswan
granite. Only one object in here: Deep-red granite sarcophagus, highly polished, no lid, no inscription. Top left-hand
corner is broken off, looks like some ancient tourist took home
a big jagged chunk. Despite the strange smell, air in here
seems better. Guide says that's because of the air shaft; this
one's located in the east wall near the floor and extends up at
a sharp angle out to the upper east side of the pyramid. Opening looks about the same size as the one in the Great Gallery.
Now the guide asks us to look up, says there are five Relieving
Chambers stacked vertically above this room, designed to
distribute the full weight of the upper part of the pyramid
away from the King's Chamber. Nice to know. Me, I go over
and inspect the sarcophagus again. Wish we had a camera, like
to strike a casual pose leaning against this thing, show the
folks back home, know what I mean? Cheops's *tomb,* John?
Yeah, sure. Deep in the bowels of the Great Pyramid over
there in ancient Egypt? Oh, yeah. Comes with the territory.

Well, as they say, everything's downhill from here. Walk
back down through the Great Gallery to the three-corridor
junction, now we bend our backs to enter the most cramped
of all corridors in the pyramid, the long one leading to the
misnamed Queen's Chamber. We're on our haunches, we're

walking like ducks in here, it's only four feet high, three feet wide, a grueling 127 feet long, but at least it's horizontal all the way. Wonder how many closet claustrophobics hit the panic button in the middle of this torture tunnel? Wonder how many mild-mannered moms from Memphis got hit with a sudden case of delirious diarrhea while waddling through this airless tube? Horrible thought. Horrible. Odor in here gives clues on such stats. Takes us three agonizing minutes to reach the Queen's Chamber, which wasn't the Queen's chamber. Relatively small room, nineteen feet long, seventeen feet wide, with a nineteen-foot-high pointed roof, all fine limestone. Nothing inside. Zero. Squat, if you'll forgive the imagery. Which is exactly what we have to do again to quack out of this place. Thought occurs to me halfway through, sweating, coughing, stumbling on my *galabiyya,* finally reduced to gagging with the odor, if old Cheops was a malicious sadist playing flat-out hardball, he'd pick a spot off this corridor for his hidden chamber. No egghead ever born could possibly work in here without tossing his cookies every hour on the hour.

Okay, we're finally outside the perfume promenade, sucking in deep breaths of musty air, all that's left on the tour are the two off-limits subterranean corridors, beginning with the one just outside. At this point, Nuz speaks quietly to our guide, who makes negative grunts deep in his throat at such blatant lawbreaking, but finally nods with great dignity. No *bakshish* changes hands at this time, of course, too undignified.

Down we go, holding the handrail, this shaft is real steep at first, but not as cramped as the odor-eater above. No electric lights in here, we're depending entirely on the flashlight now, and one fact is obvious, this passage was cut through the limestone blocks after they were in place; floor, walls, ceiling are quite rough. Even so, I'm beginning to look carefully for any sign of recent chips or scratches that might've been made last night by steel cables or equipment. Corridor seems to meander slightly once it goes underground, now it's cut through the natural bedrock of the plateau. Surprisingly, the air isn't all that bad down here, compared to what we've experienced in the pyramid proper, but maybe our lungs are adjusting to it.

Guide is tight-lipped all the way down until we're at the point where this passage joins the first Descending Corridor just outside the Subterranean Chamber, the "decoy" chamber as Farah called it. Now the old guy tells us we're exactly 100 feet below the surface of the bedrock. Leads us into the chamber, biggest one in the joint, says it's twenty-seven feet wide, forty-seven feet long, with a flat nineteen-foot-high ceiling. Damp and slippery in here. I ask the guide to move the flashlight beam slowly around the floor, walls, and ceiling. He does. Big circle of white light covers every inch. No chips, no scrapes, no errors.

Same story as we walk the entire length of the corridor, all the way up to ground level, where the fluorescent lights begin, and out to the entrance, a distance of 361 feet. Not the slightest evidence that anybody dragged, rolled, or carried cables through here last night. But he did.

And he'll be back tonight.

15

DUKE AND DORIS arrive almost on schedule, 4:39 P.M.,
but it takes another forty-three minutes to wade through Immigrations, because they both need visas. Naturally, they
breeze through Customs, they only have carry-on luggage, so
we meet them outside the crowded international arrivals area
at 5:25, not too bad. Must say, compared to the traditional
Arab garb worn by the overwhelming majority of passengers
coming through those big double doors, Doris is outrageously
chic, straight out of *Vogue,* shortish windblown blond coif
crowning the latest getaway getup going, new spirit, young
style: Gold kiss-curl earring, long-sleeved buttonless tie-wrap
white cotton shirt, medium-length pale-yellow cotton mac
with brown rayon half-collar, black velour Capri pants, gold
leather mules, matching handbag unmistakably Courrèges.
Duke towers over her, swipes back a cowlick, manages a fast
left-sided molar shower when he spots us, he's trendy-tony as
Stallone in an unzipped navy-blue windbreaker with the
Members Only label, tight white turtleneck tucked into tight

Levi's pulled over spit-polished boots, and he carries his at-taché with the first-class Egypt Air tag and the distinctive Gucci stripes; Doris should've told him there's half a necktie hanging out of it. As he clomps over to us and sticks out his mitt, it's obvious he's enjoyed more than his share of liquid refreshment. I mean, I make that observation with complete objectivity, I'm a trained observer, know what I mean?

Keeps his voice low: "Rawlings, Idrissi, nice to see ya, almost didn't recognize ya."

"Welcome, Chief," I say. "How was the—"

"Doris decided to come along at the last minute, take care of all the paperwork, y'know?"

"Happy to have her," Nuz says. "Doris, you look ravishing."

"Oh, thank you, my hair's a mess!"

"Lots of paperwork," Chief says.

"Welcome to Egypt," I tell her.

"Thank you, Little John. You look like real Egyptians in those hats and gowns, but you both need a shave."

"How was the flight?" Nuz asks.

"We haven't landed yet!" she says.

"Doris," Chief says.

"Know what?" she asks. "Actually, truth is, why I'm—paperwork? You say paperwork? Truth is, why I'm here, I mean, I'm here to *record* this collar. On *film,* I mean. Twelve *rolls* of it!"

"Doris," Chief says.

She pats her handbag. "Brought along my new automatic Nikon. Christmas present from Will, he let me open it early, y'know? I mean, it's fully automatic. Does everything."

"Foolproof camera," Chief concedes.

"Foolproof?" Doris gives me a wink. "*Fool*proof, huh? Little John, get a load of this, you won't believe this."

"Doris," Chief says, "we gotta get rollin' here."

She ignores him. "He didn't even know how to *load* it! Little John, we bought twelve rolls of film at the airport and this Rambo Bambo here couldn't even figure out how to *load* it!"

"Rawlings," Chief says, "where's your Egyptian cop?"

"Outside in the car."

"Let's roll."

Off we strut, NYPD's finest, appointment with destiny in ancient Egypt. Chief takes one fast glance at Abu's beat-to-shit old VW Bug, his jaw drops, his ears move, his bloodshot sky-blues dart to me with an unforgiving expression. Tell you what, after flying first class for twelve hours and all, I think he psyched himself into a first-class reception, a limo from the American embassy or something, maybe with a motorcycle escort, I don't know. We make the best of it, Doris has to sit on his lap, of course, no other choice, but she's got the giggles now, she's feeling no pain, she thinks this Bug's the cutest little car she's ever seen. We putter off at 5:35, it's already very dark, Shari Ramses's jammed, horn-honkers doing their stuff. Chilly night air seems to snap Vadney back to reality in no time flat. Starts asking sharp questions, Nuz and I brief him, bring him strictly to date, tell him it's odds-on that our suspect is already back at the pyramid, ready to work a thirteen-hour night.

"All right, now listen up," he says. "I got the fugitive warrant, the 'John Doe' fugitive warrant, it's all signed and legal. I'll be candid with you guys, I don't want to waste any more time on this fucker. I want his ass and I want it tonight. We know where he's at, we know what he's doin', we got a fugitive warrant, I want to go in there and take him tonight. Collar him or drop him, makes no difference to me. Now, Abu, tell me about these cops he's got outside the pyramid, they armed?"

"Yes, sir."

"They understand what a fugitive warrant is?"

"They should, sir. If they don't, I'll explain it to them in no uncertain terms. May I make a suggestion, sir?"

"Sure thing."

"I think it would be unwise for us to claim that we have the complete cooperation of Chief Kez, sir."

"Chief Kez? Why the hell not?"

Abu hesitates, chooses his words with care. "As you know, we have reason to believe that many government officials may be involved."

Chief shifts Doris on his lap, sits forward. "Now, wait a minute, Abu, let me get this straight. You sayin' Chief *Kez* might be on the take in this thing?"

"I don't know, sir. I honestly don't know."

"But you think there's a strong possibility?"

"Chief Vadney, sir, I know the workings of the Central Security Force. I know what's happened in the past. Unfortunately, police officials here are very badly paid."

"Enough said. Your branch is called the Tourist Police?"

"Yes, sir."

"And you're assigned to the Pyramids Station?"

"That's correct."

"How many officers to a shift there?"

"Normally twelve."

"Hate to ask, Abu, but can they be trusted?"

"The Tourist Police are considered an elite corps, sir. Each one is a university graduate who speaks at least two foreign languages fluently."

"Yeah, but can they be *trusted?*"

"I would trust almost any one of them with my own life, sir."

"How many of 'em could you muster to go in that pyramid with us tonight?"

"It's difficult to say. They would have to be placed on special assignment and replaced by others."

"Yeah, huh? All right, okay, Abu, you're armed yourself, right?"

"Yes, sir."

"What're you carrying?"

"Our standard-issue Colt forty-five automatic."

"And you're assigned to us full time, right?"

"Yes, sir."

Chief shrugs. "Then I don't see any problem. That's all the firepower we need for one psycho. Rawlings, Idrissi, you guys got any problem with that?"

"No, sir."

"No, sir."

"Done. Settled. Piece a cake. The four of us go in tonight. Sooner the better. We'll nail down our game plan at the hotel. Collar him or drop him, makes no difference to me. I gotta get home for Christmas."

Nice to know everything's in the bag, no problem, Walter Fosdick Molars cracks another biggie nut case, just hope Doris has enough film to satisfy the worldwide media demand. Chief sits back now, closes his eyes, takes a little snooze. Wonder why I feel so unnecessary when this guy's around?

Black silhouettes of the pyramids dominate the night sky when we arrive at Mena House, 6:05, and a thought suddenly occurs to me that makes me angry at my own stupidity; Nuz and Abu should've picked up on it too. We're all so busy rushing around, grabbing a few hours of sleep when we can squeeze it in, we're not sharp, we're not thinking logically, we're overlooking obvious facts: At 7:30 tonight, the *Son et Lumière* show starts again, it's held every night. How the hell could we forget that? Sphinx and pyramids will be lighted, hundreds of tourists will attend, as usual, whole area will be transformed into a gigantic stage. Precludes any work by our suspect until it's over, he wouldn't park that big generator truck in front of the entrance to the Great Pyramid, it's an unnecessary risk. Show lasts an hour, then it'll take another half hour or so for the crowd to clear out. My guess, this guy won't risk driving up to that pyramid until at least nine o'-clock. Cuts down on his work time every night, gives him about ten hours instead of thirteen, but it's unavoidable. Maybe that explains why he drove straight to the pyramid from the airport last night. Gave him a good leg up on the job, six hours, didn't have to wait almost a full day to get going.

Abu hasn't checked with his surveillance relief man since Nuz and I checked out of the Ramses Hilton at 3:45 this afternoon, on our way to the airport. At that time there was no movement by our suspect, he was probably still asleep. Surveillance schedule calls for the cop to call Abu at our suite, 6:15, give him an update.

We're parked in front of Mena House now, doorman's getting our luggage out of the front trunk of the VW, we're telling Vadney how we had to transfer from the Ramses Hilton, I mention nonchalantly about how Suite 315 happens to be the only vacancy they got left, so we reserved it for them, they'll have to double up. Duke and Doris exchange a quick glance, shrug, seem to take it all in stride, they'll manage somehow. Chief registers for both of them, "Walter F. Vadney & party," covers a multitude of possibilities. Get in the elevator, he's in an unusually good mood now, kids Doris about how she'll have to buy a Cleopatra outfit to go undercover with us. Doris gives him a look, says there's no way she's going to crawl around in that pyramid with us. Says there's an nine-hole golf course at this hotel, she spoke with the bell captain already, there's a pro shop, the works. She's going straight to bed, says she needs at least twelve hours' sleep to counteract the jetlag. Says she'll be up at six, have breakfast in bed, a leisurely bath, hop down to the pro shop, buy the best outfit they got, best shoes, rent the best clubs, tee off in the warm Egyptian sunshine. Chief says, "Doris, wait a minute, who the hell's gonna take the *pictures?*" She lifts an eyebrow, she says, "Walter, I'll be in the bar about noon." Says, "Have me paged." Spunky little lady, Doris. I'm telling you, this kid don't take no shit from nobody.

Step off the elevator, follow the bellhop to Suite 315, we all go in, looks like a replica of ours, except it's not on a corner. First things first, I step out on the balcony, take a quick look just to make sure. Wait for my eyes to adjust, blink, squint. What's that down there? Squint harder. No. No, I can't believe this. There it is, tiny white generator truck backed up to the entrance. Something's wrong somewhere. Why would he take that kind of risk? Now, gradually, as I look around, as I get my bearings, I understand why. Entrance to the Great Pyramid faces due north. Far beyond to my left, facing due east, is the bold silhouette of the Sphinx; I remember his words from last night: "With each new dawn I see the sun-god rise on the far bank of the Nile. His first ray is for my face, which is turned towards him." I also remember that the audience faces the Sphinx, so the audience faces due west. Therefore, only the east and south sides of the Great Pyramid are visible to the audience. The north and west sides cannot possibly be seen. My guess, they're probably not even lighted for the show. So the entrance will be in darkness throughout the night.

Go back in the living room, tell the others the truck's there, don't mention I had any doubts about it, don't want to plant any seeds that I'm dumb or disoriented, although I suspect Nuz never thought of the show either. Bellhop's got our luggage on his cart, so the three of us follow him down the hall to Suite 300, leave the Duke and Doris alone for a while, give 'em some privacy, maybe he wants to tuck her in or something, what do we know? Before it's time to tip the bellhop, I grab the binoculars, disappear out on our balcony, let Nuz do the honors. After a minute or so I finally pick up on the two kid cops in moonlight, they're sitting on a limestone block near the entrance, different spot than last night.

Almost on the dot of 6:15, Abu gets his call from the surveillance man. He's calling from a pay phone just up the road, outside the Tourist Information Office. Abu takes notes, relays the information to us. Suspect left the dorm at 5:03, wearing a black T-shirt, jeans, and sneakers. Stopped in the cafeteria for dinner, finished there at 5:23. Went directly to his truck in the lot, drove straight to the Great Pyramid, arrived 5:44, backed up to the entrance. Suspect got out of the truck, talked with two uniformed police officers, who accompanied him into the rear of the truck. At 5:46, the officers rolled two wooden spools of steel cable from the truck into the pyramid; both cables were connected to the interior of the truck. Suspect followed the officers in, carrying one piece of equipment that appeared to be heavy. All three men entered the pyramid at 5:47; the two officers came out at 6:09 and are now sitting near the truck, apparently guarding it.

Most interesting part to me, those kid cops were inside the pyramid for exactly twenty-six minutes. Of that total, let's say they were actually rolling the spools of cable for twenty minutes, which is on the conservative side, in my opinion. Now, if they rolled those things down the entire length of the descending corridor from the entrance, even all the way to the end of the subterranean decoy chamber, it wouldn't have taken them anywhere near that long, because the whole thing is only 361 feet in total length. That leaves two alternatives: (1) the first corridor down to the stairway leading to the Ascending Corridor, which they would follow for 125 feet until they reached the three-corridor junction; (2) the first corridor almost all the way to the decoy chamber, then up into the second subterranean corridor that ascends at a sharp angle and meanders up through bedrock to the three-corridor junction. I rule out the second alternative, at least the route, starting at the bottom, because the ascent would be too hard; they could enter it from the top much more easily. So that leaves the first alternative, which, in effect, takes them to the three-corridor junction. Which corridor would they take from there? Grand Gallery? Somehow I doubt it. Tell you why. Of all the corridors in the pyramid, that would be the easiest to explore, to light, to work in. No, old Cheops would never hide his burial chamber off the corridor with the most creature comforts in the joint. In my judgment, the two most difficult passages to work would be the corridor leading to the so-called Queen's Chamber, and the second subterranean corridor. From the three-corridor junction, you could roll the spools of cable into either of those passages with relative ease within the twenty-minute time frame. So it's got to be one of those.

Which one? Although the top 20 percent of that meandering tunnel is aboveground, cut through layers of limestone blocks that were already in place, all the rest of it is belowground, cut through the natural bedrock. Obviously, that would make the entrance to a hidden chamber very difficult to camouflage. Think about it. How are you going to seal up the chamber with blocks or chunks of natural bedrock and make it look like the rock is still in one piece? We could probably do a convincing job of it today, with the sophisticated materials and techniques at our disposal, but back then, no way. No, it would've been virtually impossible. On the other hand, that long and extremely narrow corridor leading to the misnamed Queen's Chamber is lined with hundreds of limestone blocks, all identical in appearance, all weighing two-and-one-half tons, the same average weight of all other blocks, and all the joints are masterpieces of precision masonry: "Not a needle nor a hair can be inserted between the joints of these stones," as our old guide said in the Great Gallery. Same is true of every block I saw. Now, that's camouflage perfection. Hidden chamber entrance could be in the ceiling or floor as easily as in the walls, every block is exactly the same. Plus it's the most cramped corridor in the entire pyramid, four feet high, three feet wide, and a torrid, almost suffocating 127 feet long. True, Ismat Farah believed the hidden chamber to be off one of the subterranean corridors, that was a key premise in his book, but he never tested his theory. Maybe this guy knows something Farah didn't know.

Chief comes in our suite about 6:45, says Doris is in bed, we can get moving now. Looks like he's ready to go bear hunting with a buggy whip. We take him out on the balcony, there's plenty of moonlight, give him the binoculars, he gets a general orientation from Abu first, seems to get his bearings fairly quickly. I brief him on where I think the steel cables lead, the approximate distances and times involved, the degree of difficulty in getting through the two narrow passages leading to the three-corridor junction. Must say, Chief listens hard, only interrupts a few times, comes up with some good sharp questions. Says he wants a detailed diagram of the pyramid now, we'll draw up a step-by-step game plan. Also, he's hungry, thank God, he wants some hot black coffee and a couple hamburgersmedium-rare with ketchup, mustard, pickles, onions, plus some fries on the side, if they got 'em here, extra ketchup, and a nice tossed salad with creamy Italian.

We go inside, sit around the old mahogany coffee table near the stone fireplace. Nuz picks up the phone, rolls his eyes, clears his throat with just a trace of indignation, says he'll see what he can do. I get out some hotel stationery and a pencil, draw a diagram of the pyramid, including the five corridors and three chambers. Abu to the rescue, uses the eraser, revises almost all the dimensions. Turns out he's a much better artist than me, I tell him to go ahead. Draws arrows out to the margins, labels everything, makes it look almost professional. Now he gets a pen, uses a broken line to trace the probable route of the cables, the route we'll follow.

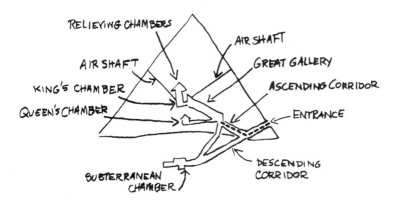

Chief studies it carefully, brows knitted. "Now, Abu, these first two corridors here, they gonna be dark, or what?"

"I think we can assume that, yes, sir."

"It's important," Chief snaps. "You sure?"

Abu runs his left hand through his thick but well-trimmed dark hair. "As I understand it, sir, the fluorescent lights in the pyramid proper are on a continuous circuit, controlled by a single master switch just inside the entrance. That switch is in a fusebox with a padlock to prevent access by tourists, kids, who might find it amusing to plunge the pyramid into darkness. So, since the entrance is dark now, as it was last night, I think we can safely assume that it's dark throughout."

"Then we'll need flashlights," Chief says.

"I'll get them from the station," Abu tells him. "If our man is working in the corridor leading to the Queen's Chamber, as John believes, it should be safe to use flashlights in the first corridor. But I would suggest to you that we really shouldn't risk flashlights in the Ascending Corridor."

Chief studies the diagram. "Yeah, I think you're right there. Little John, what kind of lights will this guy have in there?"

"I honestly don't know that, Chief. He wouldn't want to lug around heavy lighting equipment, he really wouldn't need it.

Wouldn't surprise me if the scanner and laser had built-in lights. Y'know, like they have on shoulder-mounted TV cameras?"

"So you think we can assume bright lights in that corridor?"

"That's my guess, Chief, but it's only a guess. Could be as simple as a high-powered flashlight or a six-volt lantern. Tell you something that intrigues me, though, could be important. According to—mind if I smoke?"

Gives me his cold fisheye stare, left profile.

"Windows are open," I tell him.

Takes a deep breath, crosses his legs.

"Nice cool evening breeze in here," Nuz adds quietly.

"Go ahead," Chief says. "Both of ya, it's your funeral. Just don't blow that fuckin' poison anywhere near me, huh?"

I push my armchair back, turn it toward the open balcony door, light up a Dutch Masters panetella, blow smoke toward the door, notice Nuz is doing likewise.

"That stuff can kill ya," Chief says.

I nod gravely.

"Rawlings, ya could *die* from suckin' in that shit, y'know that?"

"I rarely suck," I tell him. "But to get back to business here, as I was saying, according to Abu's relief surveillance man, who watched them unload tonight, he reported something that could be important. Says our suspect carried in one piece of heavy equipment. *One* piece of heavy equipment."

Chief nods. "So?"

I sit back, take a suck, blow it out, watch him through the thick, curling, delightfully aromatic carcinogen. "So, if he was using the scanner tonight, he'd need the computer too, they operate as a unit. Two separate but compatible pieces of high-tech equipment. Maybe three pieces, if the computer's screen is separate from the keyboard."

Chief unwraps a stick of Doublemint gum. "So?"

"He spent six hours in there last night, Chief. Obviously using the scanner and computer, first time out. Six hours. Long time—*if* he was concentrating on just that one corridor. Maybe, just maybe, he found what he was looking for."

Pops in the gum, chews, narrows his eyes.

"If so," I continue, flicking my ash, "all he'd need tonight is one piece of equipment. One piece of heavy high-tech equipment. The helium-neon gas laser drill. Plus a very substantial amount of energy from the generator truck."

Nods, chews rapidly now, eyes watering.

I turn to Abu. "How thick are those limestone blocks?"

"One-point-one-zero cubic meters, average. That's—let's see. About forty-three inches thick. In round numbers, three-and-a-half feet thick."

"Wider than the corridor," I tell him.

Abu smiles. "Exactly. And not wide enough for even a sarcophagus. For example, the one in the King's Chamber now is zero-point-nine-six meters wide, or about thirty-eight inches. Two inches too wide for the corridor. What this means in practical terms is simple. If Pharaoh Cheops actually selected that corridor for his hidden chamber, he would have had the sarcophagus placed there during the construction of the pyramid. Upon his death, the limestone blocks inside the corridor would then have to be maneuvered *inside* the chamber to admit his mummy and treasures. The blocks would then have to be maneuvered back into place, precisely, so that not the slightest difference could ever be seen. Also, of course, if this were in fact the case, there would be no formal entrance to the chamber. Therefore, there would be no need for a granite plug. In all probability, there would be only one wall of blocks between the corridor and the chamber itself. A wall three and a half feet thick."

Nuz starts stroking his mustache quickly. "Excuse me,

Abu. Excuse me, but do you realize what that means—if all of this is true? Jesus Christ. This guy could gain access to the chamber by merely drilling through *one* of the limestone blocks. *One.* Creating, in effect, a good-sized window. A window three and a half feet square. A window to climb through and take out virtually—"

"Means something else!" Chief snaps. "Rawlings, how long's he been in there so far tonight?"

"They entered at five-forty-seven. Kid cops came out at six-oh-nine." I glance at my watch. "It's now seven-fourteen. Means he's probably been on the job in there—say, at least a full hour by now."

Chief jumps up, chewing fast, grabs the binoculars, strides out on the balcony. We stand automatically, exchange glances as we follow him out. Generator truck's still there, of course, no movement that I can see. Vadney stands ramrod straight in the moonlight, we hear him breathing fast, chewing fast, he's having a hard time with the binoculars. Finally seems to have it all in sharp focus, scans around fast, then slow. Gradually, breathing slows, chewing slows.

"Nothin' doin' yet," he says. "Had me pumped up there for a minute. All right, listen up, you guys. We gotta get our asses in gear here, we gotta get in that fuckin' pyramid fast. Like the man says, drop your cocks and grab your socks, let's move it on out!"

No socks to grab, we drop our cocks, do a fast flip-flop on out at 7:17, jump in Abu's car, putter across to the station, where he picks up four traffic-control flashlights with long plastic Day-Glo hoods (no other choice), four long riot-control billy clubs with rawhide straps, three pairs of handcuffs (in case we get static from the two kid cops), and two extra clips of ammo for his Colt .45 automatic. On the one-minute drive up the plateau to the pyramid, Chief spits out his game plan in five steps: (1) Abu and Nuz identify themselves in Arabic to the two kid cops, show them the New York fugitive warrant, explain its authority if necessary, officially relieve them of duty, present them with *bakshish* of £E50 each (fresh from Vadney's pocket) as a friendly token of thanks for their cooperation with NYPD; (2) we enter the pyramid single file (Abu with .45 drawn, Chief, Nuz, me), use flashlights through the first corridor, follow the two steel cables; (3) at the stairway to the Ascending Corridor (if that's where the cables lead), flashlights are turned off, we follow Abu through the 125-foot passage as quietly as possible; (4) at the three-corridor junction, if the cables actually continue into the corridor leading to the Queen's Chamber, Abu and Vadney go in together (Nuz and I stand guard), identify themselves to the suspect, show him the fugitive warrant, arrest him, cuff him, read him his U.S. rights, lead him out; (5) transport suspect to Pyramids Station, incarcerate him, notify the appropriate police officials at headquarters in Cairo.

Sounds good to me. Soon as we pass the ticket kiosk, Abu pulls off the road, drives straight toward the entrance; generator truck looms white in his headlights against the dark mountain of rocks. Almost immediately, the two kid cops appear by the truck, wave us back with accustomed authority, all official looking in black berets, black uniforms, black gunbelts and holsters. Abu holds his ID cardholder with shield out the window before he stops opposite the truck. Kid cops see the ID, they knock off the waving, but when they sashay toward us, they're all arrogance, already yelling. That's as far as that goes. Instantly, Abu and Nuz are out of the car, shouting them down, waving the fugitive warrant. Don't know what they're shouting, it's all Arabic to me, but the message hits home, kid cops shut up, back up, arms spread in familiar body language: Hey, no problem, guys, why didn't you say so? Despite the macho mustaches, they look to be in their late teens.

Abu, he's got the psychology of authority down cold, now he's established who's in charge, he backs off just a tad, snaps questions in an almost civil tone. Chief and I climb out of the back seat, Abu tells them who we are in a voice like Peter introducing Jesus to camel stealers. Makes me blush. Chief knows his cue, rises up to his full six-three, reaches in the back pocket of his tight Levi's, eases out his new custom-made blond kidskin ID cardholder with the gold chief's shield, holds it out like a crucifix at an exorcism. Never saw this one before, kidskin's specially curved to fit the exact countour of his right cheek. Tough act to follow, I got just the standard ID cardholder with my shield, so I underplay the scene, flash it open and shut with disdain, humble street-Arab style, may your night be as black as your assholes, kids.

Abu turns to Vadney. "They freely relinquish authority to us, sir, but they deny any willful wrongdoing. They claim they were—I believe the English term is 'moonlighting,' sir."

"We won't press charges," Chief says.

"That's wise, sir."

"Abu, what're the Arab words for 'thank you'?"

"Kattar kherak."

"Come again?"

"Cat-tar care-rack."

Chief sticks his fingers in his right front pocket, pulls out two Egyptian fifty-pound notes, both new, from the currency exchange at the airport. Now he steps forward, eyes narrow to slits, left brow arches momentarily, then his forehead flattens a split second before both ears jerk back as an all-out left-sided molar shower takes twenty years off his face. Slaps a bill in his right palm, shakes the first kid's hand warmly.

"Kattar kherak!" kid says.

"Cat-tar care-rack, kid."

Same scene, take two, second kid. Now they glance at each other out of the corners of their eyes, they can't believe this dude's for real. They don't know what the hell to do at this point, so they bow humbly; Chief bows humbly. They take several steps back, bow humbly; Chief bows humbly. Off they go into the night, walking, then running, then sprinting. One small step for kid cops, one giant leap for American-Egyptian police relations. Chief looks pleased. Nothin' to it. Piece a cake.

Now, this next thing, seems unreal, I know, but it happens. Freezes my bowels every time I think of it. We're walking toward the entrance, flashlights turned on, billy clubs in hand, appointment with Death inside the Great Pyramid, suddenly this deep blue light appears in the sky, brightens slowly, and weird music starts to play. Chief, Nuz, and I stop dead in our tracks, look up fast. Whole huge jagged east edge of the pyramid is outlined in dazzling blue light, but our side remains in darkness. Sure, I know it's exactly seven-thirty and all, but somehow I just wasn't prepared for the eerie impact of this thing, spooks the piss out of me. Blue gets brighter, music gets softer, now we hear the booming voice of the narrator, sounds like Richard Burton sitting at the right hand of God: "You have come tonight to the most fabulous and celebrated place in the world. . . ."

"Holy jumpin' shit," Chief says. "Who the fuck's *that?*"

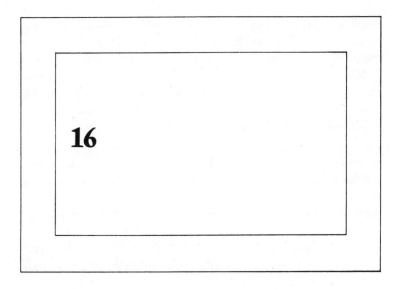

16

KNOW HOW IT FEELS to walk through long dark tunnels in an ancient tomb? Nightmarish. That's the only word for it, that's how it feels to me. Steel cables look like slithering snakes on the stone floor in the moving, overlapping, weird white circles of our flashlight beams. We're hunched over in this first corridor, almost forgot how low and narrow it is, I'm last in line, so I can't see much more than the cables and Nuz's big behind. Tunnel descends gradually for 110 feet, we struggle along in silence, all we can hear is the rhythmic scrape of Vadney's boots, the shuffle-scuffle of our sandals, and, increasingly, our own breathing, already becoming labored. Lack of oxygen? Sure, that's part of it, but this is the easy part, relatively speaking, we're going downhill. No, it's something else at this point, I can tell. I can tell by the sound, I've heard it often enough in my career. Rapid breathing like this, just starting out, I know the adrenaline's beginning to pump in each of us, fear of the unknown. I know I feel that, I'm certainly not ashamed to admit it, never have been. Cop who says he's never scared is a liar, a moron, or a fool. Me, I think I'm probably sharpest when I'm scared. Reflexes and radar seem to work better. So, anyhow, we're moving along slowly, breathing hard, I don't have a clue if any part of my time and distance theory about the cables is right or wrong until Abu finally breaks the silence and says, "Watch your step, men, stairway coming up." Says it softly, but his voice sounds like it's coming from the bottom of a well. Music to my ears, means I guessed right, cables continue up into the Ascending Corridor.

Abu stops now, keeps his voice low. "Six iron steps. Use the handrail on both sides. Cables are to your left. No talking from this point on. Flashlights out. Now."

All four flashlights click off. Total darkness. We hear Abu's sandals on the stairs. Six slow steps. Now Vadney's boots. I reach out, touch Nuz's back as he moves forward. He starts up. I feel for the handrails, find them, then stoop, feel for the cables to the left, find them. Wait for Nuz to reach the top, then start up slowly.

Surprise when I reach the top: Pinpoint of light at the end of the corridor, high in the darkness, like a distant star. I know it's coming from the three-corridor junction, 125 feet away, a steep climb, but I can't begin to tell you how reassuring it is to see that damn thing. We stand still for a while, feel around, try to get our bearings. This corridor's five feet high, I remember that, a little higher than the first, but it's the same width, three feet. I stoop, feel for the cable again, it's still on the left. There are handrails on both sides, so I hold the one to the right. Stuff the flashlight in the pocket of my *galabiyya,* grip the club in my left hand. Feel very vulnerable without a gun. You carry that thing around all your adult life, on and off the job, it's like part of you. You know it's in that little black holster on your belt, tucked into the small of your back, you know it's there, you can feel it, you know you have five friends if and when you need them, five friends you can depend on.

Now you reach back, nothing's there. Hard to adjust to that. Is that where my courage is? Could that be? Is that possible? Abu's sandals scuff softly. He's walking. Slowly. Now Vadney's boots. Nuz's sandals. I grip the club, start ahead, I'm crouched in a combat position, holding the iron handrail. Breathing, breathing, breathing. Four figures moving slowly in almost total darkness toward a pinpoint of light high in the blackness, a distant star.

And what will we find when we get there? That's what frightens me most, I admit it. What's really up there, out there, waiting? Whoever this guy is, whatever he's all about, he's totally different from anything I've ever faced before in my career. Nobody else comes even remotely close, and I've faced some very sick, grotesque, almost subhuman people. That's why I didn't like the code name for this man. You get to be my age, that word's not funny anymore. You see your friends pass away, people you knew from childhood sometimes, people you loved, people you shared a big chunk of your life with, and suddenly they're gone, and you can't believe it, it's just not possible. And you think, hell, they were too young, what's going on here? But you know what's going on. In the deepest part of you, you understand. You hate it, you won't accept it, you don't even want to think about it. But you recognize it. You know what's going on.

Rapid breathing now, all of us, slow steps, watching the pinpoint of light get slightly larger, brighter, lower as we ascend, approaching the distant star. At long last, Abu drops to his knees at the end of the corridor. Chief and Nuz do the same. I remain crouched, I can see Abu's face in silhouette now against the light, which isn't as bright as I thought it would be. Rapid breathing continues, all of us. Abu waits for his eyes to adjust, then looks around the corner to his left. Waits five seconds, then climbs out. Yellow light is coming from directly ahead, he's facing it, back to us, dark silhouette in a combat crouch. Can't see his arms, but I know from his posture he's holding the Colt .45 straight out, both hands. Remains frozen like that maybe five seconds, waits for his eyes to adjust, then removes his left hand, motions for us to come out. We do. Fast.

First thing I notice when I scramble out, the light's coming from the long horizontal corridor leading to the Queen's Chamber. Cables extend into it like silver snakes. We're standing upright at the point where the dark Great Gallery begins its ascent, we're sitting ducks in this light, we've got to take cover fast, there are two alternatives: Subterranean passage near the opening to the corridor or the Great Gallery. Abu's already decided, he's continuing up into the darkness of the Gallery, Chief on his heels, Nuz close behind. Me, I'm no hero, but for some reason I can't resist a quick look into the lighted corridor first. Opening's four feet high, three feet wide. I take a deep breath, crouch, look inside. Fine yellow dust hangs like smoke, but roughly sixty feet down the passage I can see large objects in the light. No sound, no movement, nothing. Dust makes my eyes water now. I blink, squint, try again. Objects appear to be large chunks of broken limestone. Now my eyes are adjusting more, I realize the light's not coming from the corridor itself, it's reflected out on the walls, floor, ceiling, and piles of limestone from an opening in the wall to the right. Obviously, he's done it, he's broken through to the hidden chamber. He's inside. Know my first reaction, squatting there, blinking in the dust, heart pounding, hands shaking? Admiration. Yeah. Yeah, that's right. Admiration. Only lasts a few seconds, but that's what I feel. I mean, I know he's a killer and all, totally weird, spooks the crap out of me, but I got to hand it to the son of a buck, whoever he is, he's actually done something all the eggheads couldn't do for almost five thousand years. He's found Cheops.

Shuffle up into the dark Gallery, can't wait to tell the others, I'm bursting, I feel like a kid. Whisper it, trying to catch my breath, blurt it all out in whispers, but I tell you what, I'm so excited now I'm shaking. Shaking all over, legs are shaking, hands are shaking, heart's going nineteen to the dozen, feel like laughing, feel like dancing, feel like jumping up and down. Yeah, I hear you, thought occurs to me too, maybe I'm not too old for this job after all.

"Little John," Chief whispers, "y'gotta calm down here, y'gotta get a grip on yourself, know what I mean?"

"Sorry, Chief, I just—"

"We're in a dangerous situation here, we gotta go in and collar this guy, we can't afford hysteria."

"I'm not hysterical."

"You're borderin' on it, buddy-boy. Got anything you can take for your nerves? Valium or somethin'?"

"Don't happen to have one on me."

"Well, try to stay calm. Take deep breaths, y'read me?"

I nod, take a deep breath, feel like laughing hysterically.

"Now, Abu," Chief whispers. "You okay, you all set to go in and collar this guy, wrap it up?"

"Yes, sir."

Chief glances at Nuz and me. "We follow the plan to the letter. Abu and I go in, take him, you guys wait outside, backup men. If we're not out of that chamber in three minutes, you know we're in trouble, we need help. All right, let's do it, let's take him, let's move it out."

Walk down softly, single file, Abu leads with the gun. Opening of the corridor seems to glow, pale yellow, fine dust floats through the shaft of light. We all glance in, check it out, judge the distance to the opening in the wall, just about sixty feet. Took Nuz and me three minutes to get all the way through this morning, 127 feet, so we figure roughly a minute and a half to reach the chamber. Abu cocks the .45, crouches, goes in easily. Chief hands Nuz his club and flashlight, gets down on his haunches, duck-waddles in with amazing grace for six-three. As they move ahead, their shadows stretch back huge and long on the walls and ceiling.

Most of the light is blocked now, Nuz and I squat down, I watch patterns of it move across his face and glasses. Know what he does at a time like this? Reaches in his *galabiyya,* takes out his little strand of white worry beads. Yeah. Starts massaging them in his right hand. Catches me looking at him, lifts an eyebrow indignantly like I caught him playing with himself or something. Religious people, these Arabs, they take all this stuff seriously, got to give them credit. Always wondered if they say a prayer on each bead like the Catholics do on their rosaries. Maybe not, can't see his lips moving, guess they just concentrate on worrying.

Silence is broken suddenly, Abu shouts a command, loud but muffled by Vadney's body, can't make out the words, can't see past Vadney. Their shadows are grotesque now, distorted, reaching almost all the way back to us. Abu shouts something else, I catch a fast glint of his outstretched gun as he moves into the chamber. Vadney follows him inside. They didn't have to climb over anything, they just maneuvered straight in, so there's no square window-like opening as Nuz suggested, must be more like a door. Shaft of light is back on us again, I look at my watch, 7:42, I'll give them exactly three minutes. Voices are muffled inside, I can just about distinguish between Vadney's and Abu's, the third voice is much lower, strange sounding, like he's talking through a mask of some kind, maybe an oxygen mask or a gas mask, which would make sense with the dust.

Muffled voices continue, Nuz and I just stare into the corridor, listen, watch galaxies of dust particles drift through the light like pale yellow smoke. At exactly 7:44, the unexpected happens.

Chief sticks his head out of the chamber, shouts: "Rawlings, Idrissi, listen up, do exactly like I tell ya. Drop your clubs and flashlights. Come down the corridor on your hands and knees. Enter the chamber on your knees with your hands up. Y'got that?"

"Got it," I shout. "What's happening?"

"He's got a *laser* on us! He can slice us both in half in a split second! Do like I tell ya! That's an order!"

"Does Abu still have the gun?" Nuz shouts.

"Of course not! Follow my orders, will ya?"

I go in first, get down on my hands and knees, start crawling. Instantly, seems like everything in my mind and body tells me not to do this. Know how that feels? Every nerve, muscle, impulse, instinct starts to scream: *Danger, danger, danger, stop, go back, right now, go back, get out!* Dust stings my eyes, I'm sweating, I'm shaking, I'm fighting for breath, my heart's pounding, my ears are ringing, I'm seeing sparks, I'm dizzy. I hesitate, then stop. When I start to turn, I see Nuz crawling behind me, frowning, shadows on his face. It's not too late, I can just tell him to go back, but suddenly I don't want to go back. I want to face this man, I want to know who he is, I want to know what this is all about. I wouldn't call it courage at this point. If I had to put it into words, I'd say it was just plain, dumb, stubborn curiosity. Yeah. I want to see this guy and I want to see what's in that chamber. Simple as that. Turn, start ahead again, crawling, coughing, shaking, sweating. Of course, I realize that self-preservation is supposed to be the most powerful human instinct, and my life's obviously in danger, and I don't even have a weapon to defend myself, so I must be out of my mind, right? Got to be. Temporary insanity. Triggered by a massive explosion of adrenaline pumping through my brain. If I had time to think this thing out logically, I wouldn't be here. Saturday night, December 21, I should be at Rockefeller Center with the wife and kid, looking at the Christmas tree, listening to the carols, seeing our breath in the frosty air, maybe chewing on a pretzel. Shit, I haven't even called home yet! Haven't had time! I mean, this is ridiculous! Here I am, a fifty-two-year-old man, exhausted, dirty, hungry, thirsty, unshaven, scared, shaking, sweating, coughing, crawling through a suffocating rathole tunnel in a filthy nightgown deep in the bowels of an ancient Egyptian tomb, crazed with an insatiable curiosity to meet Death. I mean, who *needs* this?

Crawling up to the chamber now, getting close, strong yellow light spills across the broken limestone rocks piled high ahead, blocking the rest of the corridor. Chamber opening is small and jagged, resembles the mouth of a cave, maybe three feet high, two feet wide. I stop crawling, try to catch my breath, look inside cautiously. Nobody in view, but the wall directly ahead is lined with statues, tall and stately, highly polished, sparkling in the light: Gold, marble, granite, painted wood; men, women, animals, birds, strange combinations, ancient gods maybe, all seem to be standing guard. Now I'm aware of a peculiar variety of odors from the room, strong, rich, like exotic perfume.

"Please come in, John," a voice says, distorted, obviously through a mask; not in the tone of a command, more like the invitation of an old friend. Tone really surprises me.

I take a deep breath, glance at Nuz approaching on my right, he looks almost as scared as me. I reach down, push the two cables to the left, go in on my knees, hands held up by my shoulders. Light seems bright in here, I have to squint at first. Chief and Abu are off to my left, kneeling; the man is over to my right, standing behind a gleaming red granite sarcophagus. He wears a black gas mask, modern design, light rubber facepiece with aviator-style lenses, outlet valve at the mouth connected to two small round cannisters at the sides. Directly in front of him, resting on the polished lid of the sarcophagus, pointed at me, is the business end of the helium-neon gas laser drill, connected to its console and tanks by two thick cables; looks like a space-age zapgun straight from a video arcade.

"Nuzhat Idrissi, please enter," the voice says calmly.

Nuz comes in on his knees, hands up, eyes darting from side to side behind glasses covered with a fine coat of dust.

"Now, all of you, please stand," the voice says, not warmly, but still not at all hostile. "Look around you at the most prized possessions of the greatest Pharaoh who ever lived. Breathe in the rare aromas—herbs, cedar oil, resin, myrrh—fragrances preserved in this once-airtight chamber, quite literally, since the dawn of history."

We stand up slowly as he speaks, glance around, pick up on the scents. Relatively big room, I'd say about twenty feet by twenty feet, maybe seven feet high, lighted by two high-intensity bulbs positioned on the shoulders of statues in the far corners. Sarcophagus occupies the center of the room, surrounded by circular rows of hundreds of art objects, countless pieces of gold jewelry inlaid with precious stones, a golden throne, dozens of statuettes, gold plates, goblets, vases, a scribe's palette, many stone tablets with hieroglyphics. Takes you back. Certainly like to get a closer look at some of this stuff. Right in front of me is a life-sized wooden statue of some Pharaoh, might be Cheops himself, carved and painted in exquisite detail. He's about five-feet-seven (I would've been a giant back then), wears the royal headdress, graceful white robe, and his skin's a ruddy brown. Thing that grabs your attention, his eyes look absolutely real, alive, watching me. Seem to be made of copper inlaid with quartz. When you face this guy head-on, his eyes glare straight into yours, burning with life, like he's either trying like hell to tell you something or he's determined to stare you down. Then—ready for this? —when you move even a fraction of an inch—*flick!*—his eyes follow you. Yeah! Me, I'm glancing around the room, taking it all in, every time I look back at this little sucker his eyes are right on me, glaring, burning, like he expects me to curtsy or something. Now I glance over at Vadney, he's standing there in his Members Only jacket, bug-eyed at all this crap, mouth open, looks exactly like he might be in the homestretch of an orgasm. Who was it said the great aphrodisiac is death? Smart man.

"Gentlemen," the distorted voice says, "tonight you are

standing in the presence of greatness, the most fabulous attempt ever made to confirm—indelibly—one's own existence. To say to countless millenniums: 'Behold my work, I have vanquished death, I have achieved immortality.' This is perhaps as close as mankind will ever come to the realization of that dream, to emerge victorious over the nemesis that has always been our most important common denominator."

Can't resist a sideward glance at the wooden Pharaoh. Still glaring at me, eyes burning with life. Spooky little guy.

"In any event," the voice continues, "tonight you are all honored. You are present at one of the greatest archaeological discoveries of all time. Your names are destined to be recorded for posterity as witnesses to this event—and unwilling participants in another historical event, one that may turn out to be far more significant."

"Wait a minute," Chief blurts out. "Are you *crazy?* We can't get all this stuff out of here! Most of it won't even fit through that hole!"

"Shut up, Vadney!" the voice snaps. "From this moment on, you will speak only when spoken to, you pompous fool. I could put an end to the pretentious posturing of your life in the blink of an eye if I wanted to, don't you realize that? Hasn't that penetrated? You represent virtually every conceit in the human animal for which I have an unaffected loathing: Vanity, arrogance, and monomaniacal egotism. In point of fact, that's precisely why you're here, why you were emotionally incapable of resisting the temptation, the opportunity I afforded you. In this room tonight, this ultimate vanity chamber, you are finally face-to-face for the first time with something commensurate with your propensity to say, 'I—I, I, I! Me! Look at me, listen to me, see how important I am!' You'll find out tonight. But to answer your question, no, I'm not crazy. I have no intention of stealing anything of any intrinsic value in this room. I'm not interested in monetary wealth. I am, however, interested in wealth of an entirely different nature: Knowledge. And there is knowledge hidden in this room. Knowledge of such colossal magnitude that it's almost beyond the imagining of man. Pharaoh Cheops, in his profound egomania and selfishness, took something to his grave that explains one of the primary riddles of this planet. Knowledge that could ignite cataclysmic changes in the fundamental philosophies of modern civilization. I intend to have that knowledge." He picks up the laser. "At any cost whatsoever. Guide yourselves accordingly. Abu Ben-Adam?"

"Yes?"

"Stand at the foot of the sarcophagus, left corner, the one nearest you."

Abu does as he's told.

"Nuzhat Idrissi, stand at the foot, right corner."

As Nuz walks over, he blows the dust off his glasses.

"Vadney, the head corner up here to my left. I want to watch you sweat at close range."

Chief's already sweating as he takes his place.

"John, to my right, please."

I walk up there slowly. Flat lid's about waist high on me.

He steps back, laser in hand. "Now, gentlemen, place your fingers under the lid. The overlap is exactly two inches on all sides, more than enough to ensure a firm grip. The lid is exactly two and one-half inches thick, solid Aswan granite, obviously very heavy. It won't be easy, but with four men it shouldn't be all that difficult. You will lift on the count of three, slide it down the side to my right, and prop it against that side. All right, get ready. One . . . two . . . three! *Lift!*"

We're straining, we're grunting, it's heavy as hell, sticks a little at first, now we got it off, we shuffle to the right, touch it against that top edge, then slide it down very slowly. Makes a horrible scraping sound, claws of King King screeching down a blackboard. Boom, hits the limestone floor. Propped solidly.

"Resume your positions," he says.

I get back up fast, can't wait to see what's inside. Strong, sweet aromas rise from a gleaming gold-plated wooden coffin inlaid with a variety of precious stones. All of us stand there in silence, staring at this beautiful thing. In the center, on a gold rectangle, are four relatively small hieroglyphic drawings cut into the gold and traced in red. From where I stand, the drawings are upside-down; seen from where Abu and Nuz stand, they read like this, left to right: (1) a circle with oblique lines drawn through it; (2) a bird with short wings standing in profile, facing the circle, which is smaller than the bird, making the circle appear to be a sunrise or sunset; (3) a short snake with its head elevated, facing the bird and sun; (4) an identical bird facing the same direction.

"This is the outermost coffin," he tells us. "There are two more inside this. The innermost coffin is solid gold and weighs about two hundred forty pounds by itself. However, the coffin lids are not sealed with any substance, at least none of the others were. They're simply fitted together with great precision. Therefore, they can each be lifted and removed. Reach down now, gentlemen, feel for the ridge in the approximate middle of the casket. When you've all located the ridge, lift the lid off, place it on the floor there to my left."

Tell you the honest truth, it's a weird feeling, reaching down in here, touching this thing, feeling for the ridge. Weird but exciting too. There's enough space between the sarcophagus and the coffin to run my right hand up and down; I find the ridge easily, so do the others. We glance up at each other, faces all sweating, nod, lift, grunt. Sticks a trifle, then comes off with surprising ease. Not all that heavy either. Could be my senses are playing tricks, but almost instantly I seem to pick up completely different aromas, all heavy and sweet, but definitely new. We shuffle to the left this time, bend, place it on the floor, top facing up, gold and jewels in shadow now.

Second coffin is also gold-plated and has the identical hieroglyphics, but this one is inlaid with at least twice as many precious stones. We work silently, feel for the ridge, glance at each other, nod, lift it off. Phew! More new aromas, these seem much stronger, sweeter, now I'm almost gagging as we carry the lid to the side, place it on the first one; it's smaller, so it doesn't fit over.

I come back quickly, take a gander. Solid-gold coffin, pale yellow, no inlaid stones, nothing but smooth gold and the now-familiar hieroglyphics cut into the middle and traced in red paint. One look, you know this thing is worth a fortune all by itself. We reach down, feel for the ridge, it's bigger than the others, allows a better grip. Lift it off, it's over a hundred pounds, of course, but not as difficult as I thought. Only one dominant aroma now, overpowers the rest, smells exactly like liniment. We have to go slow with this lid, shuffle over, place it carefully on top of the other two.

Come back, can't wait to see the mummy. Surprise! There's this gold mask over his head and chest, absolutely gorgeous, polished to a high luster. Definite resemblance to that famous golden mask of Tutankhamen, except the face is much older looking. Large eyes are dark, staring coldly from a distance of 4,630 years, lids are brown, corners extend all the way back to the temples; same deal with the brown eyebrows. Royal headdress is stunning, sacred cobra over the forehead, cowl sparkles with thick horizontal stripes of yellow and brown. Nose is aquiline, lips are full, brown goatee hangs straight from the tip of the chin like a braided ponytail. Almost identical likeness to the painted wooden statue except for the eyes. All the rest of the body is wrapped tightly in slender rolls of brown cloth.

"John," the distorted voice says from behind to my left. "The mask is joined in the middle, just behind the ears. Please remove the face."

I step over, get behind the head, reach down, feel for a ridge behind the ears. No ridge. Keep feeling with my fingertips. Can't find it. Now I apply light pressure upward from behind the ears—presto!—off comes the face and chest plate. I hand it carefully to Vadney, who's still bug-eyed at all this stuff. He places it on the floor.

"Gentlemen," the voice says, sounding almost excited for the first time, "I call your attention to the Pharaoh's hands, crossed over his chest in the traditional way. Note the convex shape of the hands? How they curve outward instead of laying flat, as if the fists are clenched? There's a good reason for that curve, that bulge. Cheops is holding a scroll in each hand. Small scrolls made of the finest papyrus of the Fourth Dynasty, the wealthiest and most powerful dynasty of all. He grips them tightly under his wrappings, as he has done for nearly five millenniums, clutching them to his sacred being, guarding their secrets with all the mystical sorcery of his great genius. For written on those two small papyrus scrolls are hieroglyphics revealing not only the riddle of how his Great Pyramid was actually built, but knowledge infinitely more significant than the secrets of all the pyramids ever built on the face of this earth. Vadney?"

"Yeah?"

"Don't turn around. Just listen."

"I'm listening."

Click! Familiar sound to me, to all cops, almost unmistakable. From the corner of my left eye, I see the gleam of a switchblade being held out shoulder-high between Vadney and me.

"Vadney!" voice says. "Hold up your right hand, palm turned to me."

Chief does. *Slap!* Handle hits his palm like a scalpel.

"Cut his hands out!" voice orders.

"Cut his—? Oh, shit, no!"

"Do it! Now! Move!"

"How'm I gonna cut through the *bone?*"

"Cut his hands *out,* not *off,* you idiot! Cut through the linen wrappings until both hands and scrolls are exposed! Obvi-

ously, you can't do it from there! Get inside and straddle his
torso!"

"Get in—? Oh, shit, *no!*"

"Do it! Get in there! Move it!"

Chief glances at me, rolls his eyes, sweat dripping from his
nose and chin now. Walks to the near side of the sarcophagus,
shrugs, hooks his left leg over the edge.

"Hold it!" voice commands. "Take those filthy *boots* off,
you moron! That mummy is a Pharaoh, a priceless artifact!"

Chief hauls his leg out, glares at the guy with seething
hatred, big cowlick over his wet forehead. Slams the switchblade on the edge of the sarcophagus, leans back against the
side, crosses his right boot over his knee, bends over, starts
pulling. He's sweating, he's grunting, he's yanking with all his
strength. Can't do it. Can't get it off.

"I need help here," he says, out of breath.

Abu walks over without a word, turns around, straddles the
right boot, starts pulling from the heel. Chief sits down, places
his left boot on the kid's ass, pushes, Abu pulls. Pop! Phew!
Now the left one. Pull, push, pop, phew!

"Now," gas mask says, "before you lower your fat, clumsy
carcass in there, you'd better be aware of a few facts. Facts
about mummification that could save us time and trouble. The
brain and entrails have been removed, their cavaties filled with
natron and a variety of spices. Do you know what natron is?"

Chief stands. "A chemical?"

"Natron is a mineral," voice says, "hydrated sodium car-
bonate. Its function during mummification is to *dehydrate*.
Keep that in mind. Next, the entire body was immersed in a
natron bath for exactly seventy days. Then, thoroughly dehydrated, it was washed in Nile water and finally wrapped in fine
linen bandages soaked in perfumes and oils. Because of the
severe dehydration of the body, there is a pronounced rigidity
of all muscle tissue, extreme rigor mortis of all muscle tissue,
including the hands and fingers. Therefore, it will take effort

to pry the fingers away from the scrolls. In addition, avoid any unnecessary pressure on the mummy's thigh areas. Try to remember that. Do not sit on his thighs, as it could cause the torso to jackknife. Do you understand?"

"Yeah."

"Lower yourself in gently!"

Chief hooks his left leg over the side, I see he's wearing white wool socks. Little hole in the big toe, but, in fairness, he did leave home in a hurry. Now he uses his strong right arm to hoist his hulk up, reaches his left hand over fast, grabs the opposite side, pulls his right leg up, tucks both knees under him. He's suspended like that for a few seconds, handstand above the mummy, looking for a place to land. Now he spreads his knees, keeps his legs tucked up as he lowers himself down slowly, slowly. He's in. He's straddling Cheops. Impressive gymnastics for a guy his size, didn't realize he was in such good shape. We're all pulling for him, of course, hoping we don't hear the brittle snap, crackle, or pop of ancient royal ribs in there. He takes a swipe at the cowlick, grabs the switchblade angrily, leans forward, begins the operation.

Can't help feeling sorry for Cheops, know what I mean? Poor old guy went to all this trouble, took him and his men twenty-two long years to build this beautiful pyramid, he pulls all kinds of tricks in the process, four crazy corridors, three phony chambers, two subterranean passages, all like that, then he puts in this top-secret hidden chamber, real stroke of genius, sticks it where nobody'd ever dream of looking, he's been safe and sound in here with his secret scrolls for 4,630 years, thinks he's got it made in the shade. Now what happens? Computerized X-ray scanner screws him through the wall, so to speak. Burns my ass. If anybody ever told old Cheops that someday some foreigners would come up with a magic way to see through solid limestone walls, he would've pissed his royal robes laughing. I just know he would've. I mean, this guy obviously had a damn good sense of humor. Which brings up another question: If he didn't want anybody to ever see what's written on these secret scrolls, why didn't he just destroy them and be done with it? Gives you pause, right? Me, I would've burned them. I mean, why'd he go to all this trouble to preserve them if he was so dead-set against anybody finding them and learning his secret? Doesn't make any sense to me, unless maybe there's some weird religious deal going on here, what do I know? Which leads to still another question: If Cheops really did have an outstanding sense of humor, a great sense of the absurd, which I'm sure he did, maybe that's why he preserved the scrolls in the first place. Right? So he could have the most imaginative last laugh in history. So five millenniums later, when some dipshit egghead came along and finally found the hidden chamber and opened the sarcophagus and removed the three sacred coffins and the solid-gold mask and cut into his wrappings and opened the secret scrolls, he'd find them *blank*. Talk about black humor, how're you going to top *that?* Or, wait a minute, how about this: Cheops leaves a message telling the egghead: "Do not embalm me, I am not dead." Huh? Or maybe he'd leave the written solution to the most profound riddle of the ages, the true definition of *stress:* "That confusion created when one's mind overrides the body's basic desire to choke the living shit out of some asshole who desperately needs it."

I mean, the possibilities are endless here.

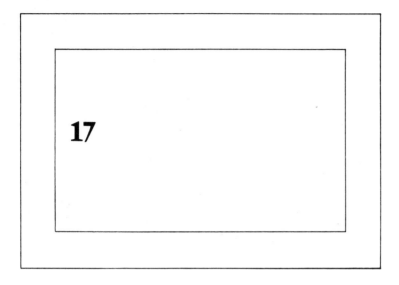

17

CHIEF'S DRIPPING SWEAT all over Cheops, working his chops off in there, linen wrappings turn out to be tough as burlap and seven layers thick. What he's doing at this point, he's thrown caution to the wind and decided to slice out a wide semicircle around each fist so he'll have two flaps to yank back, exposing the hands and scrolls. Takes him a good ten minutes to do it, then he sits back for a breather, swipes at his cowlick, looks at our friend in the gas mask. Might be my imagination, but for just an instant Vadney's eyes seem to look inward, giving rise to the possibility, however remote, that the dim outline of an idea may have bubbled up from the jungle of seaweeds in his unbalanced aquarium. Something like an amoeba breaking wind down there, but hope springs eternal in the heart of old cops like me. He's holding the long switch-blade in his right hand like a dagger, he's had to resort to brute force even with the obvious razor-sharp edges of that thing, and now he glances down at it, frowning; maybe the little bubble burst before it reached the surface, fragile thing that it was, what can I tell you?

Any event, now he places the switchblade on the edge of the sarcophagus, leans forward again, goes back to work. Yanks the flap back from Cheops's right fist. Now, I know this may be difficult to believe, but it's absolutely true, I saw it with my own eyes: Cheops's slender hand still has all the skin on it, blue-black mostly, patches of it yellow-brown, veins clearly visible, knucklebones showing under the skin. Chief takes one look, his throat makes a gasping sound, he snaps his hands back like he's touched something hot. Scroll is there, clutched in the fist, yellow papyrus wound neatly around a dark wooden cylinder with small knobs at either end.

"Take the scroll," the distorted voice says.

Chief looks at the bony hand with an expression like he's found a dead rat.

"Remove the scroll from his hand!"

"Yeah, right." Chief's nostrils twitch as he reaches down, picks up the fist gingerly, tries to pry the bony fingers away. "I think we got a problem. I think rigor mortis has set in here."

"Then cut the fingers off!"

"Cut the—? Aw, shit, I don't—wait a minute. Wait a minute, lemme try to get some leverage here." Grabs the bony wrist with his left hand, pulls it away from the body, uses all the strength in his right hand to pull the fingers away from the scroll. Ready for this? Old Cheops, he's got long fingernails. Very long. I mean, I'm talking like at least two inches, yellow, all curved in against the palm. Probably continued to grow for quite a while after he was wrapped up. Couple of tense minutes pass, they're hand-wrestling up a storm in there, mummy's long blue-black fingers keep snapping back, it's spooky to watch this, seems like the hand's still alive. Tough little guy, Cheops, two big hairy mitts against his slashing

yellow claws, but he's holding his own. Finally—*snatch!*—
Vadney's got the scroll, holds it away from the hand like he's
afraid of a desperation grab.

"Hand it to John," gas mask says. "He'll pass it to me."

When I step over and take the scroll, which is thicker than
I expected, I feel a tremendous temptation to open it just a
smidge, take a fast peek, but I don't. One reason, it might
crack or even crumble, for all I know; another reason, gas
mask here has made it a point to be almost friendly with me,
can't imagine why, and I don't want to push my luck. I turn,
hand him the scroll carefully; he takes it with his left hand,
keeps his right on the laser.

Chief's got the flap pulled back from the other fist now, he's
pumped with confidence, holds the skinny wrist in a vise-like
grip, yanks it away from the body, strains to pry the bony
fingers away from their final secrets. Long fingernails snap
back like fangs, lethal-looking things, you'd have to see this
shit in the eerie yellow light here, it's a diabolical duel. Snatch!
—*scratch!*—snatch! Chief's got it! Cheops winds up with a
fistful of air!

"Hand it to John."

I step forward, do the honors again.

Now, this next thing that happens, I'll be honest about it,
this still gives me horrible dreams. Horrible. Still wake up in
a cold sweat about this one, probably always will.

Okay, what happens, Chief's exhausted now, he's breathing
hard, he's sweating like a pig, he's undergone a grisly ordeal
here. So, of course, he sits back. Sits back hard. All 175 pounds
of him. Plop on the mummy's thighs. *SWOOSH!* Blur of
brown cloth, mummy's upper half springs bolt upright.
CONK! Skull slams into Chief's forehead like a speeding coco-
nut. *AHHHEEE!* Chief screams, sways back from the impact,
falls fast forward. *SPLAT!* Skulls and torsos collide on the
way into the coffin. *CRUNCH!* Chief crushes every rib in

Cheops's wrap. He's out cold. Whole catastrophe's over in five seconds flat. There they lie. Chief and Cheops. Strange bedfellows.

"Ho-lee shit!" Nuz says.

"Wow!" Abu says.

"Ouch!" I say.

"Poetic justice!" gas mask says. "Leave Vadney where he is, don't touch him. Follow my instructions. Abu Ben-Adam, pick up the knife by its blade, hold it out in plain sight, and bring it to me. Now. Move."

Abu moves it, hands him the switchblade carefully, returns to his place.

"Now, the three of you, listen to me. I want the lid placed back on the sarcophagus. To accomplish this, Idrissi will take his end, John will take his end, Ben-Adam will come around, position himself at the center, and lift from the bottom when the ends are first lifted. You will then slide it up over the top edge, balance it horizontally, then maneuver it back to its original position. All right, take—"

"No, sir," Nuz says. "I will not do this. The man will smother in there."

"Idrissi!" distorted voice snaps. "If you want to die instantly, I'll grant your wish. I had planned to spare all three of you. Refuse to cooperate and I'll burn a hole through your skull in a split second. It's your decision. Answer! Now!"

Nuz shrugs. "I have no choice."

"Gentlemen, take your positions. John, Idrissi, prepare to lift your ends from the bottom. Ben-Adam, go to the middle, get down, prepare to lift as soon as possible. On the count of three. Ready! One . . . two . . . three! *Lift!*"

Grunt and groan time again, three of us sweating through our dirty *galabiyyas,* my legs start to shake, I haven't had anything to eat, I feel weak, I feel sick, I feel old, but at least I know I'm not going to die, if he's telling us the truth. We slide the lid up the side edge, now King Kong's claws on the blackboard are joined by Mighty Joe Young's. Unbelievably horrible sound, sends jagged icicles up the ying-yang. When we get the lid horizontal, I take a quick last look at Vadney in the half-shadow. Hasn't moved a muscle, head's hanging over the edge of the outermost coffin, profile turned slightly to me. Cowlick's dangling near the beginnings of a mean-looking red clunker smack in the middle of his forehead. Cheops really conked him good. Makes you think twice about those legends of the mummy's curse and that, gives you pause. Chief's legs are spread in the sides of the coffin, white socks seem to glow in the dark. Awful thought flashes through my mind in these few seconds: Knowing the Duke, I'm sure he would've wanted to die with his boots on. I'm sure of it. Can't always get what you want, poor son of a buck. Back to work, now we all get over at the side of the lid, shove it across slowly, inch by inch, really straining, hollow sound of stone on stone echoes from the sarcophagus. Finally, it's in place. Sealed again. Airtight. We're leaning against it, catching our breath, I can't help thinking: What a way to go! Know what I mean? Talk about dramatic exits? Smothered inside the sacred sarcophagus of the great Pharaoh Cheops in the diabolically hidden secret chamber of the Great Pyramid in ancient Egypt. Huh? Smothered in action, in the line of duty, murdered by a weird perp in a gas mask, identity unknown, motive unknown. Okay, nobody wants to die, we all hate to see a cop buy it, anytime, anyplace, anywhere, but at least we can say the Duke went out in style. Right? I mean, he'd want it that way, I know he would.

"Empty your pockets on the lid!" gas mask orders. "Everything! Now!"

Do like the man says. Me, all I got is my wallet and NYPD cardholder with the shield. Place them on the lid. Nuz, that's all he's got too, except his worry beads; he slaps them down. Abu's got a lot more, big flashlight with the orange plastic hood, two extra clips of .45-caliber slugs, three pairs of nickel-plated handcuffs, ID holder, wallet, car keys, small ring of other keys. Plunks them down, one by one.

"Ben-Adam," gas mask says.

"Yes, sir?"

"Where are the keys to those handcuffs?"

"Right in the cuffs, sir, in the keyholes."

"Excellent," he says, lowering the laser a bit, reaching up to adjust his mask. "That solves a potential problem. I have no quarrel with you three men. Particularly you, John, and I apologize for all the inconvenience I've caused you. My intention, my basic strategy of luring you along, baiting you, was actually twofold: One, to see for myself how acute your powers of intuition really are. I'd heard good things around, you've developed quite a reputation over the past four or five years. Among career criminals, as they call themselves. Among top professionals, primarily in New York, but elsewhere too. Quite a reputation for having certain qualities that can't be taught, can't be learned, can't be gained even through long experience. Qualities like intuitive reasoning, insight, instinct. Childlike qualities. Childlike in the true sense of the term. Children are able to see things that most adults are no longer aware of. Children are able to listen to 'muses,' they're aware of such things, because they haven't yet been educated out of it. They haven't yet closed their minds to those possibilities. And I believe that if a cop is very sensitive, he can do this too. He can hear the vibrations of the invisible. Qualities such as these, in the possession of a veteran cop, are considered extremely dangerous to many people I know. Not to me. On the contrary, I find them to be refreshing, intriguing, even stimulating. You've used them wisely and added an ingredient all your own—sheer, stubborn, bullheaded tenacity. I like that. I admire that. I congratulate you, John, and I mean it sincerely. I hope our paths cross again."

This is the first time he's talked at any length, so I'm listening to the distorted voice very closely now, trying to pick up on a word, a phrase, a pronunciation, a rhythm, traces of an accent, anything that might trigger a memory—a case, a time, a place—however dim, however distant. But the voice draws a blank.

"But the second reason for the lure," he says in a different tone, "the most important reason, is probably transparent to you by now. Using my own intuitive abilities, I reasoned that if I could keep you on the line all the way to Cairo, if I could get you here and give you some perspective, just enough to convince you it was time to close in, Vadney would be here like a shot. And I was right. I assumed he wouldn't have the willpower to resist such a collar, to grab the credit, the mass-media exposure. And I was right. Make no mistake, the scrolls were always my target, my prize, my obsession for the past five years. Since the time I met Ismat Farah. The scrolls were my goal, to the exclusion of anybody and anything else. I had to have them. But when I discovered you were on the case, John —quite by accident, I admit, back in Islamorada—when I discovered that, I knew I had a chance to get Vadney. That I had an excellent chance to finally nail him after all these years, to dispose of this arrogant, contemptible piece of human garbage. Not quickly. As slowly and painfully as I could possibly manage it, within reasonable limits. I'm not a sadist, I never have been. Most sadists derive pleasure from inflicting physical pain. I prefer to inflict mental pain on an egomaniac like Vadney."

"May I ask a question?" I ask.

"Yes. I don't guarantee I'll answer it."

"What'd Vadney do to you?"

"I'm a dreamer, John, I dream dreams. I attempt to achieve goals that most people would categorically dismiss as impossible. I want knowledge. Knowledge that I can accept with my intellect. I don't want theories and legends and allegories. I want knowledge. I've spent most of my adult life trying to acquire it. Vadney attempted to stop me. He didn't succeed.

He attempted to have me hospitalized for the rest of my life. I'm a dreamer, John, I dream dreams. And the instant I saw you in Islamorada, and realized I finally had a shot at Vadney, I visualized this moment. This moment. The sarcophagus became an important part of the dream at that point, there was never any other way that would've satisfied me quite as much. Unfortunately, he wasn't conscious when the lid went back on. That spoiled it a little. I'd visualized his face in there, horrified, I'd seen his face in there a thousand times. The accident deprived me of that particular satisfaction, but the end result will be the same. He'll wake up. Sooner or later, he'll wake up in there and realize where he is. Trapped in the ultimate place of human horror: Buried alive. Like he tried to do to me. And when the overwhelming impact of shock and terror explode through his brain and central nervous system, total panic will consume him. Total hysteria. Gasping for air, screaming, kicking, clawing, crying, finally losing all control, urinating, defecating, vomiting all over himself. Buried alive. Alone with death. Finally praying for mercy. That's always been a significant part of the dream. To conjure up images of Vadney praying, screaming for mercy, suffocating in there with the greatest egotist who ever lived."

"May I point something out?" I ask.

He glances at his watch. "Certainly."

"You're inflicting severe physical pain before death. And obviously enjoying it. That's sadism in my book."

He hesitates. "All right. All right, I'll accept that from you, John. I stand corrected. It's sadistic. I suppose I've become a sadist, after all. But it was people like Vadney who made me this way. Once again, I'm sorry for having to involve you in all this. You just happened to be a convenient pawn in a dream I've been dreaming. A deadly serious dream. A lonely dream. But it's over now. I have the scrolls. I have Vadney where I want him, where he belongs. Now, gentlemen, I want you to turn around and observe the large, heavy statues against the walls of this room. Each of you will be handcuffed to one of these priceless objects, with at least two statues separating you. You'll be cuffed to an ankle of the statue, allowing you to recline, to rest, to sleep if you can, until morning, when you'll be freed. The pyramid opens every morning at eight-thirty sharp, but the government employees who work here arrive at roughly eight-fifteen. I'll leave the two electrical cables in place through the corridors, I have no further use for them or the equipment. When the employees arrive tomorrow morning and see the cables at the entrance, leading to the interior, they'll investigate immediately, of course, and the cables will lead them directly to you. So you should be found by at least eight-thirty. And freed. I'll leave the keys out in plain sight—let's see—there, on Cheops's throne there, his solid-gold throne. As I said before, I have no quarrel with you three men, I wish you no harm. John, you'll go first, pick up a pair of handcuffs, leave the key on the lid, select a statue against the wall, sit down, get comfortable, then cuff your wrist to the statue's ankle, leg, whatever's convenient. Idrissi will then do the same, selecting a statue separated from yours by at least two. Ben-Adam will follow suit. All I ask, gentlemen, is that you don't try my patience with tricks. Cuff yourselves securely but comfortably. I'll inspect your handiwork before I leave. When I do that, I'll have Ben-Adam's automatic pointed at your head—and cocked. John, go ahead, please."

I grab a pair of cuffs, open them, leave the key, cross the room, choose a painted marble statue of a young woman facing the opening in the wall. Sit down, make sure I can still see the opening, cuff my left wrist to her right ankle. Ankle's slender, but there's no way I could break it without a sledgehammer. Nuz is next, he goes four statues down the row, selects a young girl, sits down, cuffs his left wrist to her right ankle. Abu chooses a statue two past Nuz that has the head of a dog and the body of a man.

True to his word, gas mask checks us out with Abu's Colt .45 cocked. Walks back to the sarcophagus, sticks the uncocked gun in the right back pocket of his jeans, takes the three keys, places them on the seat of the solid-gold throne. Now he reaches in his left back pocket, takes out a clear plastic bag, unfolds it, places both scrolls carefully inside. Picks up his own flashlight, glances around to see if he's forgotten anything.

"May I ask a favor?" Nuz asks.

"Sure."

"Will you please leave these lights on?"

He adjusts his mask. "I'm afraid I can't do that. All the electricity is provided by the generator truck, which I need. When I disconnect the cables, you'll have no light, there's nothing I can do."

"My flashlight," Abu says. "It's on the lid there."

"All right, fine, I'll turn that on." Goes over, snaps it on, points the beam toward the opening.

"One last question?" I ask.

"Certainly, John."

"I'm just naturally curious about the scrolls. In addition to the information about how the pyramid was actually built, what else do you expect to find?"

He walks toward the opening, pauses there, turns, his flashlight in one hand, the plastic bag in the other. With the black gas mask, black T-shirt, jeans, and dark sneakers, he looks weird, especially in this light. And, of course, he sounds it: "Obviously, I don't have time to spell it out for you in detail, but essentially this is it, in layman's terms. Archaeologists, scientists, Egyptologists, and astrophysicists have been divided for a very long time about how this pyramid was built. To this day, nobody really knows. Its original height was found to be a measure directly related to the distance between the earth and the sun; the mathematics are so accurate that it's impossible to imply a coincidence. The pyramid is oriented to the cardinal directions with an error of only four degrees; in a monument of this magnitude, that accuracy is almost unbelievable. It weighs almost six million tons. The average weight of a single stone is two and one-half tons. So the riddle has always revolved around the question: How did they achieve the lift power? And, to a growing number of astrophysicists today, the only feasible answer is levitation. Levitation. They believe that the lifting machine was in fact a spacecraft. Absurd? Today, that doesn't seem as absurd as it would have, say, only twenty-five years ago. Intriguing how our collective perceptions changed so radically in such a short time. Today, astrophysicists hypothesize that at least one spacecraft, probably of vast proportions compared to our own, brought colonists to various parts of this planet some five thousand years ago. Such a hypothesis, if it could be proven beyond a reasonable doubt, would obviously have profound implications—someday. Not in the near future, certainly not in the next century, I'm not naïve enough to suggest such an unlikely awakening. The terrible joke is, we're far too primitive to grasp the significance of such knowledge today, to even dimly imagine the intelligence necessary for extraterrestrials to visit this planet five thousand years ago, or to conceive how much more advanced they must be now. We can't make the quantum leap to cosmological abstractions, because we have no finite frame of reference. It's like trying to solve differential calculus with a knowledge of basic arithmetic. But, gentlemen, I hold in my hand one of perhaps a million keys we'll need. That's all. That's all I'm saying. And, at the appropriate time, when the hieroglyphics are translated to perfection, I'll release this knowledge to the so-called academic community. Knowledge that will eventually, inexorably, perhaps a thousand years from now, help to underwrite basic changes in the fundamental philosophies of our civilization. Sorry to be so brief, John, but I hope that helps to answer your question."

"Could I have one more—a fast one?"

"Of course."

"Had you planned to tell Vadney your name?"

"No. No, because the name isn't important. The only important aspect was to rid the planet of one more egotist in a position of some authority, an egotist who tried to harm me. But I'll give you a name, John, because I suspect our paths are destined to cross again. You can call me—oh, let me think. Yes, that fits, why not? Call me Nemesis."

"Nemesis?"

"Yes. Not the Nemesis of classical mythology, of divine retribution. Nemesis in the sense of an unbeatable opponent. Because that's what I am, modesty aside, and that's what I'll remain, until you can prove me wrong. From what I've observed over the past five years, you're the only cop who has even a remote chance."

He turns, ducks, goes through the opening. I glance at my watch: 8:26. At least twelve hours before they'll find us. Don't know how much oxygen the sarcophagus holds, but common sense tells me no more than half an hour, tops. Nuz, Abu, and I glance at each other in silence. Absolutely no sound from inside the sarcophagus, Chief's been unconscious for maybe ten minutes now. Hate to think of it, but I figure that leaves him around twenty minutes. Hope he remains unconscious the whole time. That would be a blessing, to just pass away like that, like dying in your sleep, they say that's the best way to go. Can't stand the thought of him waking up in there, realizing where he is, screaming, kicking, all like that. Horrible thought. Horrible. Wonder what he'd yell? Wonder if he could hear us if we yelled back? What the hell would we say? "Sorry, Chief, we can't get you out!"? Naw. I mean, that's the wrong thing to say to a dying man, he just wouldn't want to hear that. Me, I decide to keep my mouth shut. Not only that, once he starts pounding and crying and that, I'm just going to hold my fingers in my ears. Seems more respectful that way.

At 8:31, the two high-intensity bulbs go out; he's disconnected the power. Leaves us in deep shadow behind the beam of Abu's flashlight on the sarcophagus, aimed at the opening in the wall. One of the objects that's in the partial path of the beam is that life-sized painted wooden statue of Cheops. From where I sit, he's in three-quarter profile, his shadow big and grotesque on the wall and ceiling, but his quartz eyes have followed me over here. Yeah. They're glaring right at me, burning with indignation. Can't get away from the little sucker no matter where you go. Not only that, in this light he looks more real than ever, he looks positively alive. Dawns on me, if I can't fall asleep, I'll have to put up with those spooky sparkling eyes for the next twelve hours. But I know I can't fall asleep with him glaring at me like that. Still, I'm just glad I'm not in the sarcophagus with the real thing. Now an awful thought occurs to me: If Vadney wakes up and moves his weight off the mummy's head and torso, I wonder if the rigor mortis will make it pop up again? I close my eyes at the horror of it. Now I start visualizing it, the two of them wrestling around in there, fighting for space, and the mummy's long yellow fingernails scratching at him. Tell you what, I got to get some sleep here, I think I'm losing my grip.

At 8:43, I hear a sound. Thump. Not loud, but not soft. I glance at Nuz and Abu in the shadows; they're sitting up straight, they heard it too. Only one place it could've come from. Thump. This one seems a little louder. Dread the thought of this, but it's really happening. Thump. Thump. Chief's waking up now in the pitch-black of the sarcophagus, poking around, probably still groggy, not knowing where he is. Thump. Thump. Oh, no, I can't stand this, I really can't. Please, God, don't let him suffer much, he wasn't all that bad a guy, know what I mean? Please don't let him panic and start screaming his brains out in there, wrestling around with the mummy, I don't want to remember the Duke that way. Thump! Cough! Thump!

Wait a minute, hold on here, that sound's not coming from the sarcophagus. No way. It's coming from the corridor. I look at the opening fast. Now I squint. Abu's flashlight beam extends out into the corridor a little, I can see fragments of broken limestone off to the right. Hard to be sure, but I think I saw a flash out there. *Thump! Thump!* No question, somebody's struggling through that corridor. But who? Nemesis, coming back for something? No, he's long gone. Those two kid cops, coming back for more *bakshish?* Unlikely. Who else knows we're in here? Doris, coming in to take pictures after all? No, she's fast asleep by now. Best of my knowledge, those are the only people who actually know we're in the pyramid. If it's not one of them, who the hell could it be? *Thump! Thump! Cough!*

Now I see a moving circle of light on the floor out there. Then a moving shadow. *Thump! Cough! Thump!* Footsteps stop, shadow's crouched just to the left of the opening. Silence. Five seconds. Ten.

Suddenly, a man's voice: "Who's in there?"

"Us!" Nuz shouts.

"Help!" Abu yells.

"Police!" I scream.

Figure of a large man crawls in, holding a flashlight. Full head of graying hair, white shirt open at the collar, blue blazer, gray trousers. Now he stands up in the glare of our flashlight beam, tall, lean, looks American. Familiar face, mean-looking, where have I seen this guy? Takes a deep breath, steps out of the direct glare, glances around. Penetrating eyes, big beak, thin lips, strong resemblance to Ty Cobb. Holy shit! It's Will Banks!

"Will!" I shout.

Plays his flashlight on me. "Little John!"

"Who is it?" Nuz asks.

"Will Banks, Doris's husband."

"Where's *Vadney?*" Will demands.

"We're handcuffed," Abu says. "The keys are on that—"

"Where the fuck's *Vadney?!*"

"In the sarcophagus!" Nuz says. "Please get these cuffs off!"

"Keys are on the gold throne there," I tell him.

He moves his flashlight around, spots the gold throne, walks over, grabs them, comes to me first. "What the hell's he doing in the sarcophagus?" Hands me the keys.

"Killer put him in there."

"Should've killed the little ratfucker. Save me the trouble."

"That's the general idea," I tell him, finding the right key. "Chief's smothering, we gotta get him out fast."

I'm free, I rush over to Nuz, give him the two other keys, he finds the right one quickly, scrambles up, brings the last one to Abu. Glance at my watch: 8:46. If I'm right about the half-hour oxygen capacity of the sarcophagus, Chief's time is up, either he's dead in there or he's got a matter of seconds to live.

All of us rush to the sarcophagus, get at the corners, Will and me at the head, Abu and Nuz at the foot, I give a count of three, shout, *"Lift!"* Strain, grunt, sweat, we can't get it off, can't even budge it, the three of us are too exhausted, we used all our energy. One final try, by the count, *"Lift!"* Lid moves a little, just a fraction, up by the head. *"Slide it!"* I shout. *"Slide it down from the head!"* Will puts his back into it, he's got fresh energy compared to us, he does most of the shoving. Lid squeaks, squeals, slides a few inches, a few more, then gets some momentum, slides away from the head about fifteen inches before it sticks. We stop to rest. At least it's open, oxygen's getting in now, that's the only important thing at this point. Nuz and Abu, they're so pooped they put their heads and arms down on the lid, dripping with sweat, trying to catch their breath. No sound from inside. Will gets his flashlight and plays the beam inside. Chief's in exactly the same position I saw him last. Hasn't moved a muscle. He looks dead.

Will holds the flashlight in his left hand, reaches in with his

right, pokes him in the back. "Vadney! Wake up!" No movement, no sound. Pokes him harder. "Hey, Rambo Bambo! Get
up, ya tub a puke!"

Chief's eyes open slowly in the bright circle of light. He
blinks rapidly. He frowns. Now he lifts his head, turns, looks
up into the blaze of light. "Huh? Who's that? Where am I?"

Will smiles his tight-lipped smile, lowers his head and
shoulders into the fifteen-inch gap, still holding the flashlight
in Vadney's eyes. When he speaks, it sounds like he's in an
echo chamber: *"Vadney!"*

"Huh? Who the hell's that?"

"Will Banks!"

"Will Banks? Oh, shit."

"Yeah. Yeah, you didn't think I'd be dumb enough to let
you get away with this crap, did you?"

"Now, Will, wait a minute, I can—"

"My personal problems with you can wait till later, when
I get you alone. Right now I got more important things on my
mind. Like Doris. For your information, Doris did it *again.*
She saved your butt *again*—like she's been doing for more
than two years now! She saved your incompetent butt tonight
by getting the Tourist Police to back you up outside. Just in
case. Just in case you fucked up in here. She didn't do it
obviously, of course, she waited till you were gone. She's too
sophisticated to show you up for the asshole you really are. So
she waited, then she set it up with the Tourist Police, a fail-safe
backup surveillance outside, just in case. As a result, the cops
surprised your crook, moved in to block his truck, chased him
in vehicles halfway around the pyramid, then cut him off on
the south side. At that point, he got out and started shooting.
The cops took cover and returned fire. There was only one
direction he could go—up. Up the pyramid. So he began
climbing. Now they got him trapped at the very top. They got
him surrounded from below, there's no way out. Of course,
he's still armed, they can't get near him, so now they've

reached a stalemate. And he's finally made a demand. Before he'll give himself up, he wants to talk to one man—and one man only."

Chief's voice shakes. "One man?"

"That's right. One particular man. He's selected one man to climb all the way up to the top of the pyramid and talk to him."

"Oh, my God."

"One man with *guts!*"

Chief thinks on it. "Well, okay. Help me get—"

"Obviously, that lets you out."

"Huh?"

"He'll only talk to Rawlings."

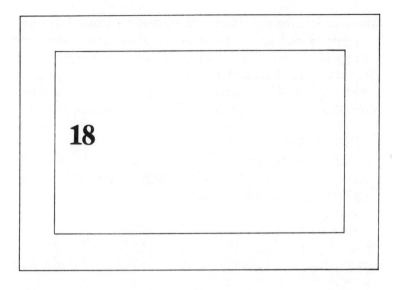

18

W<small>HEN WE GET OUTSIDE</small>, strong moonlight gives the whole area an unreal glow. It's 9:08, we're standing at the cave-like entrance, taking deep breaths of the chilly desert air, and the place is crawling with cops now because of the gunfire, dozens of uniformed Central Security kids armed with machine pistols; radios from police vehicles crackle from all sides. Also, the media boys have arrived, including TV crews with shoulder-mounted cameras at the ready, all standing behind police lines defined by white ropes that apparently surround the pyramid. Now they see us, they start shouting, waving us over, strobe lights come on, almost blinding at first, we have to squint, cameras are rolling. Chief seems to come alive, he's in his element again, instantly grasps the staggering potential for fast-breaking worldwide satellite coverage, the obvious need for a spokesman—someone, anyone—with experience in the psychology of effective press relations. Narrows his eyes, licks his chops, swipes at his cowlick, ushers Abu, Nuz, and me toward the dazzle of lights, the tangle of mikes, the media hype—*"Min fadlak, itkallim!"*—the awesome responsibility of celebrity. Suddenly occurs to me, this could be my first shot at a speaking part on TV, if I can get a word in edgewise. Arab paparazzi duck under the rope and swarm around us as we approach—*flash!-click!-whine!* Wait a minute. *Flash!-click!-whine!* How come they're only shooting Vadney? *Flash!-click!-whine!* I glance around, now I know. Standing next to the Duke here, I'm an unshaven dwarf in a filthy *galabiyya.* Look like I just crawled out of some tomb. Even the folks back home wouldn't recognize me. Probably have BO to boot, judging from the way these guys are avoiding me. Like the man says, fame is fleeting.

Nuz and Abu, they get more respect in the winner's circle here, they're interpreters. Chief stands tall in the hot glare of strobes, waits for a brief introduction by Nuz, Arabic followed by English ("Gentlemen, this is Walter F. Vadney, V-a-d-n-e-y, Chief of Detectives of the Police Department of the City of New York"), then steps up to the mikes, flashes a humble half molar shower, and launches into an opening statement; pauses at appropriate intervals for the translation, of course. Words to this effect:

"Ladies and gentlemen, tonight you're about to witness the apprehension of one of the most wanted criminals on earth, the man believed to be the mastermind behind the biggest cash robbery in history, more than eight million dollars in United States currency. But that's not all. This fugitive, who we've traveled so far to apprehend—New York to Miami to the Florida Keys to Washington to London to Cairo—eight to ten thousand miles in less than one week, this man is also suspected to be a multiple murderer. But that's not all. Not by any means. His ultimate goal went far beyond the confines of robbery and murder. Far, far beyond. This master of disguise, whose name and nationality still remain a mystery to us, actually attempted to steal the heritage, the priceless heritage, of a great nation. That's right. The priceless heritage of the great nation of the Arab Republic of Egypt. What, specifically, did he attempt to steal? I'll tell you what he attempted—unsuccessfully—to steal: The secret and sacred scrolls of the great Pharaoh Cheops."

Dozens of media men (no women) go bug-eyed at first, then glance at each other with puzzled expressions, then frown as one: What in the name of Allah is this clown talking about?

Cameras keep rolling, Chief keeps talking, slowly, savoring it, fully aware that he's finally hit the mass-media mother-lode this time, moving his right hand in an occasional gesture for the patient paparazzi (whose strobes then flash almost simultaneously), then pausing thoughtfully during Abu's fast Arabic translation, nodding as if he understood every word. Continues like so:

"Ladies and gentlemen, as we all know, nearly five thousand years have passed since the great Pharaoh Cheops was laid to rest in the Great Pyramid behind me here, the first of the seven ancient Wonders of the World. Five thousand years ago, the virtual dawn of recorded history, as it were. But, as we also know only too well, Cheops's mummy and treasures were never found. Grave robbers? That was the traditional belief. Until now. Until tonight. Remember this—" he looks up, narrows his eyes, takes a deep breath—"this cool, clear, starry night, ladies and gentlemen: Sunday, December twenty-second—"

"Saturday," Nuz corrects quietly.

"Beg your pardon, I've—I tell ya, I'm afraid I've been through quite an ordeal inside that pyramid tonight." He touches the big red bump in the middle of his forehead; strobes flash like disco beats. "In fact, I got hit pretty good, I'm still —still a little dizzy. But I think we'll all remember this night, Saturday, December twenty-first, nineteen eighty-five, because a significant discovery was made here tonight. Perhaps one of the most significant archaeological discoveries of our time, I don't know, I'll leave that to the experts. Because tonight, ladies and gentlemen, in a secret chamber inside the Great Pyramid, hidden from the world for almost five thousand years, we discovered . . . the untouched mummy and priceless treasures of Pharaoh Cheops."

A second of stunned silence, then a collective *"Ahhhhh!"* Followed by rapid Arabic chatter: *"Wallah! Wahyat en-nabi! Ya salam!"* Sounds to that effect.

"Priceless national artifacts," Chief continues. "But this—this madman only wanted to defile. To defile the mummy, ladies and gentlemen. The sacred mummy of Cheops. My men and me, we were forced to—to remove the lid of the sarcophagus."

"Wahyat abuk!" somebody moans.

"And I—forgive me if I'm a little upset, ladies and gentlemen, I—I was forced to . . . climb inside the sarcophagus and . . ."

"Ya salam!" somebody blurts out.

". . . and, uh, then I had to . . . well, cut the mummy's wrappings."

"Fen?"

"Ashshane eh?"

"Where and why?" Abu translates.

"I was forced to cut the (wrappings away from Pharaoh Cheops's hands. So I could remove the secret scrolls from his grip. That's—that's actually all I remember." Touches his forehead again. "That's when he knocked me out. I lost consciousness. Idrissi, maybe you better pick up the story at this point, huh? Ladies and gentlemen, Detective Nuzhat Idrissi, New York Police Department."

Nuz moves into the bright lights, adjusts his glasses, touches his mustache, speaks quietly, pauses, translates his own words. "Gentlemen, with Chief Vadney unconscious in the sarcophagus, the suspect forced us—there were three of us left—forced us to replace the lid on the sarcophagus. In other words, he attempted to kill Chief Vadney, to suffocate him. As you can see, he was not successful. And let me add a personal comment. I have had the pleasure of working with Chief Vadney for many years now and I can tell you from experience, he is a difficult man to kill, a courageous police officer."

Chief steps back in now, head down, shuffling his boots. "I can't take any credit for what happened here tonight, but I know who deserves the credit. Two people. Both of 'em civilians. First, the man who actually saved my life tonight in one of the most courageous civilian acts I've ever witnessed in thirty-two years of police work. Ladies and gentlemen, it's my distinct honor and privilege to introduce J.W. Banks—that's B-a-n-k-s—Banks, known to all of us affectionately as 'Will' Banks—that's W-i-l-l—Will Banks." He turns during the translation, glances around, spots Will in the shadowed crowd off to the left, standing next to Doris now, his arm around her. Chief points: "There he is over there, see if you can get a shot of him. Will, give 'em a wave, huh?"

Lights and cameras pan over to Will and Doris, Will manages an underplayed wave, but he's obviously not overjoyed; Doris steps away fast, starts applauding like crazy, the crowd around them picks up on it almost instantly, now it spreads in waves to the cops and media men. That's all the paparazzi need, they rush him, they're all over him, strobes flashing like firecrackers.

"Now keep the TV lights there," Chief commands. "Doris, stand next to Will again, huh? Ladies and gentlemen, the little lady standing next to Will there is Doris Banks, his lovely wife. That's D-o-r-i-s, Doris Banks." Waits for the translation, then: "This is the little lady who deserves the lion's share of credit for the apprehension of the master criminal who's now trapped on top of the Great Pyramid here tonight." His eyes sparkle as he waits. "Now, here's a scoop for you, listen up here. Mrs. Banks used to be my executive secretary. Until now. Until tonight. However, as a result of her superlative performance on this case, I am, as of this moment, officially promoting her to be my administrative assistant!" Waits, traces of an all-out left-sided molar shower begin to appear as he sees Doris's expression. "Ladies and gentlemen, let's hear it for the new administrative assistant to the chief of detectives, New York Police Department!"

Fast translation, then Vadney leads the applause, tries to get Doris over to say a few words, but she's surrounded by paparazzi now. Seems to be enjoying it. Will too, he's coaxed into the shots, he's even grinning a little, Ty Cobb before he spikes somebody, a detail that's not lost on Vadney.

Speaking of details, there's still a small one left, of course. I glance up at the bold black silhouette of the pyramid towering over us, take a deep breath, wonder if I have enough energy left to climb up that mountain of rocks in the dark. Wonder how long it'll take? Tell you the truth, I'm pooped just looking at it. Then, once I get up there, flat-out exhausted, falling down, all I have to do is sweet-talk Nemesis into giving himself up. Piece a cake.

Soon as the press conference breaks up, Chief takes me aside, we have a quick briefing with Commander Mohamed Bulgar, Tourist Police, who's in charge of the Pyramids Station. He's in uniform, big guy, about Vadney's height but much thinner, mid-forties, dark eyes, full mustache, left front tooth is broken off at a slight angle. Speaks almost perfect English with a British accent on certain words. Leads us to his dark blue four-door Renault, unmarked, parked near the entrance. I get in back, stretch out a little. Feels luxurious to rest my tired old bones in a cushioned seat again.

"Ordinarily," Bulgar begins, "in an operation like this, Chief Kez would take charge personally. I've been in touch with him by phone, he's fully briefed, he's given me the authority to proceed. Now, Chief Vadney, Mrs. Banks explained that you have a fugitive warrant for this man, is that correct?" He snaps on the overhead light.

"Right." Chief pulls the warrant from his jacket pocket, unfolds it. "Right, it's what we call a 'John Doe' fugitive warrant, lists his description, most of what's known about him, all the charges, particulars, everything but his name, which we still don't know."

Bulgar puts on his Ben Franklin reading glasses, takes the warrant, looks it over quickly.

"How long a climb is it?" I ask. "How long will it take me?"

He glances at me over his glasses, removes them slowly. "In daylight, the ascent from the northeast corner can be made in —anywhere from twenty to thirty minutes. Depending on one's physical condition, of course. To be perfectly frank with you, I've never seen anyone make the climb after dark, although I'm sure it's been done many times in the past. Today, the pyramid is off limits after dark. Naturally, we'll provide as much light as we can. We'll simply line up a number of our vehicles at the northeast corner and use spotlights as well as headlights. I think you'll be able to see well enough on the way up. However, under the same lighting conditions, your descent could be very difficult, because you'll be looking down into the lights."

"How high is it up there?" Chief asks.

"Four hundred fifty feet to a platform on top that's thirty-three feet square."

"Platform?" I ask.

"Yes. Originally, the pyramid was four hundred eighty feet high with a polished limestone casing and a capstone forming the apex. When the capstone was removed, probably thousands of years ago, it left the pyramid with a flat top, although it's so massive it still seems to have an actual apex."

"Little John," Chief says. "Tell the truth now, you feel up to this? That's a long climb up there, buddy-boy."

"Yeah, well, I could use a martini first."

He frowns, narrows his eyes. "A mar—? Before a dangerous climb like that? No way. Sorry, little guy, but that's simply out of the question."

"Just kidding, Chief."

"Huh? Oh." Gives me a concerned look. "You—you're absolutely sure you're up to it?"

"Yeah. Looking forward to the panoramic view."

Chief turns to Bulgar. "Tell ya what really worries me. This psycho up there is armed. We're not allowed to carry firearms here, but Rawlings has to go up and face this guy. Could be a perfect setup for a hostage situation."

"That worried me too," Bulgar says. "I brought up the subject when I talked with Chief Kez. He suggested that Rawlings should be followed, a few minutes after he starts, by at least one armed officer who would climb either the west or south side. He left the decision to me."

"Hell of a good suggestion," Chief says. "Let's do it."

"No," I tell him.

"Huh?"

I sit forward. "Send up a second cop and he's a dead man. I know this guy, Chief. He's already anticipated a move like that, plus twenty others. He's way ahead of us. Also, he's on a level platform up there, he's in the catbird's seat, he's got an unobstructed view of all four sides in strong moonlight."

"Then what do you suggest?" Bulgar asks.

"I go up alone. But I don't go all the way up to the platform until he agrees to two conditions. One, he'll have to eject the cartridge clip from the forty-five and toss it down to me; two, he'll have to eject the remaining slug from the chamber and toss it away."

"Ridiculous," Chief says. "He'll never agree."

"I *know* he'll agree," I tell him.

"*How* d'ya know?"

"Because I know the guy. And he knows me. There's no

way he'd kill me and there's no way I'd climb up on that platform unless he agreed to my conditions. So the hostage aspect doesn't worry me at all. Tell you what *does* worry me: Trying to climb up that thing in a long *galabiyya* and loose sandals."

"No problem," Bulgar says. "I'll get you a uniform and boots."

"No, no, wait a minute," Chief says. "Wait a minute, I got you covered, buddy-boy. Change clothes with me. I don't want you going up there in a uniform, that could be danger-ous, know what I mean? Change clothes with me. We'll get you some boots that fit."

"Chief, come on. You're six-three and one-seventy-five."

"Turtleneck's a stretch job, it'll fit fine. Tuck the jeans in your boots, you got it made. No arguments, that's an order. Strip!"

At 9:28, seven squad cars and two vans are parked at the northeast corner of the pyramid in relatively close proximity, motors running, high-beam headlights throwing big bright overlapping circles on an area of ragged limestone blocks maybe seventy-five feet high. Each vehicle also has a spotlight and the nine beams form a necklace of white that reaches at least halfway up the pyramid; these will be tilted higher as I climb. So, I mean, it ain't exactly a Hollywood production, more like a low-budget documentary type operation, but you can't beat the pyramid prop. Media guys and TV crews seem happy enough, they're all crowded behind the police rope at the northeast corner, bright strobe lights on the commentators now, they're ready for prime-time coverage, Saturday night live. Me, I'm ready to shine as Vadney's double, his stunt-man, I'm wearing his white turtleneck tucked into his jeans with the wide black belt pulled snug to the very last notch. Turns out Bulgar couldn't find any boots to fit me on such short notice, but he came up with sneakers belonging to one of his kid cops, they fit fine. Have to roll up these long-legged jeans, of course, show the fans some bare ankle, but teaser sex never hurt the ratings. Just hope they don't zoom in: "Oh, my *Gawd,* Arnie, lookit *dat,* get a load a dis *heah,* Chief Vadney shaves his *ankles* awready!"

Here I go, no bullhorn announcement to Nemesis that I'm coming, but I'm sure he's watching every move. Each "step" along the edge here is a limestone block that's roughly three and a half feet high, so it's something like test-course mountain climbing, getting a leg up, then hauling ass, and the combination of headlights, spotlights, and moonlight makes visibility pretty good. My shadow is long and huge on the ragged rocks above, then splintered in grotesque patterns up along the north and east sides of the pyramid. Makes me dizzy to look at those moving shadows. I try to pace myself, rest a few seconds after climbing every block, take a couple of deep breaths. One question keeps returning to my tired brain: What the hell does Nemesis want to talk about? Making a deal? No way, he's got nothing to deal, he's facing Murder-1 on top of everything else. I try to put myself in his place again as I climb. What would I want with Rawlings? What would I have to discuss with him? Don't have a clue. One thing I know for certain, Nemesis is no fool, he's got a reason for this. Think. Climb. Think. I'm tired, I'm hungry, I feel sick, I feel dizzy. *Think.* What's his angle? What's he want with you? Is he trying to buy time for something? Is he trying to distract attention? All eyes on me, while he makes his way down one of the two dark sides? Doubtful. Pyramid's completely surrounded by armed cops. There's no way out.

Then I remember the air shafts.

Two of them, the old guide pointed them out, remember that? I stop, lean against a block, head down, trying to visualize the interior again. One air shaft extends from the east wall of the King's Chamber, the bottom of the east wall, and leads out to the east side of the pyramid. The other shaft extends from the ceiling of the Great Gallery out to the west side. Both shafts have steep downward angles from the outside to the interior. Could a man of his size squeeze into one of those shafts and inch his way down? I try to remember the diagram from Farah's book. Are the shafts wide enough? Could be. Which one would he choose? First, he'd have to climb down the outside of the pyramid to reach either one of them, maybe as far as a quarter of the way down from the platform. That rules out the east side; spotlight beams are slanted across it now. West side is dark except for moonlight; it's got to be the west side. So what's he do when he gets down into the Great Gallery? Find a place to hide? Not him. Not Nemesis. He'd go straight down the Ascending Corridor, then up the corridor to the entrance. And out. Too risky? No. Why? Last place the kid cops would watch now is the entrance. All their eyes would be—

At first, from a distance, it sounds to me like a small motorboat puttering along on a lake. Know that sound? Calm, soft, tranquil. But then, as it gets closer very quickly, the sound waves are erratic, wavering, so you're not sure what the hell you're hearing, especially at night. Now, suddenly, the sound swoops down and in from the north, behind me, engine roaring, deafening. Happens so fast I don't have time to turn around, shock waves actually knock me to my knees. Fast-moving black shape of a helicopter booms overhead, no lights at all, thick clouds of dust billow all around me, swirl crazily in the spotlight beams. I'm shaking, choking, squinting in the dust, I see the blurred outline of a man grabbing a rope ladder. Gunshots from below, the rapid fire of machine pistols, every cop opens up simultaneously, hundreds of shots in a matter of seconds, but the dark cylinder is already moving away fast at a right angle, nose down, heading west.

Then, in the gradual silence, something happens that still seems to me like a slow-motion sequence, fragments from a haunting dream. I can see the silver blur of the helicopter blades in moonlight, finally, and the dark fuselage against the bright spray of stars as it climbs, and the almost invisible thread-like rope ladder with the tiny silhouette of the man, Nemesis, starting to climb up from the bottom rung. Then the right side of the rope ladder seems to sag, drop abruptly, collapsing the rungs, snapping the two side ropes together, jolting Nemesis at the bottom. He remains stationary for a while, maybe five seconds, still holding on with both hands, legs spread. And then, as his figure diminishes with distance, the other side of the rope ladder suddenly falls away. Nemesis, still holding the long rope, appears to drop slowly at first. When he releases those strands of rope, they drift away quickly, above him, and his fall seems to gain momentum.

His lonely figure is frozen in my mind now, dreamlike: He's running in the moonlight, arms and legs pumping in a slow, rhythmic, measured pace, running against a fast vertical streak of stars, like silver rain, hard silver rain, and he's running in the rain in the moonlight, running toward something, running, until his figure vanishes below the dark horizon.

Early next morning we're having breakfast at Mena House when we begin to learn some of the answers. Chief's there, Will and Doris, Nuz, Abu, me, we're sitting around a big table in the coffee shop with an excellent view of the Great Pyramid through the floor-to-ceiling windows. Story's splashed across the front page of all the Sunday papers, of course, complete with special photo sections of the evening's highlights, Vadney's puss prominent in most, but there are some flattering shots of Doris and Will, particularly in the two French-language dailies, *Le Progres Egyptien* and *Journal d'Egypte,* and the figure of yours truly appears on the front page of the English-language daily, the *Egyptian Gazette.* Yeah, front page, historic first for me. Fantastic shot of my back, taken with a telephoto lens, as I'm climbing the pyramid. Caption identifies me as "New York's Chief of Detectives Walter F.

Vadney," and the photo credit reads "United Press International/Reuter," which means it's a shoo-in for New York's Sunday editions, but old stunt-men never cry, we just have Bloody Marys for breakfast. Headline above my picture reads:

GREAT PYRAMID ROBBERY ENDS IN VIOLENT DEATH

Mummy of Cheops Discovered; Treasures in Hidden Chamber

Topic number one at breakfast: Was Nemesis's death accidental? Consensus opinion: No way. Topic number two: Who killed him? Consensus opinion: One or a number of major government officials who received generous slices of that estimated £E3.5 million cash in *bakshish* for active and/or passive cooperation in the plan. Tell you a key factor that leads us to this conclusion: Abu's considerable intelligence about the internal operations of his own police force. Example, he knows the type helicopter used, knows it cold. It's one of a fleet of U.S. Army surplus choppers owned by the Central Security Force, the same model that was used extensively in Vietnam, a Bell HH-1H, powered by a reconditioned T53-L-13B engine with 1,400 sph thrust, and a maximum speed of 138. Who operated it? Obviously, a veteran cop pilot who knew the bird and pyramids area so well he could fly at night without lights at extremely low altitudes. You don't order that type emergency duty unless you're wearing very heavy brass or unless you happen to be Chief Kez himself, who was conspicuous by his absence last night. My guess, if Kez was involved, he was following orders. Why did the "untouchables" feel they had to eliminate Nemesis? Simple fear of the unknown. If Nemesis was captured, he might very well blow the whistle on the whole conspiracy; important careers and reputations and fortunes were at risk, to say nothing of actual prison terms. No, Nemesis had to be executed, but in the guise of an escape. I think he knew that. I think he anticipated that. Can't help wondering if that's what he wanted to tell me, that he knew they'd pull all stops to prevent him from leaving Egypt alive, that highly sophisticated precautions would have to be taken to keep him alive. Yet he grabbed the rope ladder. Why? Suppose he'd refused? My opinion, they would've hit him on the spot. By grabbing it, he had at least some hope. And men need hope. Even him.

Searching for the body last night was extremely difficult because it fell in the general vicinity of Gebel el-Khashab, a mountain just southwest of Giza in the Western Desert; actually, it's less than five miles away, but the area is almost uninhabited and there are few roads leading to it. Commander Bulgar dutifully sent out two helicopters with searchlights, plus two truckloads of cops, a total of twenty-two kids, before ten o'clock. In the event the body wasn't found by six this morning (first eight-hour shift), Bulgar planned to send out two more choppers and three trucks just before sunrise at seven, and to supervise the search himself. He was very concerned because the Western Desert is subject to high winds at night, especially in the winter months, and a body could easily be buried in the sand.

Abu talked about that during breakfast. He'd checked with his station at 6:30 and learned that the ten-to-six shift had been unsuccessful. He's wearing his uniform this morning, first time we've seen him in it, thick dark hair combed neatly, smart-looking kid.

"You have to understand the desert," he tells us. "In some ways, it's like an ocean. It's constantly changing, shifting, rolling. At night, when the winds come, the—entire landscape changes radically. Last night, remember how the helicopter made a sharp right-angle turn when it left the pyramid?"

We all nod and grunt.

He sips his coffee. "It headed due west, straight for the desert. Obviously, the pilot had orders to drop the man out there. Whoever cut the rope ladder waited until they were a good five miles out."

Chief touches an index finger to the lump on his forehead; swelling's gone down some and it's turning black and blue. "Abu, let's get down to it, let's call a spade a spade here. What're the chances of the body being found?"

"All I can do is give you an educated guess, sir."

"That's good enough for me."

"All right." Abu frowns, stares down at his coffee. "If the body had been dropped in the daytime, the chances of recovery would be—improved. From several standpoints. Visibility, relative lack of high winds. Depending on how much time had elapsed, of course. At night, the chances of recovery are seriously diminished. Most of us, most of us at the station last night realized that if the initial search team didn't find anything within the first two hours, there was a strong probability that the body would never be found."

"It's now about seven-forty-five," Chief says. "What're the chances now? On a scale of one to ten?"

"In my opinion, the probability is close to zero. I'm sorry to seem pessimistic, Chief Vadney, but I'm sure you want the truth. I grew up in this area. I know this desert. I know what it's like out there at night in the winter. It can be a very hostile environment—freezing cold, high winds, gigantic drifts. Automobiles and trucks that break down or run out of gas are routinely buried out there at night. And never found. As we all know, the Sphinx itself was buried under tons of sand for hundreds of years, its existence unknown, and it's sixty-five feet high."

"The Sphinx was buried?" Doris says. "I didn't know that."

Chief nods like it's ancient history. "Well, people, I guess that wraps it up then, huh? We'll never know who this psycho was."

"Not only that," Nuz adds, "we'll never know what those scrolls said. They're buried with him."

"Chief," I say, "while you were out cold, this guy, Nemesis, he mentioned—"

"Why y'keep callin' him that?"

"Because he suggested it."

"Yeah? When? I didn't hear that."

"You were out cold," I remind him. "And during that time, Nemesis mentioned that you'd put him in a hospital some years back. Probably a mental hospital."

"Yeah?"

"Yeah. Said you tried to put him away for life."

"Yeah?"

"Yeah. Remember anybody like that?"

He smiles, shakes his head. "Little John, if I had a nickel for every yahoo I sent to a funny farm over the past thirty-two years, I'd be a multimillionaire like Will Banks here. Right, Will?"

Will gives him a fisheye that wouldn't thaw in a microwave.

Chief clears his throat. "So what else did this guy say?"

"Said he was a dreamer," I tell him. "Said he dreamed dreams. Said he tried to achieve goals that most people would call impossible."

"Yeah?" Narrows his eyes now. "What else? Anything else?"

"Said he wasn't really interested in stealing material things. Said he only wanted knowledge."

Chief thinks on it, slurps his coffee quietly, makes little hums in his throat. "Yeah. In his efforts to acquire knowledge and avoid stealing material things, he rips off eight million dollars and kills two people in the process."

"And loses his life," I add.

"Yeah. Expensive knowledge. Tell you the truth, Little John. I don't know who he was and I don't give a shit."

That last line stays in my mind for some reason, can't seem

to shake it. I'm sure it really is the truth, as he says. It has the simple, direct ring of truth to my ear. Spoken in a kind of monotone, no emphasis on any given word, no gesture of any kind, face and eyes expressionless. A guy leaning over a coffee cup, a man in his mid-fifties, a veteran cop with a hell of a lot of experience in a profession that doesn't offer many rewards, financial or otherwise. *I don't know who he was and I don't give a shit.* Simple and direct. Close the book, go home, get some rest, start on another. Because that's what it's all about. That's what you do for a living. Isn't it? *Isn't it?*

After breakfast, Nuz and I go back up to the suite. He sits in the living room and reads the papers. I sit out on the terrace and smoke a cigar. It's just past eight o'clock and the sky is overcast. There's a pleasant breeze that brings the smell of rain. Within ten minutes, it starts, just a shower. I'm sitting there, smoking the cigar, enjoying the pyramids in the rain, when Doris comes out.

"Mind some company, Little John?"

"Not at all. Pull up a chair."

She's wearing the fashionable outfit she came down in, minus the coat, and she looks lovely, as usual. Me, I'm long since back to my New York clothes, white shirt, gray trousers, real shoes. Feel almost civilized again.

"Thought you were going to play golf, Doris."

"So did I, but I'm just too tired. We didn't get to sleep till well after midnight."

"Chief find another room okay?"

"Oh, sure. It was no big deal, he didn't have anything to pack. Will and I sat out on the terrace, had a couple of nightcaps. We could see the searchlights of the two helicopters way off to the west. We had a long talk. He's in the room now, trying to get us on an afternoon flight."

"Back home so soon?"

She smiles like a kid, takes out a cigarette. "Nope." Lights up, sits back, inhales deeply. "Paris!"

"Yeah?"

"Paris. He's on the phone now."

"Fantastic, Doris. Shopping spree?"

"Yes, but it's more than that, it's—special. We need a little vacation together. We haven't had one in some time now. Years. So we decided to spend Christmas and New Year's in Paris. Ten days alone together. Then, New Year's Day, we're taking the Air France Concorde back home. We always wanted to fly on that thing, so now we're doing it."

"Only way to go."

"Did you call your wife last night?"

"Finally, yeah. Called about eleven. Five in the afternoon, her time. Talked for about twenty minutes. Hate to see the tab."

"Was she worried?"

"Yeah. Yeah, a little. Nothing really out of the ordinary. After thirty years in this racket, she's used to it."

"You haven't been home in—what, a week?"

"Close to it. Left last Tuesday."

"When was the last time you took a vacation?"

"A real one?"

"A real, honest-to-God, relaxing, all-out vacation."

I think about it. "Shit. Fourteen years."

Soft reflections of the rain move down her face as she glances away. "You guys kill me, you really do. You and Will, you have more in common than you realize. We started out with nothing, John. Nothing. Same as you. And nothing was given to us. Will worked for over thirty-five years to build a company. Built it up from six little offices to more than seven hundred. Seven *hundred* offices! And, of course, he was constantly on the road, just constantly, he had to be. There was a twenty-two-year period when he worked twelve to fifteen hours a day, seven days a week, when I never even *saw* him for months. That's no exaggeration. I kept a photo album from the time we were married back in Canton, Ohio, a chronological record of our marriage—at least, it was intended to be chronological. But somewhere in the middle, there's this big blank page representing that period of twenty-two years. Years when I didn't have any photos of us together because he was hardly ever home. So, when I gave him the album as a present, just a few years ago, I printed a little note and stuck it in that blank page. And the note read—I know it by heart—the note read: 'Due to circumstances beyond my control, you will find fewer pictures of yourself, due to the traveling years. The next few pages reveal some of my activities while you were busy on the road to becoming more successful. And more *rich!*' Looking at it now, Little John, it's like twenty-two years just—vanished. Very strange feeling. Then, when he finally made it big, when he retired, he couldn't *stop* working! No way. Now he's in the apartment most of the day, but he's studying the *Wall Street Journal,* he's on the phone for hours and hours, he's still wheeling and dealing with his brokers, his accountants, his attorneys, going out for business lunches, and he's still got the motor on his back. What I'm trying to say is, we get in ruts in our lives. Ruts! Boring ruts! We get to the point where we think work is everything, work is what we're living for. There's got to be more to it than that. I don't care what you say, there's just got to be."

We sit in silence for a while, watching the rain.

"Doris, I have to ask you a question."

"Shoot."

"It's—well, it's kind of personal."

"Fire away."

"Is Will still gonna pinch Vadney's head off?"

Gets a smile out of her. "Like a bug?"

"Like a bug."

She blows smoke out into the rain, watches it curl and vanish. "He knows the truth. He knows there's nothing between Walt and me. But he's like you, he likes to play the part of a tough guy in public. He's built a shell around himself over the years, a hard shell, because he's had to. The same as you've had to. But the truth is, he's a gentleman. In the true sense. He's a gentle man. That's why I love him."

"You don't think I'm a tough guy, huh?"

"No, Little John. I think you're a gentleman."

I'd asked the question with a sense of humor, of course, but her answer was serious all the way. She smiles then, stands up, touches my cheek, and leaves me alone.

About the Author

John Minahan is the author of fifteen books,
including the Doubleday Award–winning novel
A Sudden Silence, the million-copy best seller
Jeremy, and the first four thrillers in this series.
An alumnus of Cornell, Harvard, and Columbia,
he is a former staff writer for *Time* magazine
and was editor and publisher of *American Way*
magazine. Minahan and his wife, Verity, live in
Miami, where he is writing the fifth novel in the
series.